£21.99

Depres...e

across the lifespan

Depression care across the lifespan

Lynne Walsh

MSc, BSc (Hons) RMN, RGN, RNT Dip Prof Practice,
Cert Ed, Cert Health Promotion
Lecturer
School of Health Science
Swansea University

A John Wiley & Sons, Ltd., Publication

This edition first published 2009
© 2009 John Wiley & Sons, Ltd

Wiley-Blackwell is an imprint of John Wiley and Sons, formed by the merger of Wiley's global Scientific, Technical and Medical business with Blackwell Publishing.

Registered office
John Wiley & Sons Ltd, The Atrium, Southern Gate, Chichester, West Sussex, PO19 8SQ, United Kingdom

Editorial office
John Wiley & Sons Ltd, The Atrium, Southern Gate, Chichester, West Sussex, PO19 8SQ, United Kingdom

For details of our global editorial offices, for customer services and for information about how to apply for permission to reuse the copyright material in this book please see our website at www.wiley.com/wiley-blackwell.

Library of Congress Cataloging-in-Publication Data

Walsh, Lynne, 1961–
    Depression care across the lifespan / Lynne Walsh.
        p. ; cm.
    Includes bibliographical references and index.
    ISBN 978-0-470-51772-7 (pbk. : alk. paper)   1. Depression, Mental–Treatment.   I. Title.
    [DNLM: 1. Depression–therapy.   2. Bipolar Disorder–therapy.   3. Depressive Disorder–therapy. WM 171 W225d 2009]
    RC537.W26 2009
    616.85′27–dc22
                                                                                    2008036188

A catalogue record for this book is available from the British Library.

Set in 10/12 pt Minion by Aptara® Inc., New Delhi, India
Printed in Singapore by Fabulous Printers Pte Ltd

1   2009

Contents

Dedication

This book is dedicated to my loving father, Paul Raymond Jones (Ray), who passed away on 25th August 2007, at the age of 80 years, after living with motor neuron disease for 5 years. Dad, you were an inspiration to me giving me a good start in life, enabling me to develop a variety of skills to fulfil my potential. It has been a difficult year; however, your passing has given me the drive and motivation to complete this book. God bless you.

Acknowledgements

I thank my husband Chris and children Laura and Jonathan for their encouragement and patience whilst writing this book.

I also thank Gaynor Mabbett and team from Swansea University who have encouraged and supported me throughout the year.

Finally, I thank my mother Dorothy and also Alan and Jean who have been there during the good and not so good times.

I thank you all.

Preface

This book provides a useful and comprehensive resource for any practitioner involved in the care of people with depression. It will also be important reading for both undergraduate and postgraduate students undertaking professional qualifications in medicine, nursing and social care. It may also be of interest to informal corers and people suffering from depression.

The aim of this book is to enhance the care delivered to patients with depression throughout the lifespan. It has been estimated that mental illness will affect one in six adults in Great Britain at any one time. Depression can affect any individual at any time in their lives and is caused by a variety of both physical and psychological factors. Having cared for people with depression both from a personal and professional perspective, this book aims to make practitioners aware of the implications of dealing with people with depression.

It is important to discuss care provision in relation to evidence-based practice and this will be included as an essential component of the book. The chapters in this book will discuss the implications of depression caused by events throughout the lifespan. Because of the changes in both health and social policy, most people who have depression live within the community. Thus, treatment and care is now provided in both primary and secondary care settings. This book aims to increase knowledge and understanding of depression and to enable professionals to provide quality care to patients suffering from depression.

'... *there is no health without mental health. Mental health is central to the human, social and economic capital of nations* ...'.

Mental Health Declaration for Europe (WHO 2005)

Introduction

This book has been written as a comprehensive text on depression for doctors, nurses and primary care practitioners. Depression and mental illness are now being treated and managed within the primary care setting which is having a major impact upon health and social care provision. Depression can affect any individual irrespective of social class, age, gender or ability and can impact upon family members at various stages throughout the lifespan.

The chapters in this book take the reader through the lifespan starting with children and teenagers, through adulthood and finally old age. The book has been divided into ten chapters. Each chapter has been supported by international research studies and articles which include relevant government documents such as the National Institute of Clinical Excellence guidelines, National Service Frameworks and relevant policy initiatives. The purpose of this book is to influence practice and improve the quality of care provided by practitioner's caring for individuals suffering from depression and their families. The book is designed to be read as a whole; however, individual chapters will be of importance at different times and can be read as stand-alone chapters. Certain chapters will be more pertinent to individuals with different expertise, e.g. GPs, doctors in psychiatry, general nurses, health visitors, district nurses, CPNs and social services. This will be particularly helpful when seeking information or when addressing a specific query.

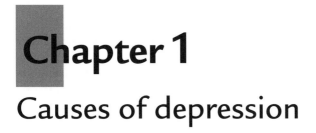

Chapter 1
Causes of depression

This chapter begins by focusing on the epidemiology of depression. Epidemiological studies are discussed in relation to depression and the concept of depression as normal in relation to some life events. It also discusses when depression becomes abnormal in the sense that it impacts upon a person's ability to function and live normally within their environment. Gender issues will be introduced and the chapter will then review mild depression, major depression, seasonal affective disorder, postnatal depression and bipolar disorder. Different beliefs about the causes of depression including cultural beliefs, lay beliefs and sociological beliefs are also discussed. This chapter concludes by discussing the importance of cultural, lay and sociological beliefs about depression.

Epidemiology of depression

It is important to consider depression from a global perspective as it affects many people across the world. The World Health Organization (1997) has predicted that by 2010, depression will be the second most common cause of disability worldwide. In 1993, the Mental Health Foundation found that clinical depression affected up to 2.3 million people in the UK at any one time. The American Psychiatric Association (1994) reported that 3% of males and 7% of females in America suffered from depressive disorder and Rorseman *et al.* (1990) reported that in Sweden every second female and every fourth male were at risk of suffering from depression at some time in their lives. More recently, the Depression Alliance (2005) has stated that depression already affects at least one in five people in the UK. A key factor to consider is that many of these reports and findings are based upon the people who have been diagnosed with a depressive illness or disorder.

A report by Lundbeck, in 1995, found that three in four cases of depression were not recognized or treated. These facts demonstrate the need for improved knowledge and understanding when recognizing symptoms of depression. This will help to ensure that patients are diagnosed and treated appropriately. Attitudes towards the illness are changing slowly as a result of the National Service Framework for Mental Health (2004) and improving education- and evidence-based approaches amongst doctors and other professionals.

Also, patients are demanding the best care and treatment as well as being part of the expert patient programmes. With the wealth of information available on the internet and in the media, patient expectations are forever increasing.

There is also more positive representation by the media when acknowledging celebrities who have suffered from mental illness. This includes sufferers from manic depression, depression, eating disorders and conditions associated with alcohol and drug abuse.

In Finland, back in 1994, Lehtinen and Joukamaa identified epidemiological studies which showed that depression was the most common mental disorder. They acknowledged that the occurrence of depression was associated with age, marital status, social class and social conditions, and that many people who suffered from depression did not get treatment. A worrying concern was that only about one-third of people suffering from depression were actually treated for their disorder in Finland.

Epidemiology must be considered from a local, national and international perspective when considering the implications of depression from a global perspective.

Gender and depression

The DH (2004) suggested that about one in five women and one in ten men get depression serious enough to require treatment. These facts also demonstrate that depression is more likely to occur in women than in men. Morris (1998) suggested that one in four women would suffer from clinical depression during their lifetime. This can potentially have major implications upon family life leading to individual, social and economic problems, resulting in a major public health problem.

There may be several reasons why women are more likely to be diagnosed with depression than men. It could be that women are more likely to report their symptoms and visit the doctor. Women are also more likely to see their general practitioner (GP) as they tend to be the main carer within the family who take children and other dependent relatives to the doctor.

Hormonal changes in women are also linked with depression, thus they may be more likely to visit their doctor. These visits often occur during pregnancy, after miscarriage, after childbirth or during changes in the menstrual cycle and the menopause (National Institute of Mental Health, 2000).

Murray and Lopez (1997) argue that depression amongst men should not be underestimated within British society as it is presently considered to be the fourth most important cause of disability worldwide. Men are more at risk of not being treated and are less likely to tell someone how they feel. This may be one reason why doctors are less likely to suspect depression in men than in women.

The National Institute of Mental Health (2000) suggested that depression in men was not recognized as it was considered to be caused by overtime at work or drinking or drug taking.

This is a worrying perception and is probably one reason why men do not report their feelings and emotions to professionals. This leads to misconceptions about men's health and can have serious implications resulting in men not being diagnosed with depression and not accessing the correct treatment. Some men may also perceive depression as a female illness and as a result feel less likely to obtain help.

This highlights the importance of the role of GPs and other mental health professionals in taking time to listen and to discuss mental health needs with men. Mental health needs to be considered of equal importance as physical health. If health needs are addressed then primary prevention will be a key feature in future health care service provision.

What is depression?

The DH (2004) described depression as a form of mental ill health. It is an emotional state that causes its sufferers to experience negative feelings about their self-image. Burns and Hartmen (2004) stated that the person can become mentally sluggish, which causes apathy and lack of interest in life generally.

Causes of depression

The National Institute of Mental Health undertook research into depression in 2000 and suggested that there are a variety of causes of depression which include:

- Death of a loved one
- Relationship breakdown
- Financial worries
- Stressful events in a person's life
- Difficult childhood experiences leading to depression in adulthood

Thus, depression can occur as a result of major life changes across the lifespan. These changes may cause feelings of inadequacy and stress. Young people may find it difficult to get a job; they may experience loss of a job and as a result of this have financial difficulties such as debt. Younger people may also experience relationship breakdown. Middle-aged people may experience a variety of loss.

Some examples include the death of parents, children leaving home, changes in financial status and moving house. An older person may lose their home, their lifelong partner, loss of income due to retirement or may experience moving into long-term care. Many of these life-changing events and experiences can potentially lead to stress and depression.

Depression is also linked to changes in the brain causing disturbances in thoughts, emotions, sleep, appetite and behaviour. The brain sends messages between the nerves using chemical neurotransmitters called noradrenaline and serotonin. Guyton and Hall (1996) suggest that depression occurs when these chemicals fail to function.

Within some families, genetic factors are also shown to cause depression where there is a family history of depression. However, for some individuals, there appears to be no known reason as to why depression occurs.

Recognizing the symptoms of depression

There are many common symptoms of depression. If a person experiences four or more of these symptoms for most of the day, nearly every day over a 2-week period, then help should be sought.

- Tiredness and lack of energy
- Persistent sadness
- Loss of self-confidence and loss of self-esteem
- Difficulty concentrating
- Not being able to enjoy things usually pleasurable or interesting
- Undue feelings of guilt or unworthiness
- Feelings of helplessness and hopelessness
- Sleeping problems, difficulties getting off to sleep or waking up much earlier than usual
- Avoiding other people, even your close friends
- Finding it hard to function at work/school/college
- Loss of appetite
- Loss of sex drive and/or sexual problems
- Physical aches and pains
- Thinking about suicide and death
- Self-harm

(Depression Alliance, 2003; National Institute of
Clinical Excellence [NICE], 2004).

Depression as normal

It must be recognized that most people will experience some of these symptoms at different times in their life but may not necessarily be suffering from depression. Many of these symptoms are normal reactions to situations in the that where one twin has been diagnosed with bipolar disorder the other twin is highly likely to develop the disorder.

Stressful life events can also trigger the disorder in people who are predisposed to manic depression. This is important as if it is established that lack of support, physical illness or stressful life events can cause increased episodes of the illness, then measures can be undertaken to provide support and help to prevent relapse. Manic depression affects women and men equally and there does not appear to be any gender-specific association with the condition. The person with bipolar disorder may suffer from extreme mood swings from mania to depression. Many sufferers of the disorder will experience varying types of mood swings; however, some sufferers will experience one or the other as an extreme.

Mental symptoms of depression experienced by people with manic depression include the following:

- Feeling unhappy
- Loss of interest
- Loss of enjoyment
- Tiredness
- Loss of self-confidence
- Irritability
- Tiredness and agitation
- Feeling hopeless and inadequate
- Thoughts of suicide
- Lack of confidence
- Inability to make simple decisions

Physical symptoms of manic depression experienced include the following:

- Early waking
- Loss of appetite
- Loss of weight
- Constipation
- Reduction in libido

The person feels unable to continue functioning with their daily routine and also finds it difficult to maintain contact with other people. Because of these feelings, it is extremely difficult for individuals to maintain employment and as a result relationships often break down. If left untreated or undiagnosed, depression can lead to suicide.

Mania

Mania is the opposite of depression. It also affects an individual's ability to function with daily living and can potentially affect employment and relationships. Mania can cause individuals to lose contact with reality and take risks and make decisions that are harmful or dangerous. Some people have spent all their savings or purchased an abundance of items.

Symptoms experienced during mania are as follows:

- Lack of insight into a condition
- Rapid speech and thoughts
- Irritation with others
- Elation and excitability
- Inability to sleep
- Unwillingness to sleep
- Hearing voices that no one else can hear
- Feelings of high importance
- Recklessness, particularly with money
- Bizarre behaviour
- Flight of ideas
- Lowered inhibitions regarding sexual behaviour
- Making unrealistic plans

Initially, the person suffering from this manic episode experiences feelings of well-being and may not listen to family, friends or carers who will have noticed this rapid change in their mood and behaviour.

This can initially cause conflict in these relationships during the manic phase. After the manic episode, the sufferer may feel a sense of guilt and embarrassment which can then lead into the depressive state of the illness. It is important to recognize warning signs of the illness so that the person can seek appropriate help before the mood and behaviour get out of hand. Helping a depressed relative or friend and knowing where to seek help is very important. Important considerations are nutrition and hygiene needs and also accessing medical help.

Seasonal affective disorder

Magnusson and Boivin (2003) suggest that seasonal affective disorder (SAD) is a relatively common condition affecting 1–3% of adults in temperate climates and is more prevalent in women. The disorder is shown by big mood swings during different seasons of the year. Sufferers from SAD usually get more depressed in the winter and may experience high moods or mania in the spring. The current criteria for SAD are that there should be at least three episodes of mood disturbance in three separate years. Baldwin and Hirschfeld (2001) state that for this diagnosis to be made the person needs to have experienced the symptoms of SAD for 2 consecutive years.

Partonen and Lonnqvist (1998) state that the recurrence of depressive episodes occurs during the winter months and even though the person does not generally warrant hospital admission, does not have psychotic symptoms or is not at risk of suicide, the person does suffer socially and also may experience impaired functioning within the working environment. The symptoms are treated with light therapy. The person sits in front of a light box for 30–120 minutes depending on the severity of the condition. Partonen and Lonnqvist (1998) found that by treating patients with bright light in the mornings and monitoring the effect every 2–3 weeks resulted in remission in two-thirds of patients with mild episodes. They also found evidence to suggest that drug therapy was also effective but there was no evidence to support the effectiveness of psychological treatments for SAD. International studies have been undertaken to establish the effectiveness of light therapy and drug therapy.

Back in 1984, Rosenthal et al. undertook research which looked at the effectiveness of light therapy on patients with SAD. Lewy et al. (1988) compared the effectiveness of morning versus evening light therapy for patients with winter depression.

Schwartz et al. (1996) undertook a follow-up study to characterize the long-term course of patients with SAD. They studied 59 patients on the National Institute of Mental Health Seasonal Studies Programme after an interval of 8 years.

The study concluded that winter depression and summer remissions remained fairly consistent over the period of time. It identified that light treatment although effective for many patients was less effective for the more severely depressed. It also concluded that non-seasonal depression in patients who suffered from SAD showed a greater severity of the illness and these patients were less likely to respond to light treatment. From this evidence, it can be determined that drug treatment would be more effective for these patients.

Lam et al. (2006) undertook a randomized control trial which compared the effectiveness of light therapy and the antidepressant drug fluoxetine in patients with winter SAD. This study showed that the light treatment had a better response earlier on and a lower rate of side effects compared to the fluoxetine; however, there were no significant differences between the two treatments and the conclusion was that both treatments were equally effective in treating SAD and that maybe the patient's preference should determine the choice of treatment.

There has also been research undertaken by Lewy et al. (2006) who considered sleep and circadian rhythm as a basis of winter depression. There has also been previous research undertaken to study the possible role of seasonal mood changes in relation to myocardial infarction.

Lurie (2006) stated that SAD is underdiagnosed in primary care and can be confused with other diagnosis. He highlighted that SAD had been linked with seasonal alcohol abuse and attention deficit hyperactivity disorder (ADHD). As a consequence of not having SAD diagnosed some patients with seasonal alcohol abuse could be self-medicating to cope with their underlying depression. This demonstrates the importance of correct investigation and diagnosis and the importance of the role of the GP and other mental health professionals.

Postnatal depression

Some women suffer from postnatal depression after childbirth. Baldwin and Hirschfeld (2001) suggested that approximately 10% of women experienced significant depression in the first few months after childbirth. Many will recover but up to half of these women will still suffer from depressive symptoms 6 months after the birth of their baby. Risk factors likely to determine if a woman will suffer from postnatal depression include:

- History of depression before conception
- History of depression during pregnancy
- Poor marital relationship
- Lack of social support
- Recent stressful life events
- Severe maternity blues in the week after delivery
- Irritability or poor motor control in the infant

Postnatal depression will be discussed in more detail throughout Chapter 3 which includes postnatal depression and depression throughout the female life cycle.

Anxiety

All people will experience anxiety at times in their lives. Anxiety can be identified as a normal reaction to stressful events. Despite this normal reaction, anxiety is often associated with depression when the experience becomes an abnormal reaction to stress. It is unsure whether the anxiety causes the depression or whether the depression causes the anxiety. Anxiety causes a person to experience physical symptoms such as headaches, dizziness, palpitations and sweating. If not treated appropriately, anxiety can cause physical exhaustion. Baldwin and Hirschfeld (2001) highlighted that a person can also experience psychological responses to anxiety which include fear, irritability, disturbed sleep, tension and poor concentration. Thus, anxiety symptoms are more significant when they are abnormally severe, prolonged, impair normal functioning and occur in the absence of stress.

Physical causes linked to depression

It is also important to recognize that depression can be caused due to an underactive thyroid. The thyroid gland produces a substance called thyroxin which helps to control metabolic rate. If there is evidence of an underactive thyroid then symptoms of depression can be experienced which include lethargy, slow movements, feelings of depression and weight gain. An overactive thyroid can also show similar symptoms to mania where the person becomes overactive, has weight loss and inability to settle and sleep (MIND, 2007).

Beliefs about depression

The move towards patient-centred health care and patient empowerment mean that patients' own perceptions and health beliefs regarding depression need to be identified and considered. Lay beliefs are beliefs that ordinary people think cause depression and can be influenced by a variety of factors. These may include previous experience of mental health, family influences, gender, social class, cultural influences, social influences and knowledge and understanding of mental health issues.

These factors require careful consideration when determining the causes of depression.

Tausig *et al.* (1999) suggested that mental illness is a social status given to people by others and goes on to suggest that when abnormal behaviour matches the criteria for depression, then the medical profession labels them as depressive.

This view needs to be treated with caution as when a person is diagnosed with depression, he or she can legitimately access treatment and care. However, it also needs to be acknowledged that some people may not wish to be labelled with a diagnosis of depression as this creates a stigma of being labelled as mentally ill. There is evidence to demonstrate that society views mental health in a negative manner. This was highlighted in a study undertaken by Evans and Jones (2001), where they undertook a survey of mental health in the Western health board in Ireland. Many changes have occurred since 2002 and with the influence of better education within both primary and secondary care services, and the influence of mental health frameworks and guidelines, it is hoped that a gradual acceptance of mental illness will be attained within society. This highlights the important role of health professionals in promoting the health of the mentally ill.

Cultural beliefs about depression

Goldbort (2006) believed that within the UK, there is cultural acceptance of certain types of intervention and treatment for depression which is primarily based upon a biomedical approach.

If people from other cultures have different beliefs and believe that their depression is caused through their living circumstances and life experiences then they may not access the treatment and care provision on offer. Studies have been undertaken across different cultures to determine beliefs about depression. One such study was undertaken by Suen and Morris (2006). This study demonstrated that Taiwanese American adults had very different beliefs about causes of depression compared with doctors in the Western world. The issue here is whether individual beliefs about the causes of depression influence the individual's ability to access appropriate health and social care provision. As a consequence, this has major implications for the diagnosis, treatment, access and provision of services.

The health beliefs of people suffering from depression are important. If the patients' beliefs are identified, it will be easier to involve them in their own care. By empowering patients to take some responsibility for their illness, they will be supported to manage their illness. This will then have an impact upon their recovery and management of their condition. This is particularly important within primary care where patients are supported in their own communities as opposed to being treated as inpatients.

Lay beliefs and depression

William and Healy (2001) undertook research into the perceptions of illness causation among new referrals to a community mental health team. They highlighted previous research which had identified explanatory models. Their research demonstrated that these explanatory models should be called explanatory maps. Their rationale being that as people expressed a variety of causes of illness and as their beliefs were changeable, it was more appropriate to refer to them as explanatory maps rather than models. These maps could then outline individual thought processes by helping them to understand reasons as to why they were experiencing particular psychological problems. Brown *et al.* (2000) supported this perception when talking about the importance of interaction between treatment and an individual's locus of control.

This was demonstrated in Brown *et al.*'s study in 2000 when patients who perceived that they had more self-control of their health and who were receiving standardized treatments experienced less depressive symptoms. This view is important as it may influence an individual's recovery rate from depression.

Lauber *et al.* (2003) undertook a study using a telephone survey with 873 interviewees in Switzerland. The survey assessed lay beliefs about causes of depressive behaviour. The study also analysed the influence of labelling and demographic factors when asking about causes of depression. The study findings showed that more than half of the respondents stated that relationship or familial difficulties were the main cause of depression, followed by occupational stress and traumatic events, depressive disorder and lastly unspecified illness. This highlights that the people in this study recognized reactive depression more than endogenous depression. However, it cannot be ignored that about a third of the study respondents acknowledged that disease or biological factors did influence the cause of depression.

Tully *et al.* (2006) undertook a study to investigate whether patient's beliefs about depression concurred with their diagnosis. It highlighted that patients were able to distinguish different causes of depression.

Sociological beliefs

Depression can affect people from all classes and groups in society; however, much of the literature has been focused upon socially and economically disadvantaged people. Poverty has been linked with depression where low income, poor life chances and chronic illness and disability can have an impact on an individual's ability to cope with everyday living.

Jorm *et al.* (2005) identified many international surveys undertaken which had asked the public about their beliefs about the causes of mental illness. Most of these respondents had identified the social environment as a strong cause of mental disorder. Jorm *et al.*'s (2005) study aimed to determine if these views had changed over time in Australia.

The findings showed that even though there was an increased belief about the genetic causes of mental disorder, the public's perception was that social causes were still the main reason for mental disorder.

Additional factors included lower family income and limited social support. Brown and Harris (1978) research looked at social origins of depression and undertook a study of psychiatric disorder in women. Their study found that lack of close, confiding relationships made women more vulnerable to depression. This demonstrates the importance of both the social environment and support networks in preventing depression. Depressed people also may find it harder to access support networks, so it is important for professionals to intervene to ensure this support is provided. It is evident from Badger's (1996) research that family support was strongly associated with improved prognosis from depression.

However, if the family is already weakened by additional factors such as poverty, unemployment and relationship issues then the prognosis may be poor and depression can take the individual into a downward spiral where they see no hope for the future. This demonstrates how some depressed people may be less able to cope, become more stressed and find it hard to solve problems.

Some individuals are more likely to suffer from depression than others and this may be due to their previous experiences, family backgrounds and ability to cope with life events. Thus, it is this inability to cope with changing life events or the inability to express feelings or inability to explore thoughts and feelings that can determine the severity of the depression.

Kessler (1997) looked at the effects of stressful life events on depression. He suggested that to determine whether stress causes depression would need to be evaluated through rigorous experiments. He suggested that previous studies undertaken had generally been undertaken using non-experimental research and as a result of methodological problems, it was difficult to determine the effects of life events on depression.

It is evident that the sociological beliefs of individuals are important to consider when determining the causes of depression upon individuals within any society.

Conclusion

The American Psychiatric Association (1994) recognized that depression affects the whole body in relation to a person's thinking, feelings, body and behaviour.

As a consequence, individual's coping strategies vary and some individuals will become a danger to themselves and may even attempt or actually commit suicide. One of the challenges for future public health is recognizing the people who do not come forward for treatment or who have not been diagnosed with a depressive illness.

If GPs, mental health workers and carers are able to recognize the early symptoms of depression and support people to seek the appropriate treatment and access the right services, then maybe depression will become less of a chronic long-term illness for some people and for others their quality of life and family relationships can be maintained.

Reflection and discussion

Why is it important to consider cultural beliefs about depression?

- *Within the UK, there is a cultural acceptance of certain types of intervention and treatment for depression which is primarily based upon a biomedical approach.*
- *If people from other cultures have different beliefs and believe that their depression is caused through their living circumstances and life experiences then they may not access the treatment and care provision on offer.*
- *Individual beliefs about the causes of depression influence the individual's ability to access appropriate health and social care provision.*
- *Poverty has been linked with depression where low income, poor life chances and chronic illness and disability can have an impact on an individual's ability to cope with everyday living.*
- *Lack of close confiding relationships make some women more vulnerable to depression. This demonstrates the importance of both the social environment and support networks in preventing depression.*

Recognize some causes of depression

- *Death of a loved one*
- *Relationship breakdown*
- *Financial worries*
- *Stressful events in a person's life*
- *Difficult childhood experiences leading to depression in adulthood*

Recognize some of the symptoms of depression

- *Tiredness and lack of energy*
- *Persistent sadness*
- *Loss of self-confidence and loss of self-esteem*

- *Difficulty concentrating*
- *Not being able to enjoy things usually pleasurable or interesting*
- *Undue feelings of guilt or unworthiness*
- *Feelings of helplessness and hopelessness*
- *Sleeping problems, difficulties getting off to sleep or waking up much earlier than usual*
- *Avoiding other people, even your close friends*
- *Finding it hard to function at work/school/college*
- *Loss of appetite*
- *Loss of sex drive and/or sexual problems*
- *Physical aches and pains*
- *Thinking about suicide and death*
- *Self-harm*

Name some of the different types of depression

Major depression
Dysthymia
Manic depression or bipolar disorder
Seasonal affective disorder (SAD)
Postnatal depression

Discuss the importance of recognizing the signs and symptoms of depression and how this influences patient care

References

American Psychiatric Association (APA). (1994). *Diagnostic and Statistical Manual of Mental Disorders (DSM-IV)*, 4th edn. Washington, DC: APA.

Badger, T.A. (1996). Living with depression. *Journal of Psychosocial Nursing, 34*, 21–29.

Baldwin, D.S. & Hirschfeld, M.A. (2001). *Fast Facts Depression*. Oxford: Health press Ltd.

Bland, R.C. (1997). Epidemiology of affective disorders: A review. *Canadian Journal of Psychiatry, 42*(4), 367–377.

Brown, G.W. & Harris, T.O. (1978). *Social Origins of Depression: A Study of Psychiatric Disorder in Women*. London: Tavistock.

Brown, C., Schulberg, H.C. & Prigerson, H.G. (2000). Factors associated with symptomatic improvement and recovery from major depression in primary care patients. *General Hospital Psychiatry, July–August*(4), 242–250.

Burns, R.B. & Hartmen, E.E. (2004). Update: A 75 year old man with depression. *JAMA*, *204*(291), 1260.

Depression Alliance (2003). *Depression Affects One in Five of Us at Some Point in Our Life*. London: Depression Allliance.

Depression Alliance. (2005). *National Depression Week*. London: Depression Alliance. Available at http://www.depressionalliance.org. Accessed 3 May 2005.

DH (2004). *Prodigy Guidance; Depression. How Do I Know My Patient Has It?* Available at http://www.prodigy.nhs.uk. Accessed 10 May 2005.

Evans, D. & Jones, J. (2001). *A Survey of Mental Health in the Western Health Board Area*. Sligo: Western Health Board.

Goldbort, J. (2006). Transcultural analysis of postpartum depression. *The American Journal of Maternal Child Nursing*, *31*, 121–126.

Guyton, A.C. & Hall, J.E. (1996). Psychotic behaviour and dementia. Roles of specific neurotransmitter systems. In: *Textbook of Medical Physiology*. Philadelphia, PA: WB Saunders.

Jorm, A.F., Christensen, H. & Griffiths, K.M. (2005). Public beliefs about causes and risk factors for mental disorders. *Social Psychiatry and Psychiatric Epidemiology*, *40*(9), 764.

Kessler, R.C. (February 1997). The effects of stressful life events on depression. *Annual Review of Psychology*, *48*, 191–214.

Lam, R.W., Levitt, A.J., Levitan, R.D., Enns, M.W., Morehouse, R., Michalak, E.E. & Tam, E.M. (May 2006). The Can–SAD Study: A randomized controlled trial of the effectiveness of light therapy and fluoxetine in patients with winter seasonal affective disorder. *American Journal of Psychiatry*, *163*, 805–812.

Lauber, C., Falcato, L., Nordt, C. & Rossier, W. (October 2003). Lay beliefs about causes of depression. *Acta Psychiatrica Scandinavica*, *108*(Suppl 418), 96–99.

Lehtinen, V. & Joukamaa, M. (1994). Epidemiology of depression: Prevalence, risk factors and treatment situation. *Acta Psychiatrica Scandinavica*, *377*, 7–10.

Lewy, A.J., Bauer, V.K., Cutler, N.L., Sack, R.L., Ahmed, S., Thomas, K.H., Blood, M.L. & Latham Jackson, J.M. (1988). Morning verses evening light treatment of patients with winter depression. *Archives of General Psychiatry*, *55*, 890–896.

Lewy, A.J., Lefler, B.J., Emens, J.S. & Baur, U.K. (2006). The circadian basis of winter depression. *Proceedings of the National Academy of Sciences of the United States of America*, *103*, 7414–7419.

Lurie, S. (2006). *American Family Physician*, *74*, 1521–1524.

Magnusson, A. & Boivin, D. (May 2003). Seasonal affective disorder: An overview. *Chronobiology International*, *20*(2), 189–207.

MIND (2007). Available at www.thyroimind.info. Accessed 27 April 2007.

Morris, K.P. (1998). *Illness and Culture in the Postmodern Age*. Berkeley, CA: University of California Press.

Murray, C.J. & Lopez, D. (1997). Regional patterns of disability-free life expectancy and disability adjusted life expectancy: Global burden of diseases. *The Lancet*, *349*, 1347–1352.

National Institute of Clinical Excellence (NICE). (2004). *Management of Depression in Primary and Secondary Care*. Clinical Guidelines 23. London: NICE. Available at www.nice.org.uk.

National Institute of Mental Health. (2000). *Depression*. Bethesda, MD: NIMH.

National Institute of Mental Health Genetics Workgroup. (1998). *Genetics and Mental Disorders*. Rockville, MD: NIMH.

National Service Framework for Mental Health Five Years On. (2004). *A Report By Professor L. Appleby*, 20th December 2004. Crown Copywright. London: DH.

Partonen, T. & Lonnqvist, J. (March 1998). Seasonal affective disorder: A guide to diagnosis and management. *CNS Drugs*, *9*(3), 203–212.

Rorseman, B., Grasback, A., Hagnell, O., Lanke, J. & Otterbeck, L., for The Lundby Study. (1990). A prospective study of first incidence depression. *British Journal of Psychiatry*, *156*, 336–342.

Rosenthal, N.E., Sack, D.A., Gillin, J.C., Lewy, A.J., Goodwin, F.K., Davenport, Y., Mueller, S., Newsome, D.A. & Werhr, T.A. (1984). Seasonal affective disorder. A description of the syndrome and preliminary findings with light therapy. *Archives of General Psychiatry*, *41*, 72–80.

Schwartz, P.J., Brown, C., Wehr, T.A. & Rosenthal, N.E. (1996). Winter seasonal affective disorder: A follow up study of the first 59 patients of the National Institute of Mental Health Seasonal Studies Programme. *American Journal of Psychiatry*, *153*, 1028–1036.

Scott, J. (1988). Chronic depression. *British Journal of Psychiatry*, *153*, 287–297.

Suen, L. & Morris, D. (2006). Depression and gender differences: Focus on Taiwanese American older adults. *Journal of Gerontological Nursing*, *32*, 28–36.

Tausig, M., Michello, J. & Subedi, S. (1999). *A Sociology of Mental Illness*. Upper Saddle River: Prentice Hall.

Thompson, T. & Mathias, P. (2000). *Lyttles Mental Health and Disorder*. Edinburgh: Bailliere Tindall.

Tully, L.A., Parker, G.B., Wilhelm, K. & Malhi, G. (2006). Why am I depressed? An investigation into whether patient's beliefs about depression concur with their diagnostic subtype. *The Journal of Nervous and Mental Disease*, 194, 543–546.

William, B. & Healy, D. (August 2001). Perceptions of illness causation among new referrals to a community mental health team: "Explanatory model" or "exploratory map"? *Social Science Medicine*, *53*(4), 465–476.

World Health Organization (1997). *The ICD –10 International Classification of Mental and Behavioral Disorders (1992)*, 10th edn. Geneva: World Health Organization.

Chapter 2

Depression in children and young people

Introduction

Childhood depression can range from a variety of symptoms from sadness and disappointment as a result of stressful life events to severe depression. The causes of depression in children can be due to a variety of factors. National Statistics (2004) found that one in ten children in the UK aged between 5 and 16 were diagnosed with a mental disorder. Mental disorder is diagnosed by the International Classification of Diseases (ICD-10), which recognizes mental disorder as a set of symptoms or behaviours causing great distress affecting daily functioning. The incidence of mental disorder in young people could be higher as these statistics consider only those children with an actual diagnosis of mental disorder. There are likely to be some children suffering from mental disorder who have not been officially diagnosed.

The National Statistics' (2004) survey undertaken between March and June 2004 commissioned by the Department of Health and the Scottish Executive found that 4% of children had an emotional disorder which included anxiety and depression. Emotional disorders in 5- to 10-year olds were similarly affecting 2.2% of boys and 2.5% of girls. However, the 11- to 16-year age group showed differences between boys and girls. The percentage increased for girls in the 11- to 16-year-old age group to 6.1% of girls compared with 4.0% of boys of the same age group. The population, which was studied, included children and young people aged between 5 and 16 years who lived in private households in the UK. If all households had been studied, the findings may have demonstrated higher incidences of mental disorder in children and young people. The study findings suggested that the prevalence of mental disorders varied due to the following familial characteristics.

Incidence of mental disorder in children

- Higher incidence in lone parent families of 16% compared with lower incidence in two-parent families of 8%.

- Higher incidence of 20% in families with neither parent working compared with lower incidence of 8% where both parents worked.
- Higher incidence in children with parents with no educational qualifications of 17% compared with lower incidence of parents with degree-level qualifications of 4%.

(Based upon the National Statistics Survey, 2004.)

Similar findings have been shown by The National Institute of Clinical Excellence (NICE, 2005) in relation to depression.

NICE (2005) stated that children who had depression were:

- Nearly twice as likely to be living with only one parent
- More than twice as likely to have both parents out of work
- More likely to have parents on low incomes and who were less educated

These findings support the view that sociological factors do have an impact and are linked with the causes of depression.

Causes of depression in young people

Birmaher *et al.* (1996) suggested that depression was more common in teenagers and at any one time, 8 in every 100 teenagers may be depressed. Reasons for older children suffering from depression may be due to hormonal influences during puberty. Burt and Stein (2002) suggest that changes in hormone levels can increase a girl's chance of becoming depressed. There is some evidence to suggest that depression is affected by gender differences. Hankin and Abramson (2001) found that up to the age of 12 years, there is an equal chance that both boys and girls will experience depression; however at puberty, nearly twice as many girls as boys will experience depression. Depression can affect how a child feels, thinks and behaves. Even though there are some similarities, there are also some differences between causes of depression in children and causes of depression in adults. Causes of depression in children may include the loss of a parent, being bullied at school or as a result of changes in the brain chemistry.

Very young children may not be able to express their feelings verbally so it is important to observe their behaviour. Jellineck and Snyder (1998) have found that these children may display a variety of symptoms which include delayed developmental milestones, failure to thrive, becoming apathetic and withdrawing from care providers. Thus, play leaders, school teachers and health professionals, particularly health visitors, school nurses and nursery nurses will all need to be observant when dealing with young children. Children may express their feelings through physical somatic complaints such as headaches, stomach upsets and anxiety. As a consequence, they may not want to go to school, become irritable and experience behavioural problems (Birmaher *et al.*, 1996).

It appears that major depressive episodes are more frequent and more severe in girls than in boys. There is also some evidence to show that there are gender differences in the type of symptoms experienced. These were shown in a study undertaken in a high school in Sweden by Olsson and Von Knorring (1997). They found that boys experienced sadness, crying and suicidal ideation whereas girls were more likely to experience guilt, fear of failure, feeling unattractive and feelings of dislike. Girls also experienced suicidal ideation.

Culture must also be considered in relation to depression in young people as the expression of symptoms may vary within different cultures. This is important as Manson (1995) stated that the diagnosis of depression is based upon the common experiences of people in different cultures. This view is supported by Choi (2002) who suggests that both culture and ethnicity influence the epidemiology of young people's depression. Culture is influenced by social conditions; therefore, professionals must be careful not to misinterpret behaviours in children from different cultures. This could have a devastating effect for young people resulting in inappropriate diagnosis and treatment of childhood depression.

From a cultural perspective, NICE (2005) suggests that under the age of 10 years, there are similar incidences of depression amongst different ethnic groups in the UK. However, there is some evidence to show that teenagers from Pakistani and Bangladeshi origins are more than twice as likely to be depressed as White, Black or Indian teenagers. Walsh (2007a) highlighted the importance of considering cultural backgrounds when dealing with people with mental illness.

Physical conditions

It is important to ensure that the correct diagnosis is given to rule out other physical illnesses such as myxoedema, which is caused through an underactive thyroid gland, glandular fever, anaemia or sleep problems, which may cause the child to display similar symptoms to depression.

It is interesting to note that Kanner *et al.* (2003) reported that young people with type 1 diabetes had significantly higher rates of depression than the general population. This needs to be investigated further with the increasing amount of children being diagnosed with childhood diabetes. If this association between diabetes and depression is proven, we could see a national increase in depression in children. This has major implications for health care provision and education and support for families.

Diagnosing depression in children

Depression will be diagnosed if the child experiences a combination of the following symptoms over a 2-week period:

- Feeling depressed most of the day, every day
- Loss of interest in most activities
- Weight loss or weight gain and appetite changes
- Inability to sleep or requiring too much sleep

- Feeling restless or sluggish
- Lack of energy and tiredness
- Feeling worthless or guilty
- Inability to concentrate or make decisions
- Thoughts about suicide or death
(NICE, 2005; *Depression in Children and Young People*, Guideline 28).

When these symptoms have been identified, the correct type of depression can be diagnosed by establishing the number of symptoms over a period of time. If the first two symptoms and two others are experienced then a diagnosis of mild depression may be given. If five or six symptoms are experienced then moderate depression will be diagnosed, whereas seven or more symptoms would indicate a diagnosis of severe depression.

Children may be diagnosed with dysthymia, if their depression has lasted for more than 2 years. Kovacs *et al.* (1994) state that dysthymia is considered a gateway disorder as it starts in early childhood and leads to an increased chance of subsequent affective disorders. This is an important factor to be considered by all health professionals.

Referral to a psychiatrist may be required if the child does not respond to treatment or if there are complicated family issues which may include a history of alcohol or drug abuse in the family, if either parent has suffered with depression or if there is poor support within the family setting.

The risk of school failure and suicide is quite high in depressed children and young people, thus it is essential to refer early on to the Child and Adolescent Mental Health Service (CAMHS) teams.

A variety of skills are required from the team and any other professionals involved when dealing with young people. The development of trust is essential with young people as they may not wish their parents to know about information they have divulged to health professionals.

This also raises the issue of confidentiality and health professionals must be clear at the start of the patient/professional relationship about what information will be shared with parents. Family influences and peer support can determine how early the young person accesses the appropriate treatment and help required.

Many young people with severe depression also suffer from substance misuse and may also pursue risky behaviour resulting in poor relationships and unwanted pregnancies. This then can lead to a downward spiral emotionally, physically and economically and has major social consequences upon their wellbeing. This potentially becomes a major public health issue providing topical debate within policy initiatives.

Support and screening within schools can provide a useful approach to depression in children and young people. Weist *et al.* (2007) advocate the importance of screening students in schools for emotional and behavioural problems. This process would help to identify potential risks, needs, support and future health planning for young people and would also help to reduce barriers to learning. This would require informing teachers about mental health and encouraging them to promote child health and well-being generally. As a consequence of this initiative, care needs to be taken to ensure that these young people whose emotional needs have been identified do not become labelled and bullied resulting in the opposite effect by making the symptoms of depression worse. This initiative would enable professionals to educate, inform and reassure parents, children and teachers about the positive aspects of mental health. There is a view that health education and health promotion should start in primary schools where children become more aware of situations that can affect both their physical and mental health. If healthy eating, childhood obesity, drug abuse and sexual health can be discussed in schools, why cannot mental health promotion be included as part of the curriculum. This would help to reduce the stigma of mental illness and also encourage children and young people to talk more openly about their feelings and emotions. This may then impact positively upon the implications of mental illness in adulthood.

Associated risk factors

Children are more likely to suffer from depression if there is a family history of depression and if there is conflict within the family setting. It must be acknowledged that depression affects all ages, social classes and genders across the lifespan and many of the symptoms of severe depression are the same for both young people and adults. Bradge et al. (1995) highlighted that the three most important factors associated with depression are loneliness, self-esteem and age.

Other factors include previous depressive occurrences, poor academic performance and anxiety disorders. Some young people may also have substance abuse disorders and may have suffered from physical, emotional or sexual abuse. For some children, there may be multiple factors influencing their depressed state. Pullen et al.'s (2000) study showed that 15- to 16-year-old girls who smoked and consumed alcohol were twice as likely to suffer from depression as non-users of alcohol. Both professionals and the family must be vigilant as these factors create their own additional risks leading to potential self-harm and suicide. Puskar et al. (1999) acknowledged the self-reported symptoms of depression by young people living in rural areas. Their perception of life events as positive or negative influenced their depressive state. These included the impact of life events in relation to losing a close friend, the death of a family member, problems with peers, being in trouble with the police and increasing arguments with parents.

One important factor that must be considered is whether a child lives with parents who suffer from mental illness. It is important that the relevant health professionals liaise appropriately to ensure that no neglect or harm comes to these children. This can result in family disruption if the child has to be taken into foster care while the parent is seeking treatment. It must be recognized that most children do not come to any harm when living in a household with parents with mental illness; however, there may be added pressures on these children to care for their ill parents. Rutter and Quinton (1984) suggested that problems were less likely for the child if the other parent did not have mental health problems, the parents had no financial problems and there was no violence within the family. Children were more likely to be at risk where there was violence within the home, the ill parent suffered from delusions or hallucinations and the child was neglected. Walsh (2007b) highlighted how adults with mental health problems suffering from acute psychotic episodes have a major impact on both their own lives and their families. These factors may also influence the incidence of these children having depression themselves in later life.

Treatment of depression in children and young people

There are a variety of treatments available to treat depression in young people including drug therapy, psychotherapy and cognitive behaviour therapy.

Drug treatment

Sung and Kirchner (2000) suggested that tricyclic antidepressants and selective serotonin reuptake inhibitors (SSRIs) have been used effectively to treat severe depression in younger people.

It is important to have a correct diagnosis of a specific type of depression before choosing drug treatment as the initial choice of treatment. Whittington *et al.* (2004) undertook a systematic review and found that even though tricyclic antidepressant drugs had been used to treat depression in young people, SSRIs have been the drug treatment of choice as they have fewer side effects. However, there has been much documented evidence which has highlighted concern about the use of SSRI antidepressants to treat depression in young people. These are shown in reports undertaken by the United Kingdom Committee on Safety of Medicines (2004), New Zealand Ministry of Health (2004) and the United States Federal Drug and Food Administration (2004). This shows that drug treatment for depression in young people has been debated on the political agendas of many countries demonstrating international concern. Within the UK, SSRIs are generally not prescribed for children and young people due to the increased association with suicidal ideas and suicide attempts. A placebo-controlled, randomized clinical trial was undertaken in America by Emslie *et al.* (2002) which considered the drug fluoxetine commonly known as Prozac as a treatment for depression in children and young people.

They concluded that fluoxetine 20 mg daily was an effective treatment for depression in children. However, Professor Gordon Duff, chair of the Committee on Safety of Medicines in the UK, in 2003, advised that most of the antidepressants known as SSRIs should not be used to treat depression in children and young people in the UK. This decision was made following a review of clinical trials by an expert group who that concerns about the risks. After considering the balance of risk, they considered flouxetine to be the only SSRI to be effective and this was only for about 1:10 of young people. As this was the main drug treatment, it caused concern amongst both patients and professionals. As Ramchandani (2004) highlighted, it also asked the question what other effective alternative treatments could be used. At that time, approximately half of the 40 000 young people in the UK were taking one of the SSRI treatments. For those children prescribed SSRIs, it was important for them to withdraw from the drugs gradually as stopping them immediately would have caused increased risk of relapse of depression. Other antidepressants used to treat depression are tricyclics. However, Hazell *et al.*'s review of tricyclic antidepressants used in young people in 1995 showed that they were no more effective than placebos. A further systematic review was undertaken by Hazell *et al.* (2003) demonstrating that tricyclic antidepressants did have some effect for young people but not for younger children. Thus, they are used with extreme caution due to their toxic effects in overdose and adverse side effects.

Therapies

Birmaher and Alexon (1998) highlighted the importance of identifying the most appropriate therapy for the age of the child. For very young children play therapy is recommended whilst for older children it would be more appropriate to undertake psychotherapy or cognitive therapy. Waslick *et al.* (2003) focused on the treatment of chronic depression in children and young people advocating psychotherapy as an effective treatment for mild to moderate depression in children and young people.

It is important that the right treatment is provided for the right age of the child and that family circumstances are taken into consideration. It is also important that the treatment from childhood depression is evidence-based. Harrington *et al.* (1998) undertook a systematic review to determine the efficacy of cognitive behavioural therapy in children and young people suffering from depression. They showed some evidence that psychological treatments were effective in treating milder depression and were usually the first line of treatment before any drug therapy was considered. Further studies have been undertaken and Possel (2005) undertook a randomized control study to determine whether a cognitive behavioural primary prevention programme reduced risk factors and symptoms of depression in young people.

This study was undertaken in six middle schools in Germany. The study concluded that in students with low self-esteem, the training programme provided by the psychologists reduced depressive symptoms. However, there were limitations to the study which included a small sample size and high levels of staff input required to enable these findings to be effective, making this study resource intensive. Before taking these findings as effective for all children in schools, larger studies would need to be undertaken.

Ellis (2004) suggests that the most effective treatment for depression is a combination of antidepressants and psychotherapy. The latter is particularly helpful for children and is often provided by experienced trained mental health nurses. Compliance with treatment regimes can be helped by involving the family and helping them to understand the child's depression. As with all age groups compliance with treatment regimes will determine future prognosis of the condition.

Substance misuse in young people

Substance misuse incorporates a variety of substances including alcohol, drugs and poisons. These substances can be swallowed and ingested, inhaled, injected or absorbed through the skin.

Alcohol is on the increase within the younger age group where within UK society there has been a huge increase in binge drinking in both young boys and girls. However, other substances liable to misuse include cannabis which is a derivative of marijuana.

Cannabis or marijuana

Cannabis or marijuana has become readily accessible in most towns, cities and rural communities. Van de Bree and Pickworth (2005) recognized that marijuana was the most commonly used illicit drug and Johnston *et al.* (2004) reported that 50% of American secondary school students had used it. Monshouwer *et al.* (2006) stated that approximately two million people in the UK smoke cannabis and half of all 16- to 29-year olds had tried it once. This evidence suggests that there is a potential problem with its use. This is demonstrated by Dennis *et al.* (2002) who found that it was the most common drug reported in arrests, emergency departments and autopsies.

The law before January 2004 stated that cannabis was a class B drug, however, it was reclassified and is currently a class C drug. This reclassification has led to uncertainty of the laws regarding decriminalization of cannabis and may have led to an increase in young people taking it, as they perceive the drug to be a harmless recreational drug taken for pleasure. For this reason, the government's Advisory Council on the Misuse of Drugs wanted to reclassify cannabis back to a class B drug; however, it currently remains a class C drug. Cannabis has a long-lasting effect staying in the bloodstream for weeks. The long-term use of cannabis reduces motivation and can lead to depression. In young people, cannabis use can lead to poor concentration and difficulty in organizing ideas. This can have a direct impact upon school and college work.

Wu *et al.* (2005) examined the association between the use of inhalants, marijuana and other drugs and recent substance use disorders amongst young people aged 12–17 years. The data were taken from National Household Surveys on

Drug Abuse. The findings showed that young people using inhalants or other drugs but not using marijuana were the least likely to report drug abuse.

However, the young people who reported using both inhalants and marijuana were more likely to be using three or more classes of drugs. It was also evident that these young people were more likely to have a past diagnosis of either alcohol and drug abuse or dependence.

Patton et al. (2002) undertook a study to determine whether cannabis use in young people predisposed higher rates of depression and anxiety in young adulthood. Daily use of cannabis in young women was associated with a fivefold increase in reporting depression in adulthood, whilst weekly use of cannabis showed that these individuals were twice as likely to report depression and anxiety in adulthood. This demonstrates that there is an increased likelihood of depression in later life caused by substance abuse in young females.

Chen et al. (1997) found that marijuana use was more frequent in younger people. This was a cause for concern because they have lower tolerance levels and a higher risk of dependence. Van de Bree and Pickworth's (2005) study highlighted three key risk factors in relation to marijuana misuse. These included the young person's peer involvement with substances, delinquency and school-related problems. There are many other factors which are associated with marijuana misuse in young people. Harrison and Narayan (2003) highlighted recognized differences in behaviour along with psychological and environmental factors. Low levels of engagement in social activities were also strongly associated with young person's substance misuse. Christie et al. (1988) demonstrated that depression and anxiety were more common in young people who misused drugs. School and family life were also very important factors as shown by Bray et al. (2000), who considered the relationship between marijuana initiation and dropping out of school and truancy. Hawkins et al. (1992) and Brook et al. (2000) provided evidence that family life was pivotal for young people and that where there was some evidence of family conflict, poor parenting and lack of structure, there was a higher risk of substance misuse.

Degenhardt et al. (2003) also explored the association between cannabis use and depression in young people. They found that heavy cannabis use and depression were associated but ruled out the suggestion that the reasons for taking it were due to social influences, i.e. social and familial causes. Risk factors need to be considered. Van de Bree and Pickworth's (2005) study considered the risk factors that predict changes in marijuana involvement in teenagers. The teenagers studied were middle school and high school students who were participating in the National Longitudinal Study on Adolescent Health. Their study showed that the strongest risk factors associated with substance abuse were delinquency, school-related problems and peer pressure.

If young people are misusing substances which affect their cognitive ability then their intellectual ability may also be affected. Fergusson et al. (2003) examined the relationship between cannabis use and young person's attainment. This was a longitudinal study taken over a period of 25 years.

The study showed that people who used cannabis were less likely to enter university and were less likely to obtain a university degree. There was some evidence to show that long-term cannabis use reduced motivation and cognitive ability. Thus, this is important in relation to depression in adulthood and the ability to seek employment.

Chassin *et al.* (2002) established that the children of parents with alcohol abuse disorders were more likely to abuse alcohol at an early age and were also more likely to have alcohol abuse disorders themselves. Clark *et al.* (1999) also found that children whose parents had substance use disorders were more likely to smoke and drink alcohol at an early age and also misuse illicit drugs and were also more likely to be diagnosed with substance use disorders.

This is not just a concern within the UK as highlighted in this chapter, but there is documented concern internationally about the mental health of teenagers who use cannabis. Rey *et al.* (2002) undertook a study funded by the Commonwealth of Australia which ascertained the prevalence of cannabis use among Australian adolescence. It also considered the association of cannabis use with mental health problems, risk behaviours and service use. This national survey in Australia consisted of 1261 young people between 13 and 17 years. A quarter of the young people surveyed had used cannabis and it was more commonly used in young people living with a single parent. This survey showed that there was an association with depression in young people who took cannabis. It also showed that these young people were more likely to smoke and drink and experience conduct problems. If behaviour is influenced by cannabis use then professionals need to work together to help these young people change their lifestyle which is having a direct impact upon both their physical and mental health. Appropriate treatments also need to be considered as shown by Kaminer *et al.* (1998) identifying that cognitive behaviour therapy was an effective treatment for young substance abusers. Self-harm and suicide must also be acknowledged amongst younger people during their lifespan.

Self-harm and suicide

Self-harm ranges from intent to communicate distress to actual suicide. Bywaters and Rolfe (2002) suggest that the average age to begin self-harming is 13 years.

The Royal College of Psychiatrists (2002) suggested that young women were seven times more likely to self-harm than young men; however, the Mental Health Foundation (2003) advocate that self-harming rates amongst boys and young men have nearly doubled since the 1980s. Hawton *et al.* (2002) identified self-harm as self-poisoning or self-injury. They estimated that 25 000 young self-harmers were admitted to general hospitals in England and Wales and that if left untreated, self-harm preceded suicide. Hawton (2005) suggests that 7–14% of young people will self-harm at some time in their lives and that 20–45% of older people will have suicidal thoughts. Richardson (2004) suggests that self-harm involves deliberately inflicting injury to one's self and may involve any of the following behaviours.

Deliberate self-harm is often referred to as parasuicide or attempted suicide, as the person may not intend to die but undertakes self-harm as a way of communicating their distress and uses this approach as a call for help. However, it must be considered seriously as some young people may actually die even though they do not mean to commit suicide. Many will overdose on paracetamol or aspirin or medication used by members of the family. The Royal College of Psychiatrists (1999) recognized deliberate self-harm in young people and highlighted the importance of mental health in young people.

Self-harming behaviour

- Excessive substance abuse
- Cutting skin
- Swallowing small amounts of toxic substances
- Burning or scalding
- Banging and scratching
- Pulling out own hair

The Mental Health Foundation (2003) identified that self-harm in the UK was the highest in Europe resulting in a UK-wide enquiry into self-harm among 11- to 25-year olds. It is important to understand the causes of self-harm so that strategic provision of education and training can be provided. The Samaritans and Centre for Suicide Oxford University (2002) reported increasing hospital admission rates amongst young people due to self-harm. A variety of situations can lead to self-harm in young people. The following have been reported by Bywaters and Rolfe (2002) including unwanted pregnancy, being bullied at school, parents' divorcing, parental conflict, abuse, rape, bereavement and entering care. Self-harm in young people has been taken seriously in the UK and was reviewed by Hawton et al. (2002) in a survey of 41 schools in England. This was a large study of 6020 young people aged 15–16 years.

The findings showed that deliberate self-harm was more common in young girls. It recommended that improved education was needed regarding mental health and that screening was needed in schools to identify those children at risk of self-harm and suicide.

Weight was an important factor linked to self-harm. Whetstone et al. (2007) acknowledged that weight perception in young people was linked to depression and low self-esteem. They undertook a study which examined the relationship between perceived weight status and suicidal thoughts and actions by gender in young people in middle schools in America. The findings showed that girls who perceived themselves as overweight were significantly more likely to report suicidal thoughts and actions, whilst boys who perceived themselves as either overweight or underweight were also significantly associated with suicidal thoughts and actions. This is surprising as even though there is a higher incidence of girls reporting these feelings, boys had considered both aspects of being over- and underweight. The study concluded that for both boys and girls perceived weight status was associated with suicidal thoughts and actions. The study did not highlight this but some of these children may have been suffering from eating disorders. Even though eating disorders are perceived as primarily female-gendered conditions, Walsh (2007b) highlighted an increased diagnosis of eating disorders amongst young males.

Self-harm is not always linked with suicide as some young people use it as a coping strategy to release feelings of anger. However, it should always be treated with caution and professionals must recognize and understand risk in relation to self-harm and suicide. NICE (2002) developed guidelines to address the physical and psychological management of self-harm.

Suicide in young people

There is a high incidence of suicide in depressed children. Hawton (2005) stated that suicide is rarely recorded in the under 15-year age group. This potentially creates a false perception as many open verdicts are actually suicides. This demonstrates that statistically the numbers of recorded suicides in young people are probably underestimated. Most young people who actually commit suicide have been suffering from depression and there are strong links between those individuals who have undertaken self-harm and suicide.

The National Institute of Mental Health (2001) stated that suicide was the most common cause of death in young people with anorexia. Stein *et al.* (2003) also suggested that anorexic young females showed suicidal tendencies which were comparable with psychiatric inpatients. This is supported by Pompili *et al.* (2004) who found that suicide was more frequent amongst young people and young adults with anorexia than amongst the general population. In future, this trend could indicate higher incidences of depression, suicide and self-harm amongst younger people.

The results of Whetstone *et al.*'s (2007) study showed the following factors.

Thinking about suicide	Girls 26%	Boys 19%
Planning suicide	Girls 12%	Boys 9%
Attempting suicide	Girls 11%	Boys 8%

There is some evidence from Hawton *et al.*'s (2003) study that school stress was associated with deliberate self-harm by overdosing on antidepressants. There were some identified gender differences where drug misuse and suicide intent were more common in boys, whilst girls were more likely to be the victim of violence and bullying. This study also identified the importance of preventative initiatives being put into place in schools. Roberts *et al.* (2004) also recognized the importance of preventing depressive symptoms in school children from rural communities. Bancilia and Mittlemore (2005) also reported a relationship between stressors and depressed mood in young people. Acne can cause stress in young people. Acne occurs as a result of hormonal changes during puberty. Purvis *et al.* (2006) found that teenagers who suffered from acne were more likely to be anxious, depressed and attempt suicide.

Purvis *et al.* (2006) study investigated 9567 young people aged 12–18 years. Those with acne problems were twice as likely to report depressive symptoms. Out of the study population 14.1% had an acne problem with 23% reporting suicidal ideas and 7.8% attempting suicide. However, a recent research suggests that the side effects of Isotretinoin, a drug used to treat acne, has been linked to more than 100 suicides and attempted suicides worldwide (NT net, 2006). Thus, both the acne and the side effects of this drug Isotretinoin can potentially cause suicide and self-harm in young people.

Risk factors associated with suicide

There are a variety of risk factors associated with suicide which may include:

- Family history of suicide
- Child abuse
- Parental divorce
- Access to fatal methods of suicide
- Previous suicidal attempts
- History of mental disorder
- Feelings of hopelessness
- Physical illness
- Isolation
- Impulsive behaviour

Beautrais *et al.* (1996) were concerned about serious suicide attempts in young people and undertook a study to establish what risk factors caused young people between the ages of 13–24 years to commit suicide. They concluded that socio-demographic factors such as low educational qualifications, low income and poor childhood experiences which included poor relationships with parents, childhood abuse and presence of mental disorders, increased the likelihood of a young person making a serious suicide attempt. Both depression and feelings of hopelessness have been linked to depression and increased risk of suicide in both young people and adults. Overholser *et al.* (1997) found that amongst young females, both depression and hopelessness were greatly associated with suicidal intent, whereas in young males depression was associated with suicidal intent. This highlights the importance of all professionals being aware of gendered factors when assessing risk and developing treatment programmes for young people who are at risk of committing suicide as a result of depression.

Conclusion

It is evident as Hazell (2004) suggests that depression in children is on the increase and that children are showing signs of depression at a younger age. This has major implications for future CAMHS provision with regard to diagnosis, treatment and support. Care provision is currently provided by a variety of multidisciplinary professionals within the CAMHS teams, which require skills in a variety of psychological approaches including cognitive behavioural therapy (CBT) and psychotherapy and in some circumstances family therapy. This highlights the importance of the role of professionals, teachers and the family when providing appropriate services for children and young people with depression. It is common for young people to be admitted to hospital following self-harm. There are a variety of factors identified by Hawton *et al.* (2002) that cause young people to self-harm. These include self-harm by family members or peers, low self-esteem, depression, anxiety and drug misuse. Knowledge and understanding of these key factors is essential in helping to prevent self-harm in young people.

Hazell (2004) indicates that most people who have suffered from depression will have had their first episode before the age of 20 years. This demonstrates how depression can begin at a very early age affecting people throughout the lifespan. Shocket and Ham (2004) advocated implementing universal school-based approaches to help prevent depression in adolescents. However, it may be equally effective to promote mental health through peer education. This can be achieved by discussing mental health issues as part of the school curriculum. This would also help to reduce the stigma of mental illness. It is clear that the experience of having an illness such as depression will affect a young person's quality of life and will require significant changes to be made in order to cope with future life events. These young people can be enabled and empowered to cope with depression with support from parents, peers, teachers, nurses, doctors and other professionals.

Reflection and discussion

What factors need to be considered when suspecting depression in children?

Depression will be diagnosed if the child experiences a combination of the following symptoms over a 2-week period:

- *Feeling depressed most of the day, every day*
- *Loss of interest in most activities*
- *Weight loss or weight gain and appetite changes*
- *Inability to sleep or requiring too much sleep*
- *Feeling restless or sluggish*
- *Lack of energy and tiredness*
- *Feeling worthless or guilty*
- *Inability to concentrate or make decisions*
- *Thoughts about suicide or death*

What other factors need to be considered?

- *A family history of depression*
- *Conflict within the family setting*
- *Previous depressive occurrences*
- *Poor academic performance*
- *Anxiety disorders*
- *Substance abuse*
- *Physical, emotional or sexual abuse*
- *Alcohol abuse*

Discuss appropriate treatments for depressed children and young people.
Reflect on the impact of substance abuse in children and young people and the impact upon their mental health.
Give examples of self-harming behaviour

- *Excessive substance abuse*
- *Cutting skin*
- *Swallowing small amounts of toxic substances*
- *Burning or scalding*
- *Banging and scratching*
- *Pulling out own hair*

Describe the risk factors associated with suicide

- *Family history of suicide*
- *Child abuse*
- *Parental divorce*
- *Access to fatal methods of suicide*
- *Previous suicidal attempts*
- *History of mental disorder*
- *Feelings of hopelessness*
- *Physical illness*
- *Isolation*
- *Impulsive behaviour*

References

Bancilia, D. & Mittlemore, M. (May 2005). Specificity in the relationships between stressors and depressed mood adolescents. *Journal of Mental Health Promotion, 7*(2), 4–14.

Beautrais, A.L., Joyce, P.R. & Mulder, R.T. (September 1996). Risk factors for serious suicide attempts among youths aged 13 through 24 years. *Journal of the American Academy of Child and Adolescent Psychiatry, 35*(9), 1174–1182.

Birmaher, B. & Alexon, A. (1998). Depression disorders in children and adolescents. In: Kagan, J. (ed) *Gale Encyclopaedia of Childhood and Adolescence.* Farmington Hills: M.I. Gale Group.

Birmaher, B., Ryan, N.D., Williamson, D.E., Brent, D.A., Kaufman, J., Dahl, R., Ronald, E., Perel, J., Nelson, J. & Nelson, B. (November 1996). Childhood and adolescent depression: A review of ten past ten years. Part 1. *Journal of the American Academy of Child and Adolescent Psychiatry, 35*(11), 1427–1439.

Bradge, D., Campbell-Grossman, C. & Dunkel, J. (1995). Psychological correlates of adolescent depression. *Journal of Child and Adolescent Psychiatric Nursing, 8,* 23–30.

Bray, J.W., Zarkin, G.A., Ringwalt, C. & Qi, J. (2000). The relationship between marijuana initiation and dropping out of high school. *Health Economics, 9,* 9–18.

Brook, J.S., Whiteman, M., Finch, S. & Cohen, P. (2000). Longitudinally foretelling drug use in the late twenties: Adolescent personality and social environmental antecedents. *Journal of Genetic Psychology, 161,* 37–51.

Burt, V.K. & Stein, K. (2002). Epidemiology of depression throughout the female lifecycle. *Journal of Clinical Psychiatry, 63,* 9–15.

Bywaters, P. & Rolfe, A. (2002). *Look Beyond the Scars: Understanding and Responding to Self Injury and Self Harm.* London: NCH and Centre for Social Justice.

Chassin, L., Pitts, S.C. & Prost, J. (2002). Binge drinking trajectories from adolescence to emerging adulthood in a high risk sample: Predictors and substance abuse outcomes. *Journal of Clinical Child Psychology, 70,* 67–78.

Chen, K., Kandel, D.B. & Davies, M. (1997). Relationships between frequency and quantity of marijuana use and last year proxy dependence among adolescence and adults in the United States. *Drug Alcohol Dependency, 46,* 53–67.

Choi, H. (2002). Understanding adolescent depression in ethno cultural context. *Advances in Nursing Science, 25,* 71–85.

Christie, K.A., Burke, J.D., Regier, D.A., Rae, D.S., Boyd, J.H. & Locke, B.Z. (1988). Epidemiologic evidence for early onset of mental disorders and higher risk of drug abuse in young adults. *American Journal Psychiatry, 145,* 971–975.

Clark, D.B., Parker, A.M. & Lynch, K.G. (1999). Psychopathology, substance use and substance related problems. *Journal Clinical Child Psychology, 28,* 333–341.

Degenhardt, L., Hall, W. & Lynsky, L. (November 2003). Exploring the association between cannabis use and depression. *Addiction, 98*(11), 1493–1504.

Dennis, M., Babor, T.F., Roebuck, M.C. & Donaldson, J. (2002). Changing the focus: The case for recognizing and treating cannabis use disorders. *Addiction, 97*(Suppl 1), 4–15.

Ellis, P. (2004). Royal Australian and New Zealand College of psychiatrists clinical practice guidelines for depression. *Australian and New Zealand Journal of Psychiatry, 38,* 389–407.

Emslie, G.J., Heiligenstein, J.H., Wagner, K.D., Hoog, S.L., Ernest, D.E., Brown, E., Nilsson, M. & Jacobson, J. (October 2002). Fluoxetine for acute treatment of depression in children and adolescents: A placebo controlled, randomized clinical trial. *Journal of the American Academy of Child and Adolescent Psychiatry, 41*(10), 1205–1215..

Fergusson, D.M., Horwood, L.J. & Beautrais, A.L. (2003). Cannabis and educational achievement. Research report. *Addiction, 98*(12), 1681–1692.

Hankin, B.L. & Abramson, L.Y. (2001). Development of gender differences in depression: An elaborative cognitive vulnerability transactional stress theory. *Psychological Bulletin, 127,* 773–796.

Harrington, R., Whittacker, J., Shoebridge, P. & Campbell, F. (1998). Systematic review of efficacy of cognitive behavior therapies in children and adolescent depressive disorder. *BMJ*, *316*, 1359–1363.

Harrison, P.A. & Narayan, G. (2003). Differences in behavior, psychological factors and environmental factors associated with participation in school sports and other activities in adolescence. *Journal School Health*, *73*, 113–120.

Hawkins, J.D., Catalano, R.F. & Miller, J.Y. (1992). Risk and protective factors for alcohol and other drug problems in adolescence and early adulthood: Implications for substance abuse prevention. *Psychology Bulletin*, *112*, 64–105.

Hawton, K. (16 April 2005). Suicide and deliberate self harm in young people. Clinical review. *BMJ*, *330*, 891–894.

Hawton, K., Hall, S., Simkin, S., Bale, L., Bond, A., Codd, S. & Stewat, A. (November 2003). Deliberate self harm in adolescents: A study of characteristics and trends in Oxford, 1990–2000. *Journal of Child Psychology and Psychiatry*, *44*(8), 1191–1198.

Hawton, K., Rodham, K., Evans, E. & Weathrall, R. (2002). Deliberate self harm in adolescents: Self report survey in schools in England. *BMJ*, *325*, 1207–1211.

Hazell, P. (2004). Depression. In: David, T. (ed) *Recent Advances in Pediatrics*. London: Royal Society of Medicine, pp. 217–229.

Hazell, P.O., Connell, D., Heathcote, D., Roberson, J. & Henry, D. (1995). Efficacy of tricyclic drugs in treating child and adolescent depression: A meta-analysis. *BMJ*, *310*, 897–901.

Hazell, P.O., Connoll, D., Heathcote, D. & Henry, D. (2003). Tricyclic drugs for depression in children and adolescents. *Cochrane Database Systematic Review*, (4), CD002317.

Jellineck, M.S. & Snyder, J.B. (1998). Depression and suicide in children and adolescence. *Pediatric Review*, *19*, 255–264.

Johnston, L.D., O'Malley, P.M., Bachman, J.G., Jerald, G. & Schulenberg, J.E. (2004). *Monitoring the Future: National Survey Results on Adolescent Drug Use: Overview and Key Findings*. Bethesda, MD: National Institute of Health. US Department of Health and Human Services.

Kaminer, Y., Burleson, J.A., Blitz, C., Sussman, J.M. & Rounsaville, B.J. (November 1998). Psychotherapies for adolescent substance abusers: A pilot study. *Journal of Nervous and Mental Disease*, *186*(11), 684–690.

Kanner, S., Hamrin, V. & Grey, M. (2003). Depression in adolescents with diabetes. *Journal of Child and Adolescent Psychiatric and Mental Health Nursing*, *16*, 15–24.

Kovacs, M., Akiskal, H.S., Gatsonis, C. & Parrone, P.L. (1994). Childhood onset dysthymic disorder. Clinical features and prospective naturalistic outcome. *Archives of General Psychiatry*, *51*, 365–374.

Manson, S.M. (1995). Culture and major depression. Current challenges in the diagnosis of mood disorders. *Psychiatric Clinics of North America*, *18*, 487–501.

Mental Health Foundation (May 2003). *Deliberate Self Harm Among Children and Young People*. London: MHF.

Ministry of Health (2004). *Review of Prescribing SSRI Antidepressants to Young People*. Wellington: Ministry of Health.

Monshouwer, K., Van Dorsselaer, S., Verdurmen, J., Ter Bogt, T., Graaf, R. & Vollebergh, W. (2006). Cannabis use and mental health in secondary school children. Findings from a Dutch survey. *The British Journal of Psychiatry*, *188*, 148–153.

National Institute of Mental Health (2001). *Eating Disorders. Facts about Eating Disorders and the Search for Solutions*. Bethesda, MD: National Institute of Mental Health. Available at www.nimh.nih.gov/publicat/eatingdisorders.cfm. Accessed 26 November 2006.

National Statistics (2004). Available at www.statistics.gov.uk. Accessed 25 May 2007.

National Institute of Clinical Excellence (NICE) (2002). *Self Harm: The Short-term Physical and Psychological Management and Secondary Prevention of Self-Harm in Primary and Secondary Care*. London: NICE. First consultation.

National Institute of Clinical Excellence (NICE). (September 2005). *Depression in Children and Young People: Identification and Management in Primary, Community and Secondary Care*. Clinical Guideline 28. Available at www.nice.org.uk/CGO28. Accessed 11 July 2006.

NT net (2006). Available at www.nursingtimes.net/behindtheheadlines. Accessed 26 September 2006.

Olsson, G. & Von Knorring, A.L. (1997). Becks depression inventory as a screening instrument for adolescent depression in Sweden: Gender differences. *Acta Psychiatrica Scandinavica, 95*, 277–282.

Overholser, J.C., Freiheit, S.R. & DiPhillipo, J.M. (May 1997). Emotional distress and substance abuse as risk factors for suicide attempts. *Canadian Journal of Psychiatry, 42*(4), 402–408.

Patton, G.C., Coffey, C., Carlin, J.B., Degenhardt, L., Lynsky, M. & Hall, W. (2002). Cannabis use and mental health in young people: Cohort study. *BMJ, 325*, 1195–1198.

Pompili, M., Mancillelli, I., Girardi, P., Ruberto, A. & Tatatelli, R. (2004). Suicide in anorexia nervosa: A meta analysis. *International Journal of Eating Disorders, 36*(1), 99–103.

Possel, P. (2005). Strategies from prevention of depression in adolescents. *Journal of Indian Association for Child and Adolescent Mental Health, 1*, 37–46.

Pullen, L.M., Modrein McCarthy, M.A. & Graf, E.V. (2000). Adolescent depression: Important facts that matter. *Journal of Child and Adolescent Psychiatric Nursing, 3*, 69–75.

Purvis, D., Robinson, E., Merry, S. & Watson, P. (2006). Acne, anxiety, depression and suicide in teenagers: A cross-sectional survey of New Zealand secondary school students. *Journal of Pediatrics and Child Health, 42*(12), 793.

Puskar, K.R., Tusaie-Mumford, K., Sereika, S.M. & Lamb, J. (1999). Screening and predicting adolescent depressive symptoms in rural settings. *Archives of Psychiatric Nursing, 13*, 3–11.

Ramchandani, P. (January 2004). Treatment of major depressive disorder in children and adolescents [Editorial]. *BMJ, 328*, 3–4.

Rey, J.M., Sawyer, M.G., Raphael, B., Paton, G.C. & Lynskey, M. (2002). Mental health of teenagers who use cannabis. Results of an Australian Survey. *British Journal of Psychiatry, 180*, 216–221.

Richardson, C. (2004). Self harm: Understanding the causes and treatment options. *Nursing Times, 100*(15), 24–25.

Roberts, C., Kane, R. & Bishop, B. (August 2004). The prevention of depressive symptoms in rural school children: A follow up study. *Journal of Mental Health Promotion, 6*(3).

Royal College of Psychiatrists (1999). *Mental Health and Growing Up: Deliberate Self Harm in Young People*. London: Royal College of Psychiatrists.

Royal College of Psychiatrists (2002). *Let Wisdom Guide. Men and Depression*. London: Royal College of Psychiatrists. Available at www.rcpsych.ac.uk. Accessed 21 March 2007.

Rutter, M. & Quinton, D. (1984). Parental psychiatric disorder: Effects on children. *Psychological Medicine, 14*, 853–880.

Samaritans and Centre for Suicide Oxford University (2002). *Youth and Self Harm: Perspectives*. London: Samaritans.

Shocket, I.M. & Ham, D. (August 2004). Universal school based approaches to preventing adolescent depression: Past findings and future directions of the resourceful adolescent programme. *Journal of Mental Health Promotion, 6*(3).

Stein, D., Orbach, I. & Shani, M. (2003). Suicidal tendencies and body image and experience in anorexia nervosa and suicidal female adolescent inpatients. *Psychotherapy and Psychosomatics, 72*(1), 16–25.

Sung, S.E. & Kirchner, J.T. (2000). Depression in children and adolescence. *American Family Physician, 62*, 2297–2308, 2311–2312.

United Kingdom Committee on Safety of Medicines (2004). *Selective Serotonin Reuptake Inhibitor (SSRI) Antidepressants.* Findings of the Committee on Safety of Medicines Working Group. London: UK Committee on Safety of Medicines.

United States Federal Drug and Food Administration (2004). *Public Health Advisory: Suicidality in Children and Adolescents Being Treated with Antidepressants.* Rockville, MD: US Federal Drug and Food Administration.

Van de Bree, M.B.M. & Pickworth, W.B. (2005). Risk factors predicting changes in marijuana involvement in teenagers. *Archives of General Psychiatry, 62*(3), 311–319.

Walsh, L. (2007a). Caring for patients who experience hallucinations. *Nursing Times, 103*(21), 28–29.

Walsh, L. (2007b). Caring for patients who have eating disorders. *Nursing Times, 103*(28), 28–29.

Waslick, B., Schoenholz, D. & Pizarro, R. (2003). Diagnosis and treatment of chronic depression in children and adolescence. *Journal of Psychiatric Practice, 9*, 354–366.

Weist, M.D., Rubin, M., Moore, E., Adelsheim, S. & Wrobel, G. (February 2007). Mental health screening in schools. *Journal of School Health, 77*(2), 53.

Whetstone, L.M., Morrissey, S.L. & Cummings, D.M. (2007). Children at risk: The association between perceived weight status and suicidal thoughts and attempts in middle school youth. *Journal of School Health, 77*(2), 59–66.

Whittington, C.J., Kendall, T., Fonagy, P., Cottrell, D., Cotgrove, A. & Boddington, E. (April 2004). Selective serotonin reuptake inhibitors in childhood depression: Systematic review of published versus unpublished data. *The Lancet, 363*(9418), 1335.

Wu, L.T., Pilowsky, D.J. & William, E. (April 2005). High prevalence of substance use disorders among adolescents who use marijuana and inhalants. *Drug and Alcohol Dependence, 78*(1), 23–32.

Chapter 3
Depression throughout the adult female life cycle

Introduction

Depression affects females throughout the life cycle and can occur due to biological, hormonal and psychosocial factors. These lifespan hormonal changes occur after puberty, during pregnancy, following childbirth during the postpartum and during the menopause. As a consequence of these factors, women are more likely to be diagnosed with depression than men.

There is also evidence to suggest that women are more likely to be diagnosed with depression at an earlier age. Burt and Stein (2002) found that females experienced first onset major depression between early adolescence and their mid-fifties. Their findings demonstrated that women had a greater chance of being depressed, compared to men, and that women were 1.7–2.7 times more likely to have depression than men.

Burt and Stein (2002) highlighted that depression could occur in young females and recognized that puberty could increase the risk of depression in young women. This was supported by previous research undertaken by Angold *et al.* (1999). Angold *et al.* (1999) acknowledged that throughout their reproductive years, women were more likely than men to suffer from depression; however, the prevalence was evident only after puberty. This questioned whether changes in hormonal levels at puberty caused depression in girls. The findings of this study concluded that the main causes of depression in young women were due to changes in hormone levels, particularly androgen and oestrogen, level rather than puberty itself. This supports the view that depression can be caused through reproductive-related hormonal changes, which is evident in some young women who complain of both physical and emotional premenstrual symptoms.

Women may also suffer from depression during pregnancy. Whilst pregnancy does not necessarily cause depression, pregnant women with a history of depression are more likely to relapse due to a reluctance to take antidepressant medication. This is supported by Macqueen and Chokka (2004) who highlighted the implications of treating and managing depression in women. They found that despite many women being reluctant to take medication during pregnancy, the effectiveness of taking antidepressant treatment far outweighed the consequences of untreated depression upon both the woman and child.

This demonstrates the important role of general practitioners (GPs), nurses, midwives, health visitors, mental health practitioners and other health professionals when educating pregnant women and their families. It also highlights the importance of considering the risks of managing and treating depression in pregnant women and empowering women to make decisions based on the best evidence and guidelines available.

However, every pregnant woman must be considered individually as there may be a variety of factors or issues influencing their decision not to take antidepressants. Nonacs and Cohen (2006) advise that further data is required on both pharmacological and non-pharmacological treatments and that currently the doctor must weigh up the risks of various treatment options in association with the patients' wishes. NICE (2007), advocates that current advice must be given on the basis of evidence-based practice and practice guidelines.

Following childbirth, there is increased risk of depression due to hormonal changes in the postpartum period. During this time, other factors such as breast-feeding may influence a mother's decision not to take antidepressants. Further discussion will need to be undertaken and decisions made in collaboration with new mothers and health professionals to promote the health of the mother and limit any risks to the baby.

Even though depression in women is more apparent during the childbearing years, Kornstein (2001) stated that when treating depression in middle-aged and elderly women, the influence of both the menopause and hormone replacement therapy must be considered. Gender-specific considerations need to be considered when dealing with depression in women. Sagud *et al.* (2002) highlighted the need for a gender-specific approach when treating and managing depression due to the influence of the menstrual cycle.

Noble (2005) identified both biological and psychological causes which predispose women to depression. These included hormonal changes, role stress, victimization and disadvantaged social status. Noble (2005) highlighted that women were also more likely to suffer from stress-induced depression and seasonal affective disorder (SAD). Noble (2005) also recognized that other reproductive events such as miscarriage, infertility, hormone replacement therapy and taking oral contraceptives can also cause depression in women. Thus, it is important to consider both biological and psychological factors in relation to depression during the female life cycle.

Premenstrual syndrome and premenstrual dysphoric disorder

Despite the occurrence of premenstrual symptoms in many women causing anxiety and changes in mood, historically, there was little interest from the medical profession in diagnosing the condition. The main reason being lack of criteria to formally diagnose the condition. Thus, many women continued to suffer from mood disorders resulting in potential social problems without any support or help.

Limosin and Ades (2001) suggested that it was after the 1983 National Institute of Mental Health Conference in America that criteria was finally developed to undertake daily assessment of symptoms experienced by women. Following on from this in 1987, the American Psychiatric Association in the DSM-III-R introduced the late luteal phase dysphoric disorder diagnosis. This was then diagnosed by the DSM-IV as premenstrual dysphoric disorder (PMDD) in 1994. Limosin and Ades (2001) stated that avoidance of social activities and the need for medical care were important criteria when diagnosing PMDD. They found that epidemiological studies demonstrated a positive correlation between a diagnosis of major depression and premenstrual dysphoric symptoms. Thus, when assessing each individual woman, it was important to understand their individual personal history and any specific psychosocial factors. Noble (2005) recognized that depression in women may develop during different phases of the reproductive cycle.

The GP or practice nurse may be the first port of call for women who may be accessing primary care services with children or family members. Thus, it is important for health professionals within primary care to recognize the signs and symptoms of depression in women.

Graze *et al.* (1990) undertook a study to assess whether premenstrual changes were likely to be considered as risk factors for future major depressive disorder. They conducted a follow-up study of 36 women who had volunteered for previous menstrual cycle studies. The study findings showed that the assessment of premenstrual depression had validity in identifying women at risk of future major depressive disorder. This demonstrates the importance of undertaking research studies to help predict the likelihood of future depression in women.

Diagnosis of premenstrual syndrome and premenstrual dysphoric disorder

It is important to obtain a correct diagnosis and appropriate treatment as premenstrual syndrome (PMS) causes distress for many women. To diagnose the chronic PMDD which is a severe form of PMS, the DSM-IV requires at least five specified symptoms. Interestingly, the ICD-10 requires only one distressing symptom to diagnose PMS. Freeman (2003) recognized that many women who required treatment fell between these two diagnostic approaches and advocated that a standard diagnostic criterion for clinically significant PMS was required.

Stearns (2001) stated that PMS is a complex cluster of symptoms occurring 7–14 days before menses and ends 1–2 days after menses. Thus to diagnose PMS, there is a need to determine the timing of symptoms in relation to the menses. A meaningful change between the severity of pre- and postmenstrual symptoms and also clinically a difference in the severity of these symptoms needs to be seen.

Diagnosis of PMS requires subjective symptom reports from prospective daily diaries. Freeman (2003) highlighted the importance of recognizing the broad range of symptoms, pattern of symptoms and most important of all the severity of the symptoms. It is the severity of the symptoms that distinguishes the diagnosis of PMS from other normal menstrual cycle changes. Stearns (2001) found that true PMS only occurred during the luteal phase of the menstrual cycle but during the follicular phase the woman was symptom-free. These symptoms can be treated by changes in lifestyle which include a healthy diet, stress management, aerobic exercise, supportive coping strategies and cognitive behaviour therapy.

Because of the severity of symptoms and limited effect achieved by lifestyle changes, some women will require medical treatment. This would normally include antidepressants such as serotonin reuptake inhibitors (SSRIs), diuretics, gonadotrophin-releasing hormone antagonists and vitamin and mineral supplements.

As can be seen from relevant literature, PMS and PMDD remain complex disorders. Other factors such as cultural and social beliefs as well as mother–daughter relationships are important aspects to consider when determining and diagnosing this particular condition. Psychological aspects which include relationships with others can also have an impact upon the intensity of depression during a woman's lifetime. This demonstrates the importance of correct diagnosis, treatment and identification of support networks when women contact primary care services.

Depression in pregnancy

Depression is more prevalent in women between the ages of 18 and 44 years and is the most likely time when women become pregnant Stewart (2005). The perinatal period is defined by the DH (2002) as the time from conception to 24 months postpartum. Deater-Deckard (1998) suggested that this is a time when some women suffer from psychological distress and mental health problems.

Stewart (2006) undertook an analysis of maternal mortality. The Confidential Enquiries into Maternal Deaths (CEMDs) in the UK reported rates of maternal deaths as far back as 1952. This was not the case in other countries. The Fifth Report of the CEMDs (2001) highlighted that women from disadvantaged groups in society were more likely to die, also non-White ethnic groups were twice as likely to die as White women and that more deaths were caused by pre-existing conditions which were increased due to pregnancy. What was very significant was that more than 40 maternal deaths occurred as a result of suicide or violence or accidental drug overdose. After thromboembolism and cardiac arrest, suicide was the third highest cause of maternal death in the UK. Stewart (2005) recognized that depression and suicide during pregnancy and the postpartum period ranged from 10 to 20%. This has major implications for public health and primary care services and needs to be highlighted to all doctors and health care practitioners dealing with pregnant women and their families.

Depression during pregnancy can influence the weight of the baby at birth. A study was undertaken by Rahman *et al.* (2007) which demonstrated that there was an association between antenatal depression and low birth weight in a developing country in South Asia. Stress and anxiety during pregnancy can also cause low birth weight in developed countries as shown by Hoffman and Hatch (2000); however in developing countries, Rahman *et al.* (2003) identified that the incidences were much higher. They found that up to 25% of mothers in South Asia suffered from depressive disorder during the third trimester of pregnancy. UNICEF and WHO (2004) also reported that the occurrence of low birth weight babies were four times more likely in underdeveloped countries. Stewart (2005) found that depressed women suffered from perturbed hypothalamus pituitary axis and beta-endorphin levels resulting in low birth weight and slow foetal development. These findings are similar to earlier research by Walker *et al.* (2000) who found that low birth weight could cause long-term health problems such as growth retardation and poor intellectual development in children and young people.

This is supported by Gale and Martyn (2004) who suggested that low birth weight babies were at an increased risk of developing depression during adolescence. These studies demonstrate the importance of diagnosing and treating depression during pregnancy and also preventing depression and physical illness in the children delivered to these women.

Feldman *et al.* (2000) demonstrated that by improving the mental health and social support of depressed women during the antenatal period the health of their babies improved. Stewart (2005) was concerned that babies born to depressed women were more likely to have poorer physical and psychological care. This could also have negative effects upon their relationships with their partners. It can also have implications upon the partner's health and well-being as shown by George (1996) who found that half of the male partners of women with postnatal depression showed signs of depression or had been diagnosed with depression themselves.

Johansson *et al.* (2000) undertook a prospective study in a North Staffordshire maternity hospital in relation to pregnancy-associated depression. The study aimed to establish the frequency of depression during pregnancy and during the postnatal period in relation to marital disharmony. The study showed a significant association between antenatal and postnatal depression. In the study, 7 out of 31 women who were depressed in the postnatal period had also been depressed during the antenatal period. Marital disharmony was strongly associated with depression in women during both antenatal and postnatal periods. Johansson *et al.* (2000) strongly recommended that the Edinburgh Postnatal Depression Scale (EPNDS) be used during pregnancy to assess for depression and to help identify depression in pregnant women.

This would help GPs to diagnose the condition. Evidence from Johansson *et al.*'s (2000) research study showed that only 5 of the 41 women with antenatal depression and 8 out of the 31 women with postnatal depression had been diagnosed by their GP with depression. To aid their diagnosis, GPs could ask pregnant women routine questions about maternal depression, violence in the home and substance misuse. This would enable doctors, midwives, health visitors and nurses to have a holistic view about family life as well as asking questions about nutrition and sleep. However, sleep and nutrition are important and it must be acknowledged that depressed pregnant women are less likely to attend antenatal clinics and are more likely to suffer from sleep problems and less likely to eat well. The CEMD (2001) highlighted that maternal mental illness was more common than most conditions that were routinely asked about during pregnancy and during the postpartum period.

Anxiety and depression during pregnancy

Anxiety and depression are often associated with each other and experienced by many pregnant women. NICE (2004a) suggests, providing psychosocial intervention for women with symptoms of anxiety or depression who do not meet the criteria for a formal diagnosis, but where symptoms interfere with their personal and social functioning. This would include individual psychotherapy, cognitive behaviour therapy and social support throughout the pregnancy.

This is an important area for future investigation and research. Heron *et al.* (2004) undertook a community study of 8323 pregnant women in England. The study identified that 11% of the women had anxiety and 13% suffered from depression during pregnancy, with 13% having both anxiety and postnatal depression. Many of the women with postnatal depression and anxiety had suffered with both during the antenatal period.

Whooley *et al.* (1997) suggested that all pregnant women should be asked two probing questions recommended by the American and Canadian Task Forces on preventative health care when assessing for depression. The questions are as follows:

Over the past 2 weeks, have you felt down, depressed or helpless?
Over the past 2 weeks, have you felt little interest or pleasure in doing things?

NICE guidelines (2007) suggest that during a pregnant woman's first contact with primary care services, whether it is by the GP, midwife or other health professional, she should be asked if she has experienced these feelings during the past month. Responses to these two questions will help doctors and other health professionals to predict depression in antenatal and postnatal women. Women's responses can then be explored in more detail throughout the assessment. Stewart (2005) identified that depression during pregnancy was the strongest predictor for postnatal depression. The terms postnatal depression or postpartum depression are used to discuss depression following childbirth.

Postpartum depression

Beck (2001) estimated that about 13% of women experienced postpartum depression. The Royal College of Psychiatrists (2004) stated that about one in every ten women will suffer from postnatal depression within a month after giving birth or up to 6 months after having a baby.

This highlights the importance for doctors, nurses and other primary care professionals in understanding both the symptoms and the reasons why women suffer with postnatal depression.

There are a variety of symptoms experienced by women with postnatal depression which include:

- Feeling depressed
- Feeling irritable
- Feeling tired
- Inability to sleep
- Not wanting to eat
- Inability to cope
- Anxiety

It is not surprising that many new mothers who do not have depression have similar feelings after giving birth, experiencing hormonal fluctuations and trying to cope with a new baby. It is usual for many women to experience baby blues after having a baby. Dennis and Creedy (2006) suggested that the baby blues were experienced by 50–80% of women usually occurring between 2 and 5 days after the birth. However, it is important to distinguish between the experience of normal baby blues which many women suffer from in the early days after birth and postnatal depression, which occurs usually after a month of giving birth. Gale and Harlow (2003) undertook a review of the clinical and epidemiological factors that influenced postpartum mood disorders. It is evident that women are more likely to suffer with postnatal depression if they have had stressful events in their lives and if they have experienced the following:

- Experienced a number of stresses over a short period of time
- Had depression/postnatal depression previously
- Had a premature or very ill baby
- Do not have a supportive partner
- Lost their mother as a child
- Been recently bereaved
- Having relationship problems
- Having financial problems
- Experiencing housing worries
    (Adapted from the Royal College of Psychiatrists, 2004).

There are a number of risk factors which doctors and health professionals can recognize when caring for women in the postpartum.

Beck (2001) undertook a meta-analysis of 84 studies published in the 1990s, looking into the relationship between postpartum depression and risk factors. Thirteen risk factors were identified with varying degrees of significance. The most likely predictors for postpartum depression were as follows:

- Prenatal depression
- Self-esteem
- Childcare stress
- Prenatal anxiety
- Life stress
- Social support
- Marital relationship
- History of previous depression
- Infant temperament
- Maternity blues
- Marital status
- Socio-economic status
- Unplanned/unwanted pregnancy

Roberston *et al.* (2004) undertook a synthesis of literature which considered the antenatal risk factors that were likely to cause postpartum depression. The findings were from a meta-analysis of 14 000 subjects and further studies of 10 000 additional subjects. They found that the following were most likely to predict postpartum depression:

- Depression during pregnancy
- Anxiety during pregnancy
- Low levels of social support
- Previous history of depression
- Stressful events during antenatal period and early puerperium

Dennis and Creedy (2006) recognized similar predictors for postnatal depression focusing upon feelings of low self-esteem, inability to cope, lack of confidence, anxiety, guilt and unrealistic expectations of motherhood. Beck's (2001) study findings also confirmed the findings from earlier studies; however, they also identified the following four new predictors of postpartum depression, which were self-esteem, marital status, socio-economic status and unplanned/unwanted pregnancy. Much of this research was undertaken in the UK. Recently, NICE (2007) developed guidelines for primary care professionals to assist with the prediction of postnatal depression. This provides the evidence base for care provided by health professionals.

Trans-cultural studies

Trans-cultural studies have been undertaken to establish whether postnatal depression is apparent in other countries and amongst other cultures.

Oates *et al.* (2004) undertook research at 15 centres across 11 different countries to establish whether postnatal depression was recognized universally. It may be apparent to some professionals that during pregnancy, women may be exposed to a variety of different cultural influences. This has already become evident as part of a multicultural society in the UK.

Oates *et al.* (2004) research study had three groups of participants, which used focus groups and interviews as methods of data collection. Focus groups were used with new mothers, interviews were undertaken with fathers and grand-fathers and also with health professionals. Participants from all the centres described feelings of morbid unhappiness following childbirth which were com-parable with experiences of postnatal depression in the UK. However, not all of the participants believed that interventions by health professionals were the most effective way to treat these feelings. This demonstrates a cultural difference of opinion compared to the UK where health professionals would see diagnosis of postnatal depression and intervention as the best way to support mothers and families. Asten *et al.* (2004) also undertook research into trans-cultural issues in relation to postnatal depression. Roberston *et al.* (2004) stated the importance of using appropriate assessment tools which recognized postpartum depression in women from different cultures.

The incidence of postnatal depression has been linked with the birth expe-rience. Parker (2004) found that if the birth was traumatic, there was more likelihood of the mother having postnatal depression. Gale and Harlow (2003) suggested that epidemiological factors could also influence the incidence of postnatal depression, i.e. poverty, social class and low income. This was also highlighted by Wickberg and Hwang (1997) who suggested that single female parents were more likely to suffer from postnatal depression. Roberston *et al.* (2004) undertook a literature review which also acknowledged the importance of examining risk factors in women from lower socio-economic backgrounds and examining risk factors relevant to teenage mothers. Doctors, midwives and health visitors need to undertake appropriate assessments to ensure that post-natal depression is recognized and treated appropriately.

Predicting risk of postnatal depression

A variety of assessment tools have been used to predict postnatal depression. These include the Beck Depression Inventory (Beck *et al.*, 1961), the reviewed Beck Depression Inventory referred to as BD1-II (Beck, 1996), the Postpartum Depression Screening Scale known as the PDSS (Beck & Gable, 2000) and the EPNDS (Cox *et al.*, 1987). The most commonly used assessment tool is the EPNDS. The questionnaire requires the mother to select the response nearest to how she has felt during the past 7 days (Cox *et al.* 1987).

Gaskin and James (2006) argued that this tool may need to be used with caution when the mother has language or literacy problems or is from a dif-ferent culture. The NICE (2006) guideline advocates that postnatal depression requires a professional diagnosis and that the EPNDS is only part of the screen-ing programme and should not be used in isolation. The NICE (2007) clinical management and service guideline makes specific recommendations regarding the identification, treatment and management of mental health disorders. The detection and management of postnatal depression is essential and provides opportunity for doctors, midwives, health visitors and nurses to assess women during routine antenatal and postnatal visits. NICE (2007) has estimated that about 1 in 7 women will experience a mental health disorder either during the antenatal or postnatal period.

Russell (2006) suggested that some mothers may be reluctant to admit that they have depression as it may make them feel inadequate, whilst other new mothers may feel that this is how they are supposed to feel after having a new baby. It is up to the health care professionals to identify the difference between normal reactions to childbirth and postnatal depression. Because of the stigma of mental illness, some women may be reluctant to seek help as they may fear being labelled with a diagnosis of mental illness. This was identified by Poole *et al.* (2006) who recognized that some mothers may be reluctant to be diagnosed with a mental illness. Some women may not feel able to discuss such personal feelings with health professionals. In fact, some women may find it difficult to discuss their feelings with their partner or close family members. This is why it is important for the family members to also be aware of the symptoms of postnatal depression as they may be able to persuade the woman to seek early intervention from the GP, midwife or health visitor.

Hall undertook a study in 2006 demonstrating that women believed that nobody would understand how they felt. This could be explored by primary care practitioners during antenatal preparation and during postnatal classes.

Pregnant women should be informed about the importance of sharing their feelings and experiences both during pregnancy and after the birth. Jomeen and Martin (2007) considered using the EPDS as a predictor of postnatal depression during the third trimester of pregnancy. However, due to the variability of the structure of the tool it was not considered a true predictor of postnatal depression during pregnancy.

Hanley (2006) highlighted the following risk factors for postnatal depression:

- Unstable or unsupportive relationships
- Previous history of depression including previous postnatal depression or clinical depression
- Anxiety during the pregnancy, concern about the well-being of the child
- History of sexual abuse
- Poor role models, particularly due to the absence of the mothers or poor parenting skills
- Obstetric intervention which involved difficult delivery or baby in special care

Postnatal depression can affect fathers and children. Thus, it is important to maintain communication and interaction with all family members.

Bloch *et al.*'s (2006) research looked at the risk factors for early postpartum depressive symptoms. They found that 6.8% of women had an EPNDS score of less than 10. Doctors, Midwives and Health Visitors need to aware that a history of mental illness including previous postpartum depression, PMDD and mood symptoms during the third trimester are closely associated with risk factors for early postpartum depression.

Puerperal psychosis

It is important to recognize puerperal psychosis and distinguish it from post-natal depression. Postnatal or postpartum depression is often used to describe mental illness following childbirth. However, there is another condition which Kumar (1990) suggested has different symptoms to postnatal depression. These symptoms include confusion, episodes of paranoid delusions and hallucina-tions, mainly auditory hallucinations, catatonic or stuporous states and mood disturbances.

Walsh (2007a) discussed the importance of understanding and caring for patients experiencing paranoia. Walsh (2007b) also discussed the care of pa-tients experiencing hallucinations. As highlighted earlier, these symptoms are different to the symptoms experienced by women with postnatal depression. Elvins and Theofrastous (1997) stated that puerperal psychosis affected less than 1% of mothers; however, it is a very incapacitating condition which usually requires hospitalization. Even though this condition occurs in some women in the postnatal period, puerperal psychosis is not classified by the WHO (1992) as a health-related problem. Neither is it identified by the American Psychiatric Association (1994) as a diagnosed mental disorder. However, the Royal College of Psychiatrists (2003) recognized that the condition occurred as a result of hor-monal changes at the end of pregnancy and at delivery. This may be one reason why postpartum depression and puerperal psychosis are often perceived to be the same condition. Even though hormones play a part in both conditions, they must be recognized as different conditions and treated differently.

Depression related to the menopause

Nicol-Smith (1996) undertook a critical review of the literature to assess if whether causal criteria could be used to determine whether the menopause caused depression. This was because depression increases significantly in women as they reach the menopause but decreases after the menopause has ended. Nicol-Smith (1996) reviewed 43 primary research articles and concluded that there was insufficient evidence at that time that the menopause caused depression. More recently, Freeman et al. (2004) undertook a prospective study over a 4-year period to determine whether there was an association between depression and the transition to the menopause. Blood samples were collected to detect hormone levels and structured interviews were undertaken to assess the general health status and behaviour of the 436 premenopausal female participants in the study. The women were assessed for major depression using the DSM-IV criteria. The findings from the study showed that depressive symptoms were more likely to be experienced during early and late transition to the menopause rather than pre- or postmenopause.

Freeman *et al.* (2004) concluded that a history of depression, severe pre-menstrual symptoms and poor sleep increased the chances of depression in menopausal women. Bosworth (2004) stated that despite many studies advocating that oestrogen therapy improves mood and cognition, evidence was not conclusive in advocating that oestrogens should be used to treat mild depressive symptoms associated with hot flushes, sleep disturbance or other symptoms. Bosworth (2004) concluded that antidepressant therapy was the only clinically effective treatment at the time.

It is important that health professionals can distinguish between depressed mood and depressive disorder. Most people experience depressed mood as feelings of sadness. Gath and Isles (1990) argued that depressive disorder is more serious and is shown by depressed mood, poor concentration, loss of interest, feelings of guilt and worthlessness, feelings of hopelessness, suicidal feelings, changes in appetite, sleep and sex drive.

Major international studies were undertaken in Sweden by Hallstrom and Samuelsson (1985), in Canada by Kaufert *et al.* (1998), in England by Gath *et al.* (1987) and in America by McKinley *et al.* (1987). They all concluded that the incidence of depression during the menopause was no more frequent than at any other times of a woman's life.

McKinley *et al.* (1972) stated that it was important to acknowledge the different stages in relation to the menopause which include premenopause, menopause and postmenopause. Premenopause or perimenopausal depression may be caused when a woman feels that she has lost her femininity as a result of her loss of fertility due to hormonal changes. However, a perimenopausal woman may also suffer from depression as a consequence of life events which are not related to the menopause. These life events would include death of parents or children leaving home. This is supported by McKinley *et al.* (1987) who considered the effect of social circumstances causing depression in middle-aged women. During the menopause, lack of oestrogen may have a biochemical effect causing the physical symptoms of hot flushes and sweats. Although this is not conclusive for all women, Gath *et al.* (1987) found that out of 500 women surveyed, there was an association between psychiatric symptoms and sweats and hot flushes. However, this does not prove a causal connection. With regard to treatment, it is important to ensure that the condition has been diagnosed correctly. Depressive disorder in perimenopausal women requires treatment with antidepressants and/or psychological therapies. Oestrogen as hormone replacement therapy may be given to relieve vasomotor symptoms. However, counselling may be the best way to deal with depressed mood as a result of life events.

Some women may not wish to take hormone replacement therapy as they may believe that there is an associated risk of causing breast cancer.

Genazzani *et al.* (2006) undertook the European Menopause Survey, which considered women's perceptions on the menopause and postmenopausal hormone therapy. Between December 2004 and January 2005, they interviewed 4201 postmenopausal women from seven European countries. The European study showed that the majority of women experienced climacteric symptoms. Their decision to comply with hormone therapy was based upon their perceived risk of breast cancer as a result of taking hormone therapy. This highlights again the importance of informing and educating patients about health risks and discussing the evidence and current guidelines.

Depression in the perimenopausal period is less likely to be associated with hormonal changes and more likely to be associated with the following risk factors:

- History of depressive disorders
- History of PMDD
- Environmental stress
- Poor physical health
                    (Robinson, 2001).

Learning disabilities and the menopause

Many women with learning disabilities have difficulty understanding and communicating their needs. This has implications for health professionals as they will need to provide additional support for these women during the menopause. Martin *et al.* (2003) identified that there is limited research into how the menopause affects women with learning disabilities, even though the menopause occurs earlier in women with learning disabilities and Downs's syndrome. They recognized that this also has implications when providing treatment as women with learning disabilities may not be given the choice or be empowered to make informed decisions about treatments available and as a result hormone replacement therapy may not be offered to them. Discussion throughout this chapter, highlights that it is not just the physical symptoms that women require support with, but of equal importance are the psychological symptoms. As a result, it may be even more difficult to diagnose depression in women with learning disabilities.

There are a variety of guidelines to help clinicians manage depression in women. The most relevant guidelines in the UK include: NICE (2007) guidelines related to antenatal and postnatal mental health, NICE (2004a) regarding the management of anxiety in adults in primary, secondary and community care and NICE (2004b) guidelines regarding the management of depression in primary and secondary care. It is important that women are given information in a way that they understand. It is also essential that health professionals build good relationships based on trust with women, their partners and families.

Depression can impact upon other members of the family and this must be considered when assessing the woman for depression.

Conclusion

As women are more likely to suffer from depression, the treatment of depression in women is a substantial public health concern. Altshuler *et al.* (2001) devised expert guidelines for the treatment of depression in women. The guidelines recommended that for the treatment of severe symptoms in all four depressive conditions in women, antidepressant medication, particularly SSRIs, alongside psychotherapy could be used. Further research was required and as a result NICE (2004b) developed guidelines on the management of depression in adults in primary, secondary and community care. NICE (2007) has also provided up-to-date guidelines and recommended treatment for antenatal and postnatal mental health. These guidelines provide appropriate direction for doctors and provide information for all health professionals and women about effective interventions for depression throughout the female life cycle.

This chapter has highlighted that women are twice as likely as men to suffer from depression after puberty, remaining constant until after the menopause. Kendler *et al.* (2004) recognized that abuse and neglect during childhood were also associated with depression in women. These could be predisposing factors to depression in adulthood. The DH (2002) acknowledged that women were very important members of the workforce in relation to caring for children and other dependents and that when a woman becomes ill, it can have major implications for both herself, her family and those she cares for. This demonstrates the impact of depression in women upon both family life and the economy.

Primary care practitioners must consider these wider implications when women of all ages across the lifespan seek their help and guidance for depression. This chapter has demonstrated that depression occurs throughout the female lifespan and requires appropriate diagnosis and intervention by members of the primary care team. This chapter has focused upon depressive conditions specific to women as highlighted by MacQueen and Chokka (2004). They include PMDD which is referred to as PMDD, depression in pregnancy, postpartum depression and depression related to the menopause.

Reflection and discussion

Discuss the importance of attaining a correct diagnosis for PMS and PMDD

- *PMS and PMDD have a major impact upon the lives of women.*
- *Epidemiological studies have shown a positive correlation between a diagnosis of major depression and premenstrual dysphoric symptoms.*

- *It is important to understand the individual personal history and any specific psychosocial factors.*

Why is it important to diagnose depression in pregnancy?

- *Depression is more prevalent in women between the ages of 18 and 44 years and is the most likely time when women become pregnant.*
- *Depression during pregnancy can influence the weight of the baby at birth.*
- *After thromboembolism and cardiac arrest, suicide was the third highest cause of maternal death in the UK.*

Why is it important to recognize postpartum depression?

- *One in every ten women will suffer from postnatal depression within a month after giving birth or up to 6 months after having a baby.*
- *Women are more likely to suffer with postnatal depression if they have had stressful events in their lives as for example,*

  Have experienced a number of stresses over a short period of time
  Have had depression/postnatal depression previously
  Have had a premature or very ill baby
  Do not have a supportive partner
  Have lost their mother as a child
  Have been recently bereaved
  Are having relationship problems
  Are having financial problems
  Are experiencing housing worries

Why is it important to consider depression during the menopause?

- *Depression increases significantly in women as they reach the menopause but decreases after the menopause has ended.*
- *A history of depression, severe premenstrual symptoms and poor sleep increases the chances of depression in menopausal women.*
- *It is important to acknowledge the different stages in relation to the menopause, which include premenopause, menopause and postmenopause.*
- *Premenopause or perimenopausal depression may be caused when a woman feels that she has lost her femininity as a result of her loss of fertility due to hormonal changes.*
- *Perimenopausal woman may also suffer from depression as a consequence of life events which are not related to the menopause.*
- *These life events would include death of parents or children leaving home.*

References

Altshuler, L.L., Cohen, L.S., Moline, M.L., Kahn, D.A., Carpenter, D. & Docherty, J.P. (2001). Treatment of depression in women: A summary of the Expert Consensus Guidelines. *Journal of Psychiatric Practice*, *7*(3), 185–208.

American Psychiatric Association (1987). *DSM-III-R Diagnostic and Statistical Manual.* Washington, DC: American Psychiatric Association.

American Psychiatric Association (1994). *Diagnostic and Statistical Manual of Mental Disorders.* Arlington, VA: APA.

Angold, A., Costello, E.J., Erkanli, A. & Worthman, C.M. (1999). Pubertal changes in hormone levels and depression in girls. *Psychological Medicine*, *29*(5), 1043–1053.

Asten, P., Marks, M.N. & Oates, M.R. (February 2004). Aims, measures, study sites and participant samples of the trans-cultural study of post natal depression. *British Journal Psychiatry*, *184*(46), s3–s9.

Beck, A.T., Ward, C.H., Mendelson, M., Mock, J. & Erbaugh, J. (1961). An inventory for measuring depression. *Archives of General Psychiatry*, *4*, 561–571.

Beck, C.T. (September–October 1996). A meta-analysis of predictors of postpartum depression. *Nursing Research*, *45*(5), 297–303.

Beck, C.T. (September–October 2001). Predictors of post partum depression: An update. *Nursing Research*, *50*(5), 275–285.

Beck, C.T. & Gable, R.K. (2000). Postpartum depression screening scale: Development and psychometric testing. *Nursing Research*, *49*, 272–282.

Bloch, M., Rotenberg, N., Koren, D. & Klein, E. (January–February 2006). Risk factors for early postpartum depressive symptoms. *General Hospital Psychiatry*, *28*(1), 3–8.

Bosworth, H.B. (2004). Commentary. *Evidence Based Mental Health*, *7*, 90.

Burt, V.K. & Stein, K. (2002). Epidemiology of depression throughout the female life cycle. *Journal of Clinical Psychiatry*, *63*(Suppl 7), 9–15.

Cox, J., Holden, J. & Sagovsky, R. (1987). Detection of post natal depression. *British Journal of Psychiatry*, *150*, 782–786.

Deater-Deckard, K. (1998). Family structure and depressive symptoms in men preceding and following the birth of a child. *American Journal of Psychiatry*, *155*, 818–823.

Dennis, C.L. & Creedy, D. (2006). Psychosocial and psychological interventions for preventing post partum depression. *Cochrane Database of Systematic Reviews*, *3*.

Department of Health (DH) (2002). *Women's Mental Health: Into the Mainstream, Strategic Development of Mental Health Care for Women.* London: DH.

Elvins, G. & Theofrastous, J. (1997). Post partum depression: A review of postpartum screening. *Primary Care Update for Obstetrics and Gynecology*, *4*(6), 24–26.

Feldman, P.J., Dunkel-Schetter, C., Sandman, C.A. & Wadhwa, P.D. (2000). Maternal social support predicts birth weight and fetal growth in human pregnancy. *Psychsomatic Medicine*, *62*, 715–725.

Freeman, E.W. (August 2003). Premenstrual syndrome and premenstrual dysphoricdisorder: Definitions and diagnosis. *Psychoneuroendocrinology*, *28*(Suppl 3), 25–37.

Freeman, E.W., Sammel, M.D. & Liu, L. (2004). Hormones and menopausal status as predictors of depression in women in transition to menopause. *Archives of General Psychiatry*, *61*, 62–70.

Gale, S. & Harlow, B.L. (December 2003). Post partum mood disorders: A review of clinical and epidemiological factors. *Journal of Psychosomatic Obstetrics and Gynaecology*, *24*(4), 257–266.

Gale, C.R. & Martyn, C.N. (2004). Birth weight and later risk of depression in a national birth cohort. *British Journal of Psychiatry, 184,* 28–33.

Gath, D. & Isles, S. (1990). Depression and the menopause. *BMJ, 300,* 1287–1288.

Gath, D., Osborne, M. & Bungay, G. (1987). Psychiatric disorder and psychological symptoms in middle aged women: A community survey. *BMJ, 294,* 213–218.

Gaskin, J. & James, H. (2006). Using the Edinburgh Postnatal Depression Scale with learning disabled mothers. *Community Practitioner, 79*(12), 392–396.

Genazzani, A.R., Schneider, H.P.G., Panay, N. & Nijland, E.A. (July 2006). The European Menopause Survey (2005): Women's perceptions on the menopause and postmenopausal hormone therapy. *Gynecological Endocrinology, 22*(7), 369–375.

George, M. (1996). Postnatal depression, relationships and men. *Mental Health Nursing, 16,* 16–19.

Graze, K.K., Nee, J. & Endicott, J. (1990). Premenstrual depression predicts future major depressive disorder. *Acta Psychiatrica Scandinavica, 81*(2), 201–205.

Hall, P. (2006). Mothers experiences of postnatal depression: An interpretative phenomenological analysis. *Community Practice, 79*(8), 256–260.

Hallstrom, T. & Samuelsson, S. (1985). Mental health in the climactereric. The longitudinal study of women in Gothenberg. *Acta Obstetricia Et Gynecologica Scandinavica, 130*(13), 8.

Hanley, J. (January 2006). The assessment and treatment of post natal depression. *Nursing Times, 102*(1), 24–26.

Heron, J., O'Connor, T.G., Evans, J., Golding, J. & Glover, G., for The ALSPAC Study Team. (2004). The course of anxiety and depression through pregnancy and the postpartum in a community sample. *Journal of Affective Disorder, 80*(1), 65–73.

Hoffman, S. & Hatch, M.C. (2000). Depressive symptomatology during pregnancy: Evidence for an association with decreased fetal growth in pregnancies of lower social class women. *Health Psychology, 19,* 53–543.

Johansson, R., Chapman, G., Murray, D., Johnson, I. & Cox, J. (June 2000). The North Staffordshire Maternity Hospital prospective study of pregnancy associated depression. *Journal of Psychosomatic Obstetrics and Gynaecology, 21*(2), 93–97.

Jomeen, J. & Martin, C.R. (May 2007). Replicability and stability of the multidimensional model of the Edinburgh Postnatal Depression Scale in late pregnancy. *Journal of Psychiatric and Mental Health Nursing, 14*(3), 319–324.

Kaufert, P., Boggs, P., Ettinger, B., Woods, N. & Utian, W. (1998). Women and menopause: Beliefs, attitudes and behaviours. The North American Menopause Society: Menopause Survey 1997. *Menopause, 5*(4), 197–202.

Kendler, K.S., Khun, J.W. & Prescott, C.A. (2004). Childhood sexual abuse, stressful life events and risk for major depression in women. *Psychological Medicine, 34*(8), 1475–1482.

Kornstein, S.G. (2001). The evaluation and management of depression in women across the lifespan. *Journal of Clinical Psychiatry, 62*(Suppl 24), 11–17.

Kumar, R. (1990). Childbirth and mental illness. *Triangle, 29*(2/3), 73–81.

Limosin, F. & Ades, J. (November–December 2001). Psychiatric and psychological aspects of premenstrual syndrome. *Encephale, 27*(6), 501–508.

MacQueen, G. & Chokka, P. (March 2004). Special issues in the management of depression in women. *Canadian Journal of Psychiatry, 49*(3, Suppl 1), 27S–40S.

Martin, D.M., Kakumani, S., Martin, M.S. & Cassidy, G. (March 2003). Learning disabilities and the menopause. *Journal of the British Menopause Society, 9*(1), 22–26.

McKinley, S., Jeffrey's, M. & Thompson, P. (1972). An investigation of age at menopause. *Journal of Biosciences, 4*, 161–173.

McKinley, J.B., McKinley, S.M. & Brambila, D. (1987). The relative contributions of endocrine changes and social circumstances to depression in middle aged women. *Journal of Health and Social Behaviour, 28*, 345–363.

National Institute for Health and Clinical Excellence (NICE) (2006). *Guidelines for Normal Post Natal Care.* Available at www.nice.org.uk. Accessed 1 August 2007.

NICE (2004a). *Management of Anxiety in Adults in Primary, Secondary and Community Care.* Clinical Guideline. London: NICE.

NICE (2004b). *Management of Depression in Primary and Secondary Care.* Clinical Guideline. London: NICE.

NICE (2007). *Antenatal and Postnatal Mental Health: Clinical Management and Service Guidance.* London: NICE.

Nicol-Smith, L. (November 1996). Causality, menopause, and depression: A critical review of the literature. *BMJ, 313*, 1229–1232.

Noble, R.E. (May 2005). Depression in women. *Metabolism, 54*(5, Suppl 1), 49–52.

Nonacs, R. & Cohen, L.S. (2006). Assessment and treatment of depression during pregnancy: An update. *Journal of Obstetrics and Gynaecology, 107*, 798–806.

Oates, M.R., Cox, J.L., Neema, S., Asten, P., Glangeaud-Freudenthal, N., Figuerido, B., Gorman, L.L., Hacking, S., Hirst, E., Kammerer, M.M., Klier, C.M., Sereviratne, G., Smith, M., Sutter-Dallay, A.L., Valoriani, V., Wickberg, B., Yoshida, K., for TCS-PND Group (2004). Post natal depression across countries and cultures: A qualitative study. *British Journal of Psychiatry, 184*, S10–S16.

Parker, J. (2004). Does traumatic birth increase the risk of post natal depression? *British Journal of Community Nursing, 9*(2), 74–79.

Poole, H., Mason, L. & Osborne, T. (2006). Women's views of being screened for postnatal depression. *Community Practitioner, 79*(11), 363–367.

Rahman, A., Bunn, J., Lovel, H. & Creed, F. (2007). Association between antenatal depression and low birth weight in a developing country. *Acta Psychiatrica Scandinavica, 115*, 481–486.

Rahman, A., Iqbal, Z. & Harrington, R. (2003). Life events, social support and depression in childbirth: Perspectives from a rural community in the developing world. *Psychological Medicine, 33*, 1161–1167.

Roberston, E., Grace, S., Wallington, T. & Stewart, D.E. (July–August 2004). Antenatal risk factors for postpartum depression: A synthesis of recent literature. *General Hospital Psychiatry, 26*(4), 289–295.

Robinson, G.E. (2001). Psychotic and mood disorders associated with the perimenopausal period: Epidemiology, aetiology and management. *CNS Drugs, 15*(10), 175–184.

Royal College of Psychiatrists (2003). *Mental Illness after Childbirth.* London: RCP. Available at www.rcpsyh.ac.uk/info/factsheets/pfacchild.htm. Accessed 22 July 2007.

Royal College of Psychiatrists (2004). Available at www.repsych.ac.uk. Accessed 4 July 2006.

Russell, A. (2006). Barriers to care in post natal depression. *Community Practitioner, 79*(4), 110–111.

Sagud, M., Hotujac, L.J., Mihaljevic-Peles, A. & Jakovljevic, M. (2002). Gender differences in depression. *Collegium Antropologicum, 26*(1), 149–157.

Stearns, S. (January 2001). PMS and PMDD in the domain of mental health nursing. *Journal of Psychosocial Nursing and Mental health Services, 39*(1), 16–37.

Stewart, D. (August 2005). Depression during pregnancy. *Canadian Family Physician,* *51*(8), 1061–1067.

Stewart, D. (January 2006). Analysis: A broader context for maternal mortality. *Canadian Medical Association Journal, 174*(3), 302–303.

The Fifth Report of the Confidential Enquiries into Maternal Deaths in the United Kingdom (2001). *Why Mothers Die 1997–1999.* London: Royal College of Obstetrics and Gynaecologists Press.

UNICEF and WHO (2004). *Low Birth Weight: Country, Regional and Global Estimates.* New York: UNICEF.

Walker, S.P., Grantham–McGreggor, S., Powell, C.A., Powell, C.A. & Chang, S.M. (2000). Effects of growth restriction in early childhood on growth: IQ and cognition at age 11–12 years and the benefits of nutritional supplementation and psychosocial stimulation. *Journal of Paediatrics, 137,* 36–41.

Walsh, L. (January 2007a). Understanding and caring for patients experiencing paranoia. *Nursing Times, 103*(1), 28–29.

Walsh, L. (May 2007b). Caring for patients who experience hallucinations. *Nursing Times, 103*(21), 28–29.

Whooley, M.A., Avins, A.L., Miranda, J. & Browner, W.S. (1997). Case-finding instruments for depression. Two questions are as good as many. *Journal of General Internal Medicine, 12*(7), 439–445.

Wickberg, B. & Hwang, C.P. (1997). Screening for post natal depression I: A population based Swedish sample. *Acta Psychiatrica Scandinavia, 95*(1), 62–66.

World Health Organization (1992). The International Statistical Classification of Diseases and Related Health Problems. Geneva: WHO.

Chapter 4

The impact of stress and depression upon work and well-being

Introduction

Individuals who suffer from work-related stress may also suffer from depression. This can potentially have implications for both employers as well as employees as it affects the worker's ability to function in the organization. Many organizations have reported increases in stress amongst their workforce leading to national concerns. Work-related stress and bullying have become such a national concern that the Health and Safety Executive (2007) commissioned a report by Goldsmiths to develop management competencies to prevent and reduce stress at work. Work stress and bullying are closely linked as demonstrated by Berry (2006) who raised concern that the health service was struggling to make any real progress in tackling bullying and harassment in the workplace. Berry (2006) reported how academic research back in 1997 highlighted bullying in the NHS Trade Unions also reported that bullying was a problem in the NHS, however, very little had been achieved in tackling the problem. It appeared that many staff were victims of corporate bullying which frequently occurred during major organizational change causing work-related pressures. The DH (2001) highlighted that tackling bullying was beneficial for the organization as it promoted the well-being of the workforce and also helped to reduce financial pressures. The DH (2001) stated that reducing the level of bullying and harassment by 1% would save the health service 9 million pounds annually. The Healthcare Commission survey (2004) stated that 16% of staff surveyed had been bullied, harassed or abused by colleagues. This accounts for approximately 200 000 workers being bullied every year, and these are the ones that have reported it. This indicates a much larger problem within the NHS than was previously anticipated.

The Healthcare Commission (2006) undertook a national survey of NHS staff in 2005. It highlighted that the attitudes of staff were very important as staff determined the effectiveness of the organization. This was also shown in previous surveys of NHS staff undertaken in 2003 and 2004 which demonstrated strong links between the attitudes of staff and outcomes in relation to both health and safety. This survey in 2005 was important; however, it only included the 570 NHS Trusts in England. A total of 209 124 NHS employees responded, which was 58% of the staff surveyed. Two of the key areas of particular importance highlighted by the study were harassment and bullying against staff and work pressure and stress. As a result of these findings, NHS staff will need reassurance that NHS organizations will be taking action to address work-related stress.

The HSE (1998) considered nursing to be the second highest most stressful occupation and is a very important factor to consider as increased stress amongst nurses will affect not only the individual nurse's physical and mental health but also impact upon the care these nurses give to vulnerable patients. Ultimately this can affect the decisions they make and the care they provide.

Causes of work-related stress and depression

Melchion and Moffit cited by Newsedge (2007) reported from their survey of young people in their early thirties, that those in high-stress jobs were twice as likely to suffer from depression or anxiety as those in low-stress jobs. It was determined that time pressure was the most likely cause of stress. The Health-care Commission (2006) survey found that 36% of NHS staff had suffered from stress related to work within the past 12 months. These figures were the same as for 2004, which demonstrates a constant incidence of work-related stress despite many human resource departments advocating that they were putting policies in place to counter work-related stress. Even though some policies provide better support for some staff, there needs to be consistency for all staff across all organizations. This can be achieved by supporting staff so that they feel their concerns about work-related stress are being listened to and addressed by managers. Also, organizations need to take a corporate view demonstrating a fair and just approach when in supporting their employees.

Bullying and harassment in the workplace

The Andrea Adams Trust (2007) stated that more than two million people are bullied in the UK every day and as a result workplace bullying is a major cause of stress-related illness. The Andrea Adams Trust (2007) is a registered charity which was set up 12 years ago to address anti-workplace bullying. The charity through its website takes approximately 70 calls every day and has dealt with suicides and nervous breakdowns as a consequence of being bullied in the workplace.

Witheridge (2007) defines bullying as an abuse of power or position and is just as likely to occur between workers of the same grade as between managers and employers. Bentley (2006) argues that if an employee perceives that he or she is being bullied then there is a problem. It is important to intervene early before the person goes off sick and tenders their resignation.

Bullying in the workplace

There are many types of abuse in the workplace, however bullying and harassment are the most common forms of abuse in many health care organizations. The types of workplace bullying include the following:

- Blocking job opportunities and developments
- Exclusion from meetings
- Overbearing levels of supervision
- Malicious rumours or actions
- Undermining and victimizing employees
- Increasing unrealistic expectations
- Setting timescales that are unachievable
- Setting unrealistic workloads

As a consequence of being bullied, many workers will suffer from depression and will be unable to continue working. This has major implications upon their physical and mental health, personal and working relationships and financial circumstances.

Depression and the ability to work

Murray and Lopez (1997) predicted that depression will become the second major cause of functional disability after ischemic heart disease by the year 2010. This demonstrates the devastating impact that depression has upon a person's ability to work. Kessler and Frank (1997) highlighted the impact of psychiatric disorders upon days lost in the workforce. This is supported by Druss et al. (2000) who demonstrated that by suffering from depression, a person was more likely to lose days off from work resulting in reduced productivity for employers. Broadhead et al. (1990) demonstrated that depression was the most important factor associated with sickness absence from work in America. This has been supported more recently by European studies by the ESEMeD (2004) project. This study looked at disability and quality of life in relation to the impact of mental disorders across Europe.

Kessler et al. (2003) suggested that within the USA between 5 and 25% of Americans will suffer from depression at some time during their lives. This is important as many of these people are part of the workforce. It is in both employer's and employee's interests to ensure that depression is recognized early and that employers offer support to enable their employees to return to work. Kessler et al. (2003) also suggested that only about 20% of people suffering from depression were treated appropriately, however if treated appropriately the depressed person can return to productive work.

Both Zhang *et al.* (1999) and Simon *et al.* (2001b) have undertaken studies to demonstrate that it was both beneficial and more cost effective to treat depressed workers as soon as possible. Simon *et al.* (2001a) have also demonstrated the comparative costs of treatment versus non-treatment for workers with depression. There have also been comparisons made between depressed and non-depressed workers. Elinson *et al.* (2004) undertook a study involving depressed people who worked and depressed people who did not work. They identified causative factors in relation to depressed people in the workplace. The study found that depressed people who worked were more likely to be younger males who were better educated and living alone in urban or suburban areas. What is interesting is that these depressed workers did not perceive themselves as unable to work. This demonstrates different perspectives of illness as these young men did not perceive themselves as being ill and they continued working and getting on with their daily lives. It also highlights how individual beliefs about health can determine ability to function. It could be argued that Elinson *et al.*'s (2004) study demonstrated a male gender-specific belief about health. This study also found that more men worked than women and as a result may have influenced men's beliefs about illness and work particularly if they were the main breadwinner in the family. The findings may have been very different if undertaken in another country or culture. However, this study concluded that working depressed people were healthier than non-working depressed people.

Studies have been undertaken to review the impact of redundancy in the workplace. Workplace redundancies can also cause mental health problems. A large study was undertaken in Finland highlighted by Ford (2007) consisting of 26 500 municipal workers between 1994 and 2000. It found that men who kept their jobs in downsized organizations were approximately 50% more likely to be prescribed psychotropic medication than those working in organizations that were not downsized. They found that women who worked in downsized organizations were also 12% more likely to be prescribed prescription drugs. This demonstrates the impact of stress in the workplace as a consequence of others losing their jobs and also the pressure placed upon those left in the organization who continued to work there. The study also showed that women were more likely to be prescribed anxiolytics whilst men were more likely to be prescribed sleeping pills. This also demonstrates a potential-gendered approach to prescribing by doctors.

Compliance with prescribed medication may also affect recovery rates from depression. This was highlighted by Lingham and Scott (2002) who found that inadequate treatment and poor adherence to treatment by workers hindered their recovery from depression and contributed to functional work disability.

Families, health care professionals and employers all have an important role to play in supporting depressed people by recognizing causes of work-related stress and offering appropriate advice, support and, if required, by ensuring they get the right treatment. For many employers, it should be about preventing stressful situations occurring in the first place. What needs to be prevented is long-term disability caused through depression.

Rytsala *et al.* (2007) undertook a prospective study to identify the predictors of long-term work disability in major depressive disorder. They found that slow recovery from depression was one of the most likely factors affecting a person's ability to work. Other factors included feelings of hopelessness amongst older workers.

Rytsala *et al.* (2007) acknowledged that early intervention and treatment was effective in reducing long-term disability. Both employees and employers must take responsibility for identifying causes of work-related stress which can lead to depression and identify ways of preventing depression amongst the workforce. Risk assessments can be undertaken to determine risks from both physical and mental health perspectives. Risk assessments often determine health and safety and physical risks but there must be an equal focus upon risk assessment when identifying factors that impact upon worker's psychological health and well-being.

This highlights the importance of employers putting in place strategies to prevent psychological problems and mental illness when considering changing working practices within their organizations. As already highlighted, depression and work-related stress both have personal and economic implications for health care organizations. Surely, the cliché 'who cares for the carers' is a concept that must be considered and addressed.

The economic impact of stress and depression in the workplace

The economic impact of work-related stress and depression in the workplace is of great significance. The HSE (2007) stated that 6.5 million days are lost in the UK every year as a result of stress. These workdays which are lost due to stress have been estimated to cost the UK's economy approximately 7 billion pounds per year. This can lead to overreliance on agency workers which inevitably incurs even higher costs when staffing organizations. Stewart *et al.* (2003) demonstrated that work disability had high costs for employers, employees and society in general. Cuijpers *et al.* (2007) undertook a population-based study in 2003 to determine the economic costs of minor depression in the Netherlands. They concluded that the economic costs associated with minor depression were considerable and almost as much as the economic costs of major depression. Pincus and Perrett (2001) also considered the societal costs of major chronic depression.

Rapaport and Judd (1998) acknowledged the impact of minor depression on the quality of life of patients and Cuijpers and Schoevers (2004) highlighted the high risk of these patients developing major depressive disorder. Conti and Burton (1994) also considered the economic impact of depression in the workplace. This is supported by earlier research undertaken by Broadhead *et al.* (1990) who discussed the impact of depression, disability days and days lost from work due to depression. Simon *et al.* (2001b) highlighted the implications of depression upon work productivity. Similar issues were addressed by Thomas and Morris

(2003) who undertook a study in 2000 to determine the total cost of depression amongst adults in England in the year 2000. Thomas and Morris (2003) stated that the cost of depression in the UK was estimated at £3.5 billion pounds almost a decade ago. They recorded data on the health service use by patients with depression. This was analysed and the cost of treating patients was calculated. The cost of working life lost was estimated from sickness benefit claims and by the number of registered deaths from patients with depression. The findings of the study showed that the total cost of adult depression was estimated at over £9 billion pounds. It was interesting that out of this amount, £370 million pounds was for direct treatment costs. Thomas and Morris (2003) concluded that there were 109.7 million working days lost and 2615 deaths due to depression in England in the year 2000. This highlights that depression has a severe impact upon both individuals and society in relation to capacity to work.

Improving health and well-being and employer's responsibility

Employers must become more aware of bullying in the workplace and recognize that this problem occurs in a variety of organizations. Acknowledging that bullying occurs is the first step towards a healthy working environment. It is important to have an approach where bullying is discussed openly in the organization. It is also important to ensure that appropriate policies are in place to deal with both the bully and the bullied and also options on how to deal with bullying. Making staff aware at all levels that it will not be tolerated is the right approach as it gives commitment from managers at all levels to promote a healthy workforce. If staff are adequately prepared and trained for their roles then bullying may be reduced. A press release was made on 28 February 2006 by NHS employers in response to the Royal College of Nursing (RCN) Survey Working Well – at breaking point suggesting that they had already introduced initiatives to improve the working lives of their staff.

They introduced the following initiatives to improve work/life balance of their employees:

- Flexible working
- Changes in staff rostering
- Improved childcare provision
- Launched a stress campaign
- Organization of workshops to help trusts to identify problems and help staff to address problems
- Developing guidance to help managers identify bullying in the workplace
- Develop and implement bullying and harassment policies
- Provide a framework or NHS trusts to deal with staff incidents

Employers must recognize that depression in their workforce has a serious impact on the workplace in relation to lower productivity, absenteeism and short- and long-term disability costs. This was recognized by Goetzel *et al.* (2002) who advocated that employers must care for the mental health and well-being of their employees. The CSIP NIMHE (2005) have developed good practice guidelines to reduce mental health-related unemployment and enable people with depression to return to work. There are nine public mental health key areas and measures for success. However, the key actions with regard to employment are as follows:

■ To reduce mental health-related unemployment
■ For all workplaces to adopt HSE stress management standards
■ To provide support to enable people off work with mental health problems to return to work

(CSIP NIMHE, 2005).

Various organizations in the UK have produced information to support employees in the workplace. These include the RCN (2003) which produced guidance for dealing with bullying and harassment in the workplace. The RCN (2005a) produced Working Well Initiative which considered bullying and harassment at work, RCN (2006) produced Annual Workforce Survey and more recently, a study to determine morale entitled Holding On: Nurses Employment and Morale (RCN, 2007). Previously, the WHO (2000) developed good practice guidelines to promote good mental health at work. The WHO (2000) considered the importance of work for an individual's mental health and focused upon the workplace and mental well-being. It also highlighted job stress and stressful characteristics in the workplace, the consequences of mental health problems in the workplace as well as the implications of mental health and unemployment.

The WHO (2000) provides good practice examples in America, Canada, the UK, Finland and China demonstrating that mental health in the workplace is an international health concern and that health policy can be developed from a worldwide perspective.

Depression in the workplace affects both men and women. However, men are less likely to seek help despite depression being the main reason for taking time off work.

Men and depression

There is no evidence of a separate type of male depression; however, there is evidence that some symptoms of depression are more common in men. The following symptoms have been recognized by the Royal College of Psychiatrists (2006):

■ Irritability
■ Sudden anger
■ Increased loss of control
■ Greater risk taking

- Aggression
- More likely to commit suicide
    (Royal College of Psychiatrists, 2006).

Men are more likely to try to deal with their depression themselves and often take drugs and alcohol. Thus, it is not surprising that statistics show that men are more likely to abuse drugs and alcohol than women. Despite men suffering from depression due to them not seeking help, they are not always diagnosed with depression and as a consequence do not receive the correct treatment. This highlights the importance for all health care workers in both primary and secondary care and their families to recognize the symptoms and causes of depression in men and to support them to seek early diagnosis and intervention. It is likely that some men are misdiagnosed and as a result are treated for drug and alcohol problems but the underlying depression goes untreated. This has major implications across the male lifespan not just in terms of work but also in terms of relationships with partners, children and society as a whole. Shiels *et al.* (2004) undertook a study of depression in men who had attended a rural general practice. They considered factors associated with prevalence of depressive symptoms and diagnosis. They were aware that doctors were more likely to diagnose depression in women than in men. The study explored the reasons why this happens in rural communities. The study also compared and contrasted primary care doctors with male patient's ratings of perceived depression.

Even though many patients with severe symptoms of depression seek help from their general practitioner (GP), Davidson and Meltzer Brody (1999) and Anderson *et al.* (2000) found that there was evidence of underdiagnosis of depression.

Shiels *et al.*'s (2004) study demonstrated wide disparities between GPs and patients ratings of depression. Patients were more likely to consider themselves depressed than their doctors. Again this has implications for treatment. This study suggests that even though male patients were accessing their GP, they were not being diagnosed with depression. Sociological factors such as employment status, housing tenure, type of work and family structure did not appear to be significant in predicting male depression. What was significant in relation to male depression was lack of enjoyment in paid work in Shiels *et al.*'s (2004) study.

Some depressed men may be reluctant to talk about their feelings and may focus more upon their work rather than their relationships and family life. This can cause conflict and can lead to separation or divorce which is associated with depression. The Royal College of Psychiatrists (2006) has highlighted that some divorced men are more likely to commit suicide due to losing their main relationship. The following factors may be the cause of depression in men whose relationships have broken down:

- Losing contact with children
- Moving away from the family home
- Financial problems
    Adapted from Royal College of Psychiatrists (2006).

It must be recognized that some of these men may have already suffered from depression prior to the relationship breakdown and this could be the final straw which leads them to contemplate suicide. As already identified, there are many life events which can lead to depression across the male lifespan. The perinatal period is an important time for both women and men; however, the psychological aspects for some men during the perinatal period is rarely discussed as it is considered to be a time of increased likelihood of mental health and emotional problems for women due to hormonal changes after childbirth.

Paternal perinatal mental health

Because of changes in parental employment and diversity in family structures some men are having more involvement with the care of their children. Shemilt and O' Brian (2003) suggested that fathers are currently providing about one-third of total parental childcare. Draper (2003) supports this view by suggesting that the roles of women and men have changed significantly over the past few years and it is evident that men are generally becoming more involved with the care of their children. There are many reasons for this, including more women in paid employment and some women in higher paid jobs than their partners. Also, many families have financial pressures with high mortgages, and with the desire to have a better quality of life both partners choose to continue to work when their children are very young. Draper (2003) highlighted how these changes have evolved in society comparing them with the previous role of men as the breadwinner. There are risk factors that can help to determine the likelihood of depression in men before and after childbirth. Alexander (2001) found that a poor relationship with their partner, a history of depression in either themselves or their partner and lack of a close confiding relationship all contributed to the likelihood of depression in men. This supports the view of Gjerdingen and Centre (2003) that stable relationships contribute to improved mental health for both men and women. It is not surprising that childbirth puts extra strain on relationships when individuals are trying to balance the needs of a new baby, their partner's needs as well as employment needs. This is equally relevant for both men and women in paid employment.

Unemployment and retirement

The Royal College of Psychiatrists (2007) states that for some men who have experienced relationship difficulties, unemployment is the second most likely cause of depression in men. Becoming unemployed may create role changes in their family circumstances affecting not just their lifestyle but also their feelings of self-worth. In these situations, men suddenly become the unpaid child carer while their partner becomes the main breadwinner. They may feel lack of self-worth, insecure and become depressed. This may be reinforced if they are unable to find another job. Whilst suffering from depression, it will become more difficult to find the motivation to apply for jobs and the illness may also limit the types of jobs applied for.

Even though many people cannot wait to retire and perceive retirement as a positive stage in their lives, for others it can be a time of uncertainty and loneliness. Retirement can cause a variety of feelings and can be stressful for some men. Reasons may be loss of status, finance, security, friendships and is often a time when they lose their partners.

Following recent events across the world and the UK, posttraumatic stress disorder (PTSD) is on the increase and is evident amongst a variety of professions. The final part of this chapter will explore the implications of PTSD and will discuss the impact upon both men and women and their families.

PTSD in men and women

PTSD occurs as a result of exposure to traumatic events when an individual experiences extreme psychological emotions. Many soldiers, police, firemen and ambulance workers have witnessed trauma following accidents during their employment. Nursing Times (2006) reported that psychological trauma can occur as a result of war experiences, accidents, rape, witnessing violent death or abuse. This is supported by the Royal College of Psychiatrists (2005) which also included the following:

■ Being a prisoner of war
■ Being taken hostage
■ Terrorist attack
■ Serious road accidents
■ Violent personal attacks including robbery, mugging, physical attack, sexual abuse
■ Military combat
■ Natural or man-made disasters
■ Being diagnosed with a life-threatening illness

(Royal College of Psychiatrists, 2005).

Green (2003) undertook research into the symptom profiles of 65 men and 38 women who were suffering from PTSD. Over half the participants in his study had been in a motor vehicle accident, a third had experienced a personal assault, and the remainder had been involved in occupational traumas such as falls, electrocution and gas explosions. Acute stress reactions (ASRs) were evident in 90% of the participants. The study concluded that men with PTSD were more likely to suffer symptoms of irritability and to drink more alcohol than women. It was also evident that PTSD diagnosis was more likely after the person had experienced ASRs or disorders.

It was not until recent years that PTSD became a recognized condition warranting appropriate treatment. Lasiuk and Hegadoren (2006) identified how, historically, prisoners of war and soldiers who had fought in wars had suffered psychological effects from their experiences but very little had been done to help them cope with the psychological trauma.

As can be seen from the above list, there are a variety of causes of PTSD. It is not clear why some individuals suffer from PTSD and others do not but the following factors are relevant:

- Previous experience of depression or anxiety
- Family history of mental health problems
- History of child abuse
- MRI scans have shown differences in parts of the brain responsible for memory. This could explain why some individuals suffer from flashbacks
- People who suffer from PTSD continue to release adrenaline after the event
                                                                (Nursing Times, 2006).

Persistent symptoms experienced by PTSD sufferers

- Flashbacks
- Intrusive thoughts
- Difficulty in concentrating
- Feelings of alienation and numbing of emotions
- Memory loss regarding parts of the event
- Loss of interest in daily living
- Sleep difficulties
- Feelings of guilt
- Alcohol and drug abuse
- Relationship difficulties
- Excessive alertness to potential danger
- Compromised immune system
                    (NICE, 2005; Nursing Times, 2006).

The Royal College of Psychiatrists (2006) states that there is a difference between normal life stress caused through lack of money, relationship problems or relationship problems and PTSD. Normal life stress makes people feel anxious, depressed and tired and is often associated with physical symptoms such as headaches, palpitations, feelings of panic and irregular heart beats. PTSD is different as the symptoms are continual for more than 6 weeks after the event. The symptoms include flashbacks, avoidance and numbing and continually being on guard. Van de Kolk *et al.* (1996) reviewed the effects of traumatic stress upon the mind, body and society.

Hoge *et al.* (2007) reviewed the impact of women in combat and the risk of PTSD and depression. Kessler *et al.* (2005) found that women were more likely to suffer from both depression and PTSD than men. Similar findings have been shown by Hoge *et al.* (2002) and Riddle *et al.* (2007) in the military. A study was undertaken by Rona *et al.* (2006) to consider the mental health trends in the UK armed forces. This study reviewed men and women deployed to the Iraq war. The study showed that 26.7% of women compared with 19.8% of men reported high levels of psychological distress measured using the General Health Questionnaire (GHQ).

The GHQ is relevant as it asks questions which are pertinent when measuring depression.

Even though much has been written about PTSD in the armed forces and police, Ohayon and Shapiro (2000) and Stein *et al.* (2000) highlighted that PTSD was a disorder affecting 2.5% of the general population. Stein *et al.* (2000) was concerned about the lack of knowledge of PTSD in the primary care setting. They recognized that many primary care patients were either going untreated or receiving inadequate treatment. Weissman *et al.* (2005) undertook research into gender differences in PTSD amongst primary care patients following the World Trade Centre attack in New York on 11 September 2001. Both sexes had exposure to high lifetime stress events as well as direct exposure to the World Trade Centre attack. The increased number of women with PTSD following September 11 was influenced by their social and economic circumstances. These included living alone, no permanent relationship, poor education and low income. The increased rate of major depressive disorder (MDD) in women appeared less relevant compared with their economic circumstances. It is recognized that there needs to be more research undertaken regarding gender differences and mental disorders.

Robinson *et al.*'s (1997) research focused upon duty-related stressors and PTSD symptoms in suburban police officers where a 13% prevalence rate of PTSD was identified. Robinson *et al.* (1997) argued that this had significant implications upon morale, absenteeism, occupational health, early retirement and family functioning. Green (2003) found that police suffering from PTSD were more likely to have had antidepressant medication as treatment and were also more likely to have received counselling. Calhoun *et al.* (2000) found that military personnel with PTSD were also more likely to take antidepressants to reduce their symptoms. Green (2004) advocates the reason why police officers are more likely to receive treatment and counselling is due to occupational health protocols being implemented in their organization. However, Rose *et al.* (1999) argued that counselling and incident debriefing was not productive in the treatment of PTSD.

This is supported by the Cochrane review undertaken by Rose in (2002) who advocated that compulsory debriefing after traumatic incidents should cease. Ursano *et al.* (1995) have shown evidence that exposure to traumatic death increases the likelihood of stress, hostility, PTSD and depression. This is supported by Hyer *et al.* (1999) who suggested that depression is frequently linked with PTSD and the combination of both of them can be long lasting.

A traumatic incident is an incident that occurs outside normal experiences, but it must not be automatically assumed that exposure to traumatic incidents will always cause PTSD and/or depression. This will depend very much upon an individual's coping strategies and support. ASRs are common in a variety of psychological disorders including anxiety, PTSD and depressive disorders. RCN (2005b) developed guidance on managing traumatic stress in the health care sector. Employers have a responsibility to support their staff which is demonstrated in organization that undertake risk assessments and critical incident analysis

Conclusion

The first part of this chapter has focused primarily upon the impact of stress and depression suffered by employees in the workplace. The causes of work-related stress including bullying and harassment have been reviewed and discussed and also the impact this has upon their ability to work and function in the organization. Health policy, risk assessments and various guidelines and documents have been discussed in relation to the well-being of employees and also the importance of the employer's responsibility towards their workforce. There is currently a focus on national and international health policy agendas in relation to both the economic impact of stress and depression in the workplace and also on improving the health and well-being of the workforce. The second part of the chapter has reviewed the impact of men and depression and has identified key times during the male lifespan when depression and stress is likely to occur. Finally, PTSD has been reviewed from both male and female perspectives. This is important as many men and women undertake similar roles in the police, army, health service and ambulance service and are both likely to experience stress during their employment. Stress and depression have a major impact upon the relationships of individuals, families and the work environment. The issues discussed in this chapter will highlight important issues and hopefully help individuals and professionals to care for themselves and others.

Reflection and discussion

What causes work-related stress and depression?

- *People working in high stress jobs are twice as likely to suffer from depression or anxiety as those in low stress jobs.*
- *Time pressure is the most likely cause of stress.*
- *Work stress and bullying are closely linked.*
- *Many staff can become victims of corporate bullying which frequently occurs during major organizational change.*

Describe the types of workplace bullying

- *Blocking job opportunities and developments*
- *Exclusion from meetings*
- *Overbearing levels of supervision*

- *Malicious rumours or actions*
- *Undermining and victimising employees*
- *Increasing unrealistic expectations*
- *Setting timescales that are unachievable*
- *Setting unrealistic workloads*

How can employers help to improve health and well-being?

- *Acknowledging that bullying occurs is the first step towards a healthy working environment.*
- *It is also important to ensure that appropriate policies are in place to deal with both the bully and the bullied and also options on how to deal with bullying.*
- *Making staff aware at all levels that it will not be tolerated is the right approach, as it gives commitment from managers at all levels to promote a healthy workforce.*
- *If staff are adequately prepared and trained for their roles then bullying may be reduced.*

How do you ensure that depression in men is addressed?

Some symptoms of depression are more common in men. These include:

- *Irritability*
- *Sudden anger*
- *Increased loss of control*
- *Greater risk taking*
- *Aggression*
- *More likely to commit suicide*
- *Men are more likely to try to deal with their depression themselves and often take drugs and alcohol*
- *Men are more likely to abuse drugs and alcohol than women*
- *Despite men suffering from depression, due to them not seeking help they are not always diagnosed with depression and as a consequence do not receive the correct treatment*
- *It is important to support men to seek early diagnosis and intervention*
- *It is likely that some men are misdiagnosed and as a result are treated for drug and alcohol problems but the underlying depression goes untreated*
- *This has major implications in terms of work, relationships with partners, children and society as a whole*

Why is it important to understand posttraumatic stress disorder (PTSD)?

- *PTSD occurs as a result of exposure to traumatic events when an individual experiences extreme psychological emotions.*

■ *Psychological trauma occurs as a result of war experiences, accidents, rape, witnessing violent death or abuse.*

It is not clear why some individuals suffer from PTSD and others do not but the following factors are relevant:

■ *Previous experience of depression or anxiety*
■ *Family history of mental health problems*
■ *History of child abuse*
■ *MRI scans have shown differences in parts of the brain responsible for memory. This could explain why some individuals suffer from flashbacks*
■ *People who suffer from PTSD continue to release adrenaline after the event*

References

Alexander, J. (2001). Depressed men: An exploratory study of close relationships. *Journal of Psychiatric and Mental Health Nursing, 8*(1), 67–75.

Anderson, I.M., Nutt, D.J. & Deakin, J.F.W. (2000). Evidence based guidelines for treating depressive disorders with antidepressants: A review of the British Association for Psychopharmacology guidelines. *Psychopharmacology, 14,* 3–20.

Andrea Adams Trust (2007). Available at www.BanBullyingatWork.com. Accessed 21 August 2007.

Bentley, R. (November 2006). Bullying at work: What are employers doing to tackle it? *Personnel Today.* Available at www.personneltoday.com. Accessed 21 August 2007.

Berry, M. (2006). NHS bullying fight back falters. *Personnel Today.* Available at www.personneltoday.com. Accessed 20 August 2007.

Broadhead, W.E., Blazer, D.G. & George, L.K. (1990). Depression, disability days, and days lost from work in a prospective epidemiological study. *JAMA, 264,* 2524–2528.

Calhoun, P.S., Samson, W.S. & Bosworth, H.B. (2000). Drug use and validity of substance use self reports in veterans seeking help for post traumatic stress disorder. *Journal of Consulting and Clinical Psychology, 68,* 923–927.

Conti, D.J. & Burton, W.N. (1994). The economic impact of depression in the workplace. *Journal of Occupational Medicine, 36,* 983–988.

CSIP NIMHE (2005). *Making It Possible: Improving Mental Health and Well Being in England.* Executive summary. London: DH.

Cuijpers, P. & Schoevers, R.A. (2004). Increased mortality in depressive disorders: A review. *Current Psychiatric Reports, 6,* 430–437.

Cuijpers, P., Smit, F., Oostenbrink, J., de Graaf, R., Ten Have, M. & Beekman, A. (2007). Economic costs of minor depression: A population based study. *Acta Psychiatrica Scandinavica, 115,* 229–236.

Davidson, J.R.T. & Meltzer Brody, S.E. (1999). The under recognition and under treatment of depression: What is the breadth and depth of the problem? *Journal of Clinical Psychiatry, 60*(Suppl 7), 4–9.

DH (2001). Cited by Berry M (2006) NHS bullying fight back falters. *Personnel Today.* Available at www.personneltoday.com. Accessed 20 August 2008.

Draper, J. (2003). Men's passage to fatherhood: An analysis of the contemporary relevance of transition theory. *Nursing Inquiry, 10*(1), 66–78.

Druss, B.G., Rosenheck, R.A. & Sledge, W.H. (2000). Health and disability costs of depressive illness in a major US Corporation. *American Journal of Psychiatry, 157*, 1274–1278.

Elinson, L., Houck, P., Marcus, S. & Pincus, H.A. (January 2004). Depression and the ability to work. *Psychiatric Services, 55*, 29–34.

Ford, S. (January 2007). *Redundancies Increase Mental Health Problems.* Available at steve.ford@emap.com. Accessed 25 June 2007.

Gjerdingen, D.K. & Centre, B.A. (2003). First time parent's prenatal to postpartum changes in health, and the relation of postpartum health to work and partner characteristics. *Journal of the American Board of Family Practice, 16*, 304–311.

Goetzel, R.Z., Ozminkowski, R.J. & Sederer, L.I. (2002). The business case for quality mental health services: Why employers should care about the mental health and well being of their employees. *Journal of Occupational and Environmental Medicine, 44*, 320–330.

Green, B. (2003). Post traumatic stress disorder: Symptom profiles in men and women. *Current Medical Research and Opinion, 19*(3), 2324–2328.

Green, B. (2004). Post traumatic stress disorder in UK police officers. Brief Report. *Current Medical Research and Opinion, 20*(1), 2324–2328.

Health and Safety Executive (1998). *From Accidents to Assaults – How Organisational Responses to Traumatic Incidents Can Prevent PTSD in the Workplace.* Sudbury: HSE Books.

Health and Safety Executive (2007). *Management Competencies for Preventing and Reducing Stress at Work.* Identifying and developing the management behaviors necessary to implement the HSE management standards. Research report RR553. London: HSE.

Healthcare Commission for Healthcare Audit and Inspection (March 2006). *National Survey of NHS Staff 2005.* London: Healthcare Commission.

Hoge, C.W., Clark, J.C. & Castro, C.A. (2007). Commentary: Women in combat and the risk of post traumatic stress disorder and depression. *International Journal of Epidemiology, 36*(2), 327–329.

Hoge, C.W., Lesiker, S.W. & Guevera, R. (2002). Mental disorders among US military personnel in the 1990s: Association with high levels of health care utilization and early military attrition. *American Journal of Psychiatry, 159*, 1576–1583.

Hyer, L., Stranger, E. & Boudewyns, P. (1999). The interaction of post traumatic stress disorder and depression among older combat veterans. *Journal Clinical Psychology, 55*, 1073–1083.

Kessler, R.C., Bergland, P., Demler, O., Jin, R., Koretz, D., Merikangas, K.R., Rush, A.J., Walters, E.E. & Wang, P.S. (2003). The epidemiology of major depressive disorder: Results from the National Co morbidity Survey Replication (NCS-R). *JAMA, 289*, 3095–3105.

Kessler, R.C., Chiu, W.T., Demler, O. & Walters, E.E. (2005). Prevalence, severity and co morbidity of 12 month DSM-IV disorders in the National Co morbidity Survey Replication. *Archives of General Psychiatry, 62*, 617–627.

Kessler, R.C. & Frank, R.G. (1997). The impact of psychiatric disorders on work loss days. *Psychological Medicine, 27*, 861–873.

Lasiuk, G.C. & Hegadoren, K.M. (2006). Post traumatic stress disorder. Part 1. Historical development of the concept. *Perspectives in Psychiatric Care, 42*(1), 13–20.

Lingham, R. & Scott, J. (2002). Treatment and non-adherence in affective disorders. *Acta Psychiatrica Scandinavica, 105*, 164–172.

Melchion and Moffit (2007). Cited in Newsedge (2007) High stress jobs double chances of developing depression. Available at www.psychiatry24×7.com. Accessed 6 August 2007.

Murray, C.J.L. & Lopez, A.D. (1997). Alternative projections of mortality and disability by cause 1990–2020: Global Burden of Disease Study. *Lancet, 349,* 1498–1504.

NHS Employers (February 2006). Press release: NHS employer's response to RCN Survey Working Well – at breaking point. Media Centre. Available at www.nhsemployers.org. Accessed online on 22 August 2007.

NICE (2005). *CG26. Post Traumatic Stress Disorder.* NICE Guidelines. London: NICE.

Nursing Times (April 2006). Post traumatic stress disorder. *Nursing Times, 102,* 15. Available at www.nursingtimes.net. Accessed 4 July 2006.

Ohayon, M.M. & Shapiro, C.M. (2000). Sleep disturbances and psychiatric disorders associated with PTSD in the general population. *Comprehensive Psychiatry, 41*(6), 469–478.

Pincus, H.A. & Perrett, A.R. (2001). The societal costs of chronic major depression. *Journal of Clinical Psychiatry, 62*(Suppl 6), 5–9.

Rapaport, M.H. & Judd, L.L. (1998). Minor depressive disorder and subsyndromal depressive symptoms: Functional impairment and response to treatment. *Journal of Affective Disorder, 48,* 227–232.

RCN (2003). *Dealing with Harassment and Bullying at Work. A Guide for RCN Members.* London: RCN. Publication code 001 302.

RCN (2005a). *Working Well Initiative. Bullying and Harassment at Work. A Good Practice Guide for RCN Negotiators and Health Care Managers.* London: RCN.

RCN (2005b). *RCN Working Well Initiative Guidance on Traumatic Stress Management in the Health Care Sector.* London: RCN.

RCN (2006). *Annual Workforce Survey.* London: RCN.

RCN (2007). *Holding On: Nurses Employment and Morale.* Employment Research Ltd. London: RCN.

Riddle, J.R., Smith, T.C. & Smith, B., for the Millennium Cohort Team (2007). Millennium Cohort: The 2001–2003 baseline prevalence of mental disorders in the US Military. *Journal of Clinical Epidemiology, 60,* 191–202.

Robinson, H.H., Sigman, M.R. & Wilson, J.P. (1997). Duty-related stressors and PTSD symptoms in suburban police officers. *Psychological Reports, 81,* 835–845.

Rona, R.J., Fear, N.T., Hull, L. & Wessley, S. (2006). Women in novel occupational roles: Mental health trends in the UK armed forces. *International Journal of Epidemiology, 36,* 319–326.

Rose, S. (2002). Psychological debriefing for preventing PTSD. *Cochrane Database Systematic Review,* CD000560.

Rose, S., Brewin, C.R., Andrews, B. & Kirk, M. (1999). A randomized controlled trial of individual psychological debriefing for victims of violent crime. *Psychological Medicine, 29,* 793–799.

Royal College of Psychiatrists (2005). *Post Traumatic Stress Disorder (PTSD).* Available at www.rcpsych.ac.uk. Accessed 14 July 2007.

Royal College of Psychiatrists (2006). Available at www.rcpsych.ac.uk. Accessed 4 July 2007.

Royal College of Psychiatrists (2007). Available at www.rcpsych.ac.uk. Accessed 25 August 2007.

Rytsala, H.J., Melartin, T.K., Leskela, U.S., Sokero, T.P., Lestela-Mielonen, P.S. & Isometsa, E.T. (2007). Predictors of long term work disability in Major Depressive disorder: A prospective study. *Acta Psychiatrica Scandinavica, 115,* 206–213.

Shemilt, I. & O' Brian, M. (2003). *Working Fathers, Earning and Caring.* Research Discussion Series. Available at www.eoc.org/.uk/cseng/research/ueareport.pdf. Accessed 4 July 2006.

Shiels, C., Gabbay, M., Dowrick, C. & Hulbert, C. (2004). Depression in men attending a rural general practice: Factors associated with prevalence of depressive symptoms and diagnosis. *British Journal of Psychiatry, 185,* 239–244.

Simon, G.E., Barber, C. & Birnbaum, H.G. (2001a). Depression and work productivity: The comparative costs of treatment versus non-treatment. *Journal of Occupational and Environmental Medicine, 43,* 2–9.

Simon, G.E., Katon, W.J., VonKorff, M., Unutzer, J., Lin, E.H.B., Walker, E.A., Bush, T., Rutter, C., Ludman, E. (October 2001b). Cost effectiveness of a collaborative care program for primary care patients with persistent depression. *American Journal of Psychiatry, 158*(10), 1638–1644.

Stein, M.B., McQuaid, J.R., Pedrelli, P., Lennox, R. & McCahill, M.E. (July–August 2000). Post traumatic stress disorder in the primary care medical setting. *General Hospital Psychiatry, 22*(4), 261–269.

Stewart, W.F., Ricci, J.A., Chee, E., Hahn, S.R. & Morganstein, D. (2003). Cost of lost productive work time among US workers with depression. *JAMA, 289*(23), 3135–3144.

Thomas, C.M. & Morris, S. (2003). Cost of depression among adults in England in 2000. *British Journal of Psychiatry, 183,* 514–519.

Ursano, R.J., Fullerton, C.S. & Norwood, A.E. (1995) Psychiatric dimensions of disaster: Patient care, community consultation and preventative medicine. *Harvard Review Psychiatry, 3,* 196–209.

Van de Kolk, B.A., Mcfarlane, A.C. & Weisaeth, L. (1996). *Traumatic Stress: The Effects of Overwhelming Experience on Mind, Body and Society.* New York: Guildford Press.

Weissman, M.M., Neria, Y., Das, A., Feder, A., Blanco, C., Lantigua, R., Shea, S., Gross, R., Gameroff, M.J., Pilowsky, D. & Olfson, M. (June 2005). Gender differences in posttraumatic stress disorder among primary care patients after the World Trade Centre attack on September 11th 2001. *Gender Medicine, 2*(2), 76–87.

Witheridge (November 2007). Cited by Bentley R (2006) Bullying at work: What are employers doing to tackle it? *Personnel Today.* Available at www.personneltoday.com. Accessed 21 August 2007.

WHO (2000). *Mental Health and Work: Impact, Issues and Good Practices.* Geneva: WHO.

Zhang, M., Rost, K.M. & Fortney, J.C. (1999). A community study of depression treatment and employment earnings. *Psychiatric Services, 50,* 1209–1213.

Chapter 5

Depression in chronic disease and long-term conditions

Introduction

The DH (2004) identified that chronic disease was the biggest problem facing health and social care services with 60% of adults in England alone reporting a chronic health problem. Chronic diseases are conditions which cannot be cured but are controlled by medical interventions. In England in 2004, there were 8.8 million people with a long-term illness severely affecting their daily living and coping ability.

Many people with chronic physical disease also suffer with mental health problems. This affects 1 in 6 of the UK population, including 1 in 10 children (DH, 2004). The British Household Survey (DH, 2001) demonstrated that within the UK, many people will have three or more chronic ill health problems at any one time. These people have complex needs requiring support from both health and social care services.

Major depressive disorder is considered to be a chronic condition when depressive episodes recur without full recovery and the total duration of the illness is 2 years or more (Tossani *et al.*, 2005). Thus, depression can become a very disabling and debilitating chronic illness in its own right.

This chapter focuses upon the links between depression and chronic illness and long-term conditions. It discusses the impact of depression in relation to coronary heart disease (CHD) and myocardial infarction, stroke, chronic obstructive pulmonary disease, kidney disease, diabetes, cancer and neurological conditions. The management of depression and physical illness will be discussed as well as approaches to assessment in palliative care. The role of the clinical nurse specialist in caring for palliative care patients with depression will also be reviewed.

Murray and Lopez (1997) recognized that without treatment, depressive disorder will develop into a chronic condition predicted to be the second highest chronic illness in the world by the year 2020. This highlights the importance of identifying the causes and symptoms of depression which may have developed as a result of chronic physical illness or may already have been established prior to the onset of physical illness. MacHale (2002) identified a variety of biological and psychological factors which contributed to increased risk of depression in physical illness. Biological factors include electrolyte imbalance, hormonal and endocrine abnormalities, brain disease, nutritional deficiencies and side effects of medication. Bazire (2001) recorded many drug treatments with side effects that caused depression. Some of these included steroids, beta-blockers and non-steroid anti-inflammatory drugs. Psychological factors linked with increased risk of depression include poor self-esteem, sense of loss, poor ability to maintain relationships and inability to work.

This sense of loss may be associated with the person's inability to function normally due to pain, disfigurement or being diagnosed with a life-threatening illness. Being unable to work adds extra stress by lowering self-esteem resulting in potential relationship disharmony and financial difficulties.

Chapman *et al.* (2005) undertook a study in America which focused upon the chronic diseases which had the most likely incidence of morbidity and mortality amongst adults. They identified depression in patients with the following chronic diseases:

▪ Cardiovascular disease
▪ Asthma
▪ Diabetes
▪ Cancer
▪ Arthritis
▪ Obesity
    (Chapman *et al.*, 2005).

Similar findings were shown by MacHale (2002) who identified that depression was more common in patients with physical disorders, particularly diabetes, cardiac and neurological diseases. This view was also acknowledged by Rodin and Voshart (1986) who had previously reviewed depression in medically ill patients.

Being depressed can affect the compliance rates of treatment as some patients may feel unwilling or unable to take certain medication or undertake investigations. This has implications for the type of treatment prescribed for individual patients. Also, if a patient is prone to depression, doctors will need to consider alternatives if side effects are likely to cause depression. Physical chronic conditions associated with depression will now be discussed.

Depression and coronary heart disease

Cuijpers and Schoevers (2004) recognized that depressive symptoms were associated with disability, morbidity and mortality. Rugulies (2002) undertook a systematic review which showed that depressive symptoms were closely associated with the development of CHD in previously healthy people. Carney *et al.* (2002)

identified that depression was a risk factor associated with cardiac mortality and morbidity. They identified the following associations:

- Higher prevalence of cardiac risk factors such as cigarette smoking, diabetes or hypertension
- Non-compliance with cardiac medication
- Inflammation

(Carney *et al.*, 2002).

Similar risk factors regarding depression and cardiovascular disease (CVD) were established by Haywood (1995) in relation to smoking and physical inactivity. In fact, Nemeroff *et al.* (1998) established that people with depression were much more likely to develop coronary artery disease.

Both Rugulies (2002) and Wulsin and Singal (2003) showed that the risk of developing heart disease in people with depression or having depressive symptoms was 1.6 times higher than that for non-depressed people. This highlights the importance of assessing depressive symptoms in patients with CHD and also ensuring that they receive the correct treatment. This was also advocated by Glassman *et al.* (2002) who undertook a randomized trial into the treatment of acute myocardial infarction patients with the antidepressant sertraline. However, Pickering *et al.* (2004) debated whether depression was a risk factor for CHD and studies undertaken by van de Brink *et al.* (2002) considered whether treating depression after myocardial infarction had any impact at all upon cardiac prognosis and quality of life.

However, results from an earlier study showed that for the first year following myocardial infarction some patients suffered with depression and reduced quality of life, thus the ENRICHD (2003) trial was undertaken. This trial showed that by treating depression the symptoms reduced significantly. Pratt *et al.* (1996) looked into the risk factors related to myocardial infarction and found that people with a history of depression were four times more likely to have a myocardial infarction compared to those people who did not have depression. These findings were supported by Barefoot and Schroll (1996) who established in their community study that the symptoms of depression were linked with acute myocardial infarction. It has to be acknowledged that it is difficult for some depressed patients to adhere to treatment regimes and make lifestyle changes. This is particularly relevant in relation to cardiac rehabilitation.

Cardiac rehabilitation is important but non-compliance with treatment can have detrimental effects. Milani and Lavie (1998) highlighted how cardiac rehabilitation improved depressive symptoms in older people who had experienced CHD. This is also highlighted in a number of research studies undertaken link depression with heart disease.

CIHI (2002) reported that cardio-vascular disease (CVD) was the main cause of death in both men and women in Canada and found that depression contributed to both incidence and recovery rates from CVD.

Nolen Hoeksema *et al.* (1999) stated that this was particularly relevant for women who experienced twice the rate of depression compared with men.

Beaudet (2001) found that Canadians aged between 55 and 74 years who had experienced depression during the previous 12 months were three times more likely to suffer from CVD within the next 4 years compared to Canadians who had never experienced depression. CVD patients who suffered from depression whilst in hospital were also more likely to experience long-term chronic illness. These patients were also more likely to have more advanced cardiac disease. Ford (2006) cited a report in the Netherlands stating that patients who experienced their first episode of depression after a heart attack were at greater risk of future heart problems.

The study included 468 patients who were in hospital after suffering from a heart attack. The patients were assessed for depression whilst in hospital and after 3 and 12 months following their heart attack. The study recommended that all patients should be screened for depression in ICU following a heart attack. This highlights the important role of health care professionals in helping to predict future depressive illness in cardiac patients. These patients who are of a higher risk of depression require support to help them to cope. Park et al.'s (2006) research found that focusing upon social support and helping people to cope were useful strategies when alleviating depression in people with congestive heart failure (CHF).

McCall (1992) highlighted that CHF was a chronic progressive disease impairing the heart's ability to maintain normal blood circulation causing both physical and psychological problems for patients. These physical and psychological problems can impact greatly upon a patient's quality of life. This is supported by Freedman and Carney (2000) who found that depression had negative effects upon patient's ability to function, their quality of life and the overall prognosis of CHD. Park et al. (2006) highlighted that due to depression having such a negative impact upon health, the causes of depression need to be identified so that help and support could be provided. As MacMahon and Lip (2002) suggested the two most important psychological factors which influence recovery from depression are social support and coping processes. Studies undertaken by Holahan et al. (1997) into patients with cardiac problems also demonstrated that social support helped patients to cope with depression.

Depression and stroke

Stroke is the third biggest cause of death in the UK and the largest cause of severe disability (DH, 2007a). The government aim to reduce the death rate from stroke, CHD and related diseases in people aged under 75 years by 40% by the year 2010.

A consultation document on the new National Stroke Strategy, DH (2007a) addressed some of the challenges faced by stroke services in England.

Stroke can affect a person's physical and mental health and has major consequences upon their quality of life. The implications of physical disability are addressed during poststroke rehabilitation; however, it is equally important to address the psychological implications following a stroke. This includes recognizing the symptoms of depression in poststroke patients at an early stage. Both primary and secondary care nurses are in an optimal position to look for these symptoms in stroke patients to ensure appropriate treatment is offered.

Research undertaken in Australia by Seana (2006) demonstrated a high incidence of depression in stroke patients. The study included 289 patients in the North East Melbourne Stroke Incidence Study. The findings showed that 17% of patients were depressed 5-year poststroke and that only 22% of them were taking any antidepressants for their depression. This suggests that it was the stroke that caused the depression. However, for many other people it may be that depression was apparent before the stroke and that as a result of the stroke the depression becomes worse.

There is also evidence to suggest that having depression increases the chance of having a stroke. This was demonstrated by Jonas and Mussino (2000) who highlighted that people with symptoms of depression were more likely to suffer a stroke. Ohira et al.'s (2001) research found that Japanese people with significant depressive symptoms were twice as likely as people who had fewer depressive symptoms to suffer a stroke within 10 years. This is important and demonstrates that if depressive symptoms are recognized early then long-term physical chronic illness and disability may be prevented.

This does not only have implications for the individual patient but also has implications for resources within the health and social care sectors. Inevitability, this would impact upon the overall economic funding of services and certainly impact upon secondary care services. Thus by focusing upon primary care and preventative services, chronic illness and disability for some patients can be avoided.

It must also be recognized that there may be other factors and variables that influence these findings such as lifestyle, social class, education and family support. This is where primary care and public health can be utilized and is of influence early on in people's lives.

Depression following a stroke is called poststroke depression and can cause delays in the rehabilitative process. Berg et al. (2003) found that more than half of the stroke patients reported depressive symptoms within 18 months of having a stroke. Treatment of depression in stroke patients must be considered and antidepressants have been effective in both treating the depression, helping with cognitive function and increasing survival rates (Jorge et al. (2003) Kimura et al. (2000).

Ramasubbu and Patten (2003) have demonstrated that there is clear evidence to demonstrate that depression is associated with increased risk of stroke morbidity and mortality.

Depression and chronic obstructive airways disease

Depression is common in patients with chronic obstructive airways disease (COPD). Stage et al. (2006) recognized that approximately 40% of COPD patients were likely to suffer from severe symptoms of depression.

They highlighted the importance of screening for depressive symptoms in COPD patients as this affected the quality of life of patients with this long-term chronic disease.

Anxiety is often associated with depression and can impinge upon a person's ability to recover from depression. Mikkelsen *et al.* (2004) undertook a review of anxiety and depression in patients with COPD. They stated that existing studies showed a prevalence of depressive symptoms and anxiety in about 50% of patients studied and that treatment with antidepressants demonstrated an improvement in both the physical and psychological state of patients. Norwood (2006) stated that depression rates in patients with COPD ranged from 20 to 60%. Roundy *et al.* (2005) undertook a study in the primary care setting which showed that the rate of depression in COPD patients was 54%. This study was undertaken by patient focus group discussion and highlighted to the GPs that depression was not being managed appropriately within their practice. It can be determined from the findings of these studies that over 50% of patients with COPD were likely to suffer from depression.

Stage *et al.* (2005) focused on the survival of patients with depression and COPD. This was achieved by determining whether the presence of depression in COPD patients had any impact upon mortality.

Health professionals need to be aware that depression causes lack of motivation and can deter people from taking part in their rehabilitation. Simon *et al.*'s (2005) research established that patients with chronic medical illness and co-morbid depression showed significant improvement in mood, social and emotional functioning and disability following commencement of treatment for depression. They suggested that depression might be a more likely cause of disability than the chronic disease. Thus, by treating the depression the chronic disease becomes more manageable for some people and they are more able to cope with their daily lives.

Depression and renal disease

It has been difficult to diagnose depression in patients with renal disease due to similarity of both signs and symptoms. These include appetite loss, weight loss, loss of interest, insomnia and loss of energy (Abbey *et al.*, 1990).

Tossani *et al.* (2005) highlighted that very few studies had been undertaken to explore the prevalence of depression in patients with kidney disease despite depression being the most likely mental health disorder in end stage renal disease (ESRD).

Kim *et al.* (2002) found that approximately 20–30% of renal dialysis patient's suffered with depression and there appeared to be an increased likelihood of morbidity and mortality in depressed ESRD patients. Similar findings were found by Kimmel *et al.* (2000) in their longitudinal study of outpatients with chronic haemodialysis. It is not surprising that being diagnosed with a long-term condition as well as having to undergo dialysis over long periods of time on a regular basis causes stress and anxiety for many patients. As a consequence, some of these patients will suffer from depression. As Kimmel and Peterson (2006) highlighted, depression is a persistent problem for some ESRD patients which does not just occur as a reaction to being diagnosed with a chronic illness. It is the endurance of the treatment that can lead to chronic depression. Kimmel and Peterson (2006) suggested that more research was needed to include a variety of factors in relation to depression in patients with ESRD. The relationship between the family, doctors and dialysis personnel is important.

However, the following factors could be considered when undertaking future research:

- Age
- Gender
- Ethnic background
- Socio-economic status
- Residence
- Marital status
- Satisfactory relationships
- Patient compliance
    (Kimmel *et al.*, 2000).

More studies are required regarding treating depression in renal failure, however, for ESRD patients if low doses of medication are given depressive symptoms can be reduced.

Depression and diabetes

Depression in people with diabetes is often severe with frequent reoccurrence. Anderson *et al.* (2001) stated that patients with diabetes were twice as likely to suffer from depression as patients with non-diabetes.

They also highlighted that there was a higher incidence of depression in women with diabetes than men.

Lustman *et al.* (1992) identified the major implications of depression in diabetes, which included the effect upon glycemic control causing diabetic complications. These were caused by obesity, inactivity, and non-compliance which all contributed to insulin resistance. Despite some similarity of symptoms in diabetes and depression, e.g. fatigue and weight loss, sad mood and significant loss of interest or pleasure these two latter symptoms are not used to diagnose diabetes. However, they are essential symptoms identified by the DSM-IV in diagnosing depression. Therefore, if these symptoms are apparent then depression would be diagnosed. Some antidepressants can be helpful in treating depression, however, they can cause potential side effects and affect glycemic control in people with diabetes so may need to be used with caution. Lustman *et al.* (1992) suggested that even after treatment for depression, less than 10% of diabetic patients will be free from depression during the following 5 years.

There has been some debate about whether type 1 or type 2 diabetics are more likely to suffer from depression. Literature reviews were undertaken by Ali *et al.* (2006) to determine the prevalence of depression in adults with type 2 diabetes. They found that there was evidence to support raised rates of depression in people with type 2 diabetes; however, there was little evidence to support the effective treatment of these people. They also stated that more, better-controlled studies were required. Barnard *et al.* (2006) reviewed literature regarding the prevalence of depression in adults with type 1 diabetes.

They concluded that there were variations in the studies reviewed and that due to the small number of study participants and different methods of diagnosis that the results should be treated with caution. They recommended that a controlled study using diagnostic interviewing techniques should be undertaken to determine levels of depression in people with type 1 diabetes. What is clear is that there is an association between depression and diabetes complications in both type 1 and type 2 diabetes. de Groot *et al.*'s (2001) meta-analysis demonstrated that out of the 27 studies included in the review depression was significantly associated with the following diabetic complications: retinopathy, nephropathy, neuropathy, macrovascular complications and sexual dysfunction.

Having both depression and diabetes can also affect a person's chances of having other chronic conditions. Georgiades' (2007) research in America which advocated that having both diabetes type 2 and depression increased the risk of dying from cardiovascular disease.

The study researched 933 heart patients over a 4-year period and concluded that patients with type 2 diabetes with high depression scores had an increased risk of dying by up to 30% compared with patients with type 2 diabetes who did not suffer from depression. This demonstrates an association between depression and diabetes and the severity of these chronic long-term conditions.

Zhang *et al.* (2005) stated that depressed people with diabetes died sooner than other people, irrespective of their lifestyle or health status.

Brown *et al.* (2006) were concerned about studies showing the incidence of depression in type 2 diabetes. As a result, they conducted a population-based retrospective cohort study which evaluated the incidence of new onset depression in people with diabetes. They also compared this with people who did not have diabetes. They found that depression increased the risk of diabetes rather than diabetes causing depression, which was also supported by previous studies undertaken by Lustman *et al.* (1992), Anderson *et al.* (2001) and Nichols and Brown (2003).

Brown *et al.* (2006) concluded that people with diabetes were at no greater risk of developing depression than people without diabetes. What needs to be treated with caution is whether some of these patients had depression prior to being diagnosed with diabetes as this was not apparent to the researchers. What has to be acknowledged is that this was a very large study undertaken over a length of time.

It is evident that depression is associated with hyperglycemia and increased risk of diabetic complications. However, as Anderson *et al.* (2001) highlighted, there needs to be an accurate estimation of depression rates to ensure that depression is managed and treated effectively in people with diabetes.

Depression and cancer

Many people with terminal cancer also suffer from depression; however, depression in patients with terminal cancer is treatable. It is important to seek help and ensure a correct diagnosis at an early stage. This is advocated by the European Association for Palliative Care. If people are anxious about being diagnosed with cancer they may be less likely to go to the doctors, which inevitably leads to a delay in diagnosis. Spiegel (1996) suggested that a delay in diagnosis reduces the long-term prospects of cancer survival by up to 20%. Spiegel (1996) also found that cancer patients who were treated for depression reported fewer symptoms and appeared to cope better with their illness. Earlier studies by Massie and Holland (1990) suggested that approximately 25% of hospitalized cancer patients were likely to be diagnosed with major depression or have depressed mood.

They suggested that the following patients were most at risk from depression:

- History of affective disorder or alcoholism
- Advanced stages of cancer
- Poorly controlled pain
- Having treatment with medication
- Concurrent illnesses that caused depressive symptoms
                    (Massie and Holland, 1990).

It is important for health professionals to use a holistic approach when assessing cancer patients. The following aspects are of equal importance: physical symptoms, mental health symptoms as well as the effectiveness of the cancer treatment. This is important as Somerset *et al.* (2004) highlighted that depression in women with breast cancer was both underdiagnosed and undertreated. As already mentioned, depression affects quality of life and compliance with treatment and ultimately survival rates.

Reeve *et al.* (2007) undertook a study in Merseyside to determine the prevalence of depression in a primary care population with terminal cancer.

They recommended further research into evidence-based palliative care within the primary care setting. Limitations of the study were that it was a small study and different depression tools were used during the two phases of the research.

Katon *et al.* (2007) highlighted that primary care patients with anxiety and depression often experienced multiple physical symptoms. They reviewed studies which had been undertaken in patients suffering from both chronic medical illness and anxiety and depression.

They reviewed 31 studies involving 16 922 patients with chronic medical disorder and anxiety and depression.

The four categories of medical disorder included:

- Diabetes
- Pulmonary disease
- Heart disease
- Arthritis
    (Katon *et al.*, 2007).

They found that somatic symptoms were strongly associated with depression and that by decreasing the somatic symptoms the depression improved. They advocated the importance of correctly diagnosing depression in patients with chronic medical illness.

The most frequently used assessment tool to predict depression is the Hospital Anxiety and Depression Scale (HADS) developed by Zigmund and Snaith (1983), which consists of 14 questions relating to anxiety and depression. This was reviewed by Hotopf *et al.* (2002) during their systematic review of depression in advanced disease. An American study reported in *Annals of Oncology* (2006) that cancer patients were twice as likely to commit suicide as the general population. An analysis of 1.3 million cancer patients found that 19 out of every 1000 male cancer patients and 4 out of every 1000 female patients had committed suicide. The highest suicide rates were in patients with lung, bronchus, bladder, head and neck cancer. These statistics show as with most suicides that it is more common amongst the male population.

Pirl (2004) provided an evidence-based report on the occurrence, assessment and treatment of depression in cancer patients. There were very few studies undertaken on head and neck cancer patients despite these patients having one of the highest rates of depression. Morton *et al.*'s (1984) study reviewed quality of life in head and neck cancer patients.

The HADS was the scale used in many studies to detect depression rates in people with cancer. These studies included Pinder *et al.* (1993) which considered psychiatric disorder in patients with advanced breast cancer; Roth *et al.* (1998) which considered psychological distress in men with prostrate cancer; Groenvold *et al.* (1999) which considered anxiety and depression in breast cancer patients; and Hopwood and Stephens (2000) which considered depression in patients with lung cancer. The DSM criteria are the standard used for diagnosing major depressive disorder and other depressive disorders in all patients including those with cancer. Pirl (2004) recommended that longitudinal studies were needed to determine the incidence of depression prior to the diagnosis of cancer. Pirl (2004) also suggested that a meta-analysis of treatment studies regarding depressed patients is required.

The role of the clinical nurse specialist in palliative care

The clinical nurse specialist has an important role in caring for palliative care patients as depression affects the quality of life of both patients and their families.

Williams and Payne (2003) found that up to 80% of psychological and psychiatric morbidity in cancer patients is unrecognized and untreated because cancer patients are reluctant to talk about their symptoms. Williams and Payne (2003) undertook a qualitative study to determine clinical nurse specialists' views on depression in palliative care patients. Some of the issues highlighted included nurses finding it difficult to talk about depression and also their lack of training in identifying psychological and psychiatric symptoms.

It is evident from this study that palliative care nurses would benefit from training in psychological assessment and management of palliative care patients. Maybe there should be more dual-registered nurses caring for palliative care patients to ensure that their holistic needs are equally addressed. Also, more opportunities for multidisciplinary learning should be encouraged through shared case studies and patient scenarios. Peer clinical supervision could also be developed to enable good practice to be shared and discussed.

Neurological conditions

There are a variety of neurological conditions including multiple sclerosis (MS), motor neurone disease (MND) and Parkinson's disease (PD). The National Service Framework on long-term (neurological) conditions was launched in March 2005 focusing upon person-centred care planning, information and support, self-care and case management. Many conditions are illustrated in the framework using case studies (DH, 2007b).

Williams *et al.* (2003) undertook a study to determine the prevalence and impact of depression and pain in neurology patients. They found that there was an increased chance of having depression in patients suffering from pain and in those patients with a cognitive or cerebrovascular diagnosis. It was recognized that neurologists were more likely to treat the pain than the depression. It must be highlighted that both pain and depression are common in newly diagnosed neurology patients and that both have detrimental effects upon an individual's physical and mental health.

Isaksson *et al.* (2007) undertook a study in Sweden which explored sorrow and the presence of depression in people with MS. People with MS experience a variety of losses due to this chronic progressive neurological condition. Some of these losses include loss of bodily control, loss of freedom, loss of faith, loss of health, loss of freedom and loss of social relations. Sorrow appeared to be constantly present. These are similar losses experienced by people with other neurological conditions. It is important that nurses and doctors provide psychological support to promote hope and a sense of control for patients with chronic neurological conditions. Siegert and Abernethy (2005) undertook a review of depression in people with MS. They found that there was a lifetime prevalence of depression in 50% of patients with MS. There has been much debate about the effectiveness of new drug treatments in patients with MS, some being beneficial whilst others have limited effect.

Previously, Tedman *et al.* (1997) compared depression in 40 patients with MND with 92 patients with MS who attended the same neurology clinic. At that time there was very little published evidence regarding depression in patients with MND. The study concluded that patients with MND and those patients with other neurologically disabling conditions suffered equally from depression as patients with MS. It is important that both professionals and home carers understand that depression and pain are significant in patients with MND irrespective of their physical disability.

It is also important for professionals caring for patients with neurological conditions to consider depression and depressive symptoms and their effect upon the person's well-being. Hickards (2005) suggested that more evidence and research is required regarding treating depression in neurological disorders.

Evidence regarding long-term conditions

Long-term conditions are conditions which cannot be cured but can be treated with medication and other therapies. The DH (2007b) highlighted current evidence regarding long-term conditions which included the following important factors:

- People with long-term conditions are the most intensive users of the most expensive services
- Due to an ageing population there are more recognized and diagnosed long-term conditions
- Health inequalities and lifestyle choices have led to more chronic illness
- People with long-term conditions are high users of specific acute services, emergency care, primary care, social care and community care
- Long-term conditions are the leading cause of mortality in the world
- Better health for individuals and a more effective health and social care economy will be achieved by the effective management of long-term conditions
- Ill health in the workforce puts a burden on health and social care

(DH, 2007b).

Conclusion

This chapter has focused upon a variety of chronic long-term conditions and has highlighted that depressive illness is more common in patients with physical illness than those patients without physical illness. Health care professionals must be able to recognize both the biological and psychological factors which contribute to an increased risk of depression in physical illness. The management of depression in long-term chronic illness is also very important as highlighted by

MacHale (2002) who suggested that medical patients with depression were more likely to use health care resources. It has been acknowledged that many long-term chronic physical conditions will cause depression and it was also recognized by Bazire (2001) that the treatments for some of these physical conditions may cause depressive illness. MacHale (2002) suggested that some physical conditions may trigger depression if the condition is disabling, disfiguring or fatal.

Some patients with chronic illness may already have a previous depressive illness; others may have increased physical disability due to the depression, whilst for other patients both the depression and physical illness may trigger each other. One example is stress which may cause both a stroke and depression.

Keller and Boland (1998) highlighted that untreated depressive illness is a chronic disorder in its own right and if left untreated will add to the burden of physical chronic illness and disease. It has been identified that due to the similarity in symptoms of some physical illness and depression that depression may be difficult to diagnose in patients with physical illness. This highlights the importance of assessment using a holistic approach to care. Three important symptoms were identified by Hawton *et al.* (1990) when diagnosing depression in medical patients. These included depressed mood, morning depression and feelings of hopelessness.

Some depressed patients may also refuse treatment or not comply with prescribed medication. This has an impact upon physical and mental health and well-being. Non-compliance may ultimately lead to deterioration in physical health and symptoms and as a result lead to increased depressive symptoms. Health professionals need to understand the reasons for non-compliance in patients and also help patients to understand the long-term consequences of non-compliance and the effects on their health and well-being. It may be that alternative treatments or options need to be considered as some patients with chronic long-term conditions make their own decisions about the quality of their lives. Health care professionals and carers must also be aware that patients who are in pain and who have a chronic physical illness are at an increased risk of committing suicide. The importance of risk assessments and observation is important, however, equally important is the ability to enable patients to be pain free.

For some patients, an assessment may need to be undertaken to assess their mental capacity. As shown in the new Mental Capacity Act (2005), capacity is evident if the patient is able to understand, retain and believe the information about the treatment they are required to have. The patient needs to be able to weigh up the options and make a decision based on informed consent.

This chapter has focused upon the key long-term conditions identified by the DH (2004) and DH (2007b). These chronic conditions have an impact upon the lives of many individuals across the UK and in many other countries. It is evident from this chapter that research has been undertaken internationally across a variety of nations worldwide.

Long-term conditions and chronic diseases must be made a priority for health and social care and where possible further research needs to be undertaken to address key issues identified in this chapter. Do not underestimate the importance of primary care and public health in educating the public and professions about prevention rather than cure.

Reflection and discussion

Discuss the impact of depression on long-term conditions

Give some examples of chronic diseases where depression is evident

- *Depression and CHD*
- *Depression and stroke*
- *Depression and COPD*
- *Depression and renal disease*
- *Depression and diabetes*
- *Depression and cancer*
- *Depression and neurological conditions*

Discuss the importance of the role of the clinical nurse specialist in palliative care

References

Abbey, S.E., Kennedy, S.H., Kaplan, A.S., Toner, B.B. & Garfinkel, P.E. (1990). Self report symptoms that predict major depression in patients with prominent physical symptoms. *International Journal Psychological Medicine, 20*, 247–248.

Ali, S., Stone, M.A., Peters, J.L., Davies, M.J. & Khunti, K. (November 2006). The prevalence of co-morbid depression in adults with type 2 diabetes: A systematic review and meta analysis. *Diabetes Medicine, 23*(11), 1165–1173.

Anderson, R.J., Freedland, K.E., Clouse, R.E. & Lustman, P.J. (June 2001). The prevalence of co morbid depression in adults with diabetes: A meta analysis. *Diabetes Care, 24*(6), 1069–1078.

Annals of Oncology (2006). Online publication. DO1.1093/annonc/mdl85.

Barefoot, J.C. & Schroll, M. (1996). Symptoms of depression, acute myocardial infarction and total mortality in a community sample. *Circulation, 94*, 3123–3129.

Barnard, K.D., Skinner, T.C. & Peveler, R. (April 2006). The prevalence of co-morbid depression in adults with type 1 diabetes: Systematic literature review. *Diabetes Medicine, 23*(4), 445–448.

Bazire, S. (2001). *Psychotropic Drug Directory: The Professional's Pocket Handbook and Aide Memoir.* Lancaster: Quay Publishing Limited.

Beaudet, M. (2001). *Depression and Incident Heart Disease.* Toronto: Annual Epidemiology Conference.

Berg, A., Palomaki, H., Lehtihalmes, M., Lonnqvist, J. & Kaste, M. (2003). Post stroke depression: An 18 month follow up. *Stroke, 34,* 138–143.

Brown, L.C., Majumdar, S.R., Newman, S.C. & Johnson, J.A. (July 2006). Research: Type 2 diabetes does not increase risk of depression. *CMAJ, 175*(1), 42–46.

Carney, R.M., Freedland, K.E. & Miller, G.E. (2002). Depression as a risk factor for cardiac mortality and morbidity: A review of potential mechanisms. *Journal of Psychosomatic Research, 53,* 897–902.

Chapman, P.D., Perry, G.S. & Strine, T.W. (2005). The vital link between chronic disease and depressive disorder. *Preventing Chronic Disease, 2*(1), 14.

CIHI (Canadian Institute of Health Information) (2002). *Hospital Mortality Database.* Ottawa: CIHI.

Cuijpers, P. & Schoevers, R.A. (2004). Increased mortality in depressive disorders: A review. *Current Psychiatric Report, 204*(6), 430–437.

de Groot, M., Anderson, R., Freedland, K.E., Cloude, R.E. & Lustman, P.J. (July–August 2001). Association of depression and diabetes complications: A meta analysis. *Psychosomatic Medicine, 63*(4), 619–630.

DH (2001). *British Household Survey.* London: DH. Available at www.doh.gov.uk. Accessed 11 October 2007.

DH (May 2004). *Chronic Disease Management: A Compendium of Information.* London: DH.

DH (July 2007a). *A New Ambition for Stroke: A Consultation on a National Strategy.* London: DH.

DH (2007b). *Long Term Conditions.* Available at www.doh.gov.uk. Accessed 4 October 2007.

Ford, S. (2006). Depression after MI indicates future problems. Cited in: *Journal of the American College of Cardiology.* Online publication. DOI: 10.1016/j.jacc 2006. 06.077. Available at steve.ford@e-map.com. Accessed 28 June 2007.

Freedman, K.E. & Carney, R.M. (2000). Psychosocial considerations in elderly patients with heart failure. *Clinical Geriatrics, 16,* 649–661.

Georgiades, R. (2007). Diabetes and depression together increase risk for heart patients. Science News. *Science Daily,* 11 March 2007. Available at www.scisncedaily.com/releases/2007. Accessed 25 July 2007.

Glassman, A.H., O'Connor, C.M. & Califf, R.M. (2002). The sertraline antidepressant heart attack randomised trial (SADHEART) group. Sertraline treatment of major depression in patients with acute MI or unstable angina. *JAMA, 288,* 701–709.

Groenvold, M., Fayers, P.M., Sprangers, M.A., Bjorner, J.B., Klee, M.C. & Aaronson, N.K. (1999). Anxiety and depression in breast cancer patients at low risk of recurrence compared with the general population: A valid comparison? *Journal of Clinical Epidemiology, 52,* 523–530.

Hawton, K., Mayou, R. & Feldman, E. (1990). Significance of psychiatric symptoms in the general medical patient with mood disorder. *General Hospital Psychiatry, 12,* 296–302.

Haywood, C. (1995). Psychiatric illness and cardiovascular disease risk. *Epidemiology Review, 17,* 129–138.

Holahan, C.J., Moos, R.H., Holahan, C.K. & Brennan, P.L. (1997). Social context, coping strategies and depressive symptoms: An expanded model with cardiac patients. *Journal of Personality and Social Psychology, 7,* 918–928.

Hopwood, P. & Stephens, R.J. (2000). Depression in patients with lung cancer, prevalence and risk factors derived from quality of life data. *Journal of Clinical Oncology, 18*, 893–903.

Hotopf, M., Chidgey, J., Addington-Hall, J. & Lan, L.K. (2002). Depression in advanced disease: A systematic review. Part 1: Prevalence and case findings. *Palliative Medicine, 16*(2), 81–97.

Isaksson, A.K., Gunnarson, L.G. & Ahlstrom, G. (November 2007). The presence and meaning of chronic sorrow in patients with multiple sclerosis. *Journal of Clinical Nursing, 16*(11), 315–324.

Jonas, B.S. & Mussino, M.E. (2000). Symptoms of depression as a prospective risk factor for stroke. *Psychosomatic Medicine, 62*, 463–471.

Jorge, R.E., Robinson, R.G., Arndt, S. & Starkstein, S. (2003). Mortality and post stroke depression: A placebo controlled trial of antidepressants. *American Journal of Psychiatry, 160*, 1823–1829.

Katon, W., Lin, E.H.B. & Kroenke, K. (March–April 2007). The association of depression and anxiety with medical symptom burden in patients with chronic illness. *General Hospital Psychiatry, 29*(2), 147–155.

Keller, M.B. & Boland, R.J. (1998). Implications of failing to achieve successful long term maintenance treatment of recurrent unipolar major depression. *Biological Psychiatry, 44*(34), 360.

Kim, J.A., Lee, Y.K., Huh, W.S., Kim, Y.G., Kim, D.J., Oh, H.Y., Kang, S.A., Kim Moon, Y.H., Kim, H.W. & Kim, J.H. (2002). Analysis of depression in continuous ambulatory peritoneal dialysis patients. *Journal of Korean Medical Science, 17*(6), 790–794.

Kimmel, P.L. & Peterson, R.A. (2006). Depression in patients with end stage renal disease treated with dialysis: Has the time to treat arrived? *Clinical Journal of the American Society of Nephrology, 1*, 249–352.

Kimmel, P.L., Peterson, R.A., Weihs, K.L., Simmens, S.J., Alleyne, S., Cruz, I. & Veis, H. (2000). Multiple measurements of depression predict mortality in a longitudinal study of chronic hemodialysis outpatients. *Kidney International, 57*, 2093–2098.

Kimura, M., Robinson, R.G. & Kosier, J.T. (2000). Treatment of cognitive impairment after post stroke depression: A double-blind treatment trial. *Stroke, 31*, 1482–1486.

Lustman, P.J., Griffiths, L.S., Gavard, J.A. & Clouse, R.E. (1992). Depression in adults with diabetes. *Diabetes Care, 15*(11), 1631–1639.

MacHale, S. (2002). Managing depression in physical illness. Advances in psychiatric treatment. *British Journal of Psychiatry, 8*, P297–P305.

MacMahon, K.M.A. & Lip, G.Y.H. (2002). Psychological factors in heart failure: A review of the literature. *Archives of Internal Medicine, 162*, 509–516.

Massie, M.J. & Holland, J.C. (July 1990). Depression and the cancer patient. *Journal of Clinical Psychiatry, 51*(Suppl), 12–17, 18–19.

Mental Capacity Act (2005). Available at www.directgov.uk. Accessed 25 October 2007.

McCall, D. (1992). Recognition and management of asymptomatic patients with left ventricular dysfunction. *American Journal of Cardiology, 69*, 139G–140G.

Milani, R.V. & Lavie, C.J. (1998). Prevalence and effects of cardiac rehabilitation on depression in the elderly with coronary artery disease. *American Journal of Cardiology, 81*, 1233–1236.

Mikkelsen, R.L., Middelboe, T., Pisinger, C. & Stage, K.B. (January 2004). Anxiety and depression in patients with chronic obstructive airways disease (COPD). *Nordic Journal of Psychiatry, 58*(1), 65–70.

Morton, R.P., Davies, A.D., Baker, J., Baker, G.A. & Stell, P.M. (1984). Quality of life in treated head and neck cancer patients: A preliminary report. *Clinical Otolaryngology*, 9, 181–185.

Murray, C.J. & Lopez, D. (1997). Regional patterns of disability-free life expectancy and disability adjusted life expectancy: Global burden of diseases. *The Lancet*, 349, 1347–1352.

Nemeroff, C.B., Musselman, D.L. & Evans, D.L. (1998). Depression and cardiac disease. *Depression and Anxiety*, 8(Suppl 1), 71–79.

Nichols, G.A. & Brown, J.B. (2003). Unadjusted and adjusted prevalence of diagnosed depression in type 2 diabetes. *Diabetes Care*, 26, 744–749.

Nolen Hoeksema, S., Larson, J. & Grayson, C. (1999). Explaining the gender difference in depressive symptoms. *Journal of Personality and Social Psychology*, 77(5), 1060–1072.

Norwood, R. (2006). Prevalence and impact of depression in chronic obstructive pulmonary disease patients. *Current Opinion in Pulmonary Medicine*, 12(2), 113–117.

Ohira, T., Iso, H., Satoh, S., Sankai, T., Tanigawa, T. & Ogawa, Y. (2001). Prospective study of depressive symptoms and risk of stroke among Japanese. *Stroke*, 32, 903–908.

Park, C.L., Fenster, J.R., Suresh, D.P. & Bliss, D.E. (December 2006). Social support, appraisals, and coping as predictors of depression in congestive heart failure patients. *Psychology and Health*, 21(6), 773–789.

Pickering, T.G., Davidson, K. & Shimbo, D. (2004). Is depression a risk factor for coronary heart disease. *Journal of the American College of Cardiology*, 44, 472.

Pinder, K.L., Ramirez, A.J., Black, M.E., Richards, M.A., Gregory, W.M. & Rubens, R.D. (1993). Psychiatric disorder in patients with advanced breast cancer: Prevalence and associated factors. *European Journal of Cancer*, 29A, 524–527.

Pirl, W.F. (2004). Evidence report on the occurrence, assessment and treatment of depression in Cancer patients. *JNCI Monographs*, 2004(32), 32–39.

Pratt, L.A., Ford, D.E., Crum, R.M., Armenian, H.K., Gallo, J.J. & Eaton, W.W. (1996). Depression, psychotropic medication and risk of myocardial infarction. Prospective data from the Baltimore ECA follow up. *Circulation*, 94, 3123–3129.

Ramasubbu, R. & Patten, S.B. (2003). Effects of depression on stroke morbidity and mortality. *The Canadian Journal of Psychiatry*, 48, 250–257.

Reeve, J., Lloyd-Williams, M. & Dowrick, C. (2007). Depression in terminal illness: The need for primary care specific research. *Family Practice*, 24, 263–268.

Richards, H. (2005). Depression in neurological disorders: Parkinson and RSQUO-S disease, multiple sclerosis and stroke. *Journal of Neuro Surgery and Psychiatry*, 76, 148–152.

Rodin, G. & Voshart, K. (1986). Depression in the medically ill: An overview. *American Journal of Psychiatry*, 143, 696–705.

Roth, A.J., Kornblith, A.B., Batel-Copel, I., Peabody, F., Scher, H.I. & Holland, J.C. (1998). Rapid screening for psychological distress in men with prostrate carcinoma: A pilot study. *Cancer*, 82, 1904–1908.

Roundy, K., Sully, J.A. & Stanley, M.A. (2005). Are anxiety and depression addressed in primary care patients with chronic obstructive pulmonary disease? A chart review. *Primary Care Companion Journal of Clinical Psychiatry*, 7(5), 213–218.

Rugulies, R. (2002). Depression as a predictor of coronary heart disease: A review and meta analysis. *American Journal of Preventive Medicine*, 23, 51–61.

Seana, P. (2006). Cited in: *Stroke*. Online publication. D0I: 10.1161/01.STR.0000244806.05099.52.

Siegert, R.J. & Abernethy, D.A. (2005). Depression in MS: A review. *Journal of Neurology, Neurosurgery and Psychiatry*, 76, 469–475.

Simon, G.E., Von Korff, M. & Lin, E. (February 2005). Clinical and functional outcomes of depression treatment in patients with and without chronic medical illness. *Psychological Medicine, 35*(2), 271–279.

Somerset, W., Stout, S.C., Miller, A.H. & Musselman, D. (2004). Breast cancer and depression. *JNCI Monographs, 2004*(32), 105–111.

Spiegel, D. (June 1996). Cancer and depression. *British Journal of Psychiatry Supplement,* (Suppl 30), 109–116.

Stage, K.B., Middelboe, T. & Pisinger, C. (2005). Depression and chronic obstructive pulmonary disease (COPD). Impact upon survival. *Acta Psychiatrica Scandinavica, 111*(4), 320–323.

Stage, K.B., Middleboe, T., Stage, T.B. & Sorenson, C.H. (2006). Depression in COPD. Management and quality of life considerations. *International Journal of COPD, 1*(3), 315.

Tedman, B.M., Young, C.A. & Williams, I.R. (October 1997). Assessment of depression in patients with motor neurone disease and other neurologically disabling illness. *Journal of the Neurological Sciences, 152*(Suppl 1), 75–79.

The ENRICHD Investigators (2003). The effects of treating depression and low social support on clinical events after myocardial infarction: The enhancing recovery in coronary heart disease patients (ENRICHD) randomised trial. *JAMA, 289,* 3106–3116.

Tossani, E., Cassano, P. & Fava, M. (March 2005). Psychological factors in patients with chronic kidney disease. Depression and renal disease. *Seminars in Dialysis, 18*(2), 73–81.

van de Brink, R.H., van Melle, J.P. & Honig, A. (2002). Treatment of depression after myocardial infarction and the effects on cardiac prognosis and quality of life: Rationale and outline of the myocardial infarction and depression – intervention trial. (MIND-IT). *American Heart Journal, 144,* 219–2125.

Williams, L.S., Jones, W.J., Shen, J., Robinson, R.L., Weinberger, M. & Kroenke, K. (2003). Prevalence and impact of depression and pain in neurology outpatients. *Journal of Neurology, Neurosurgery and Psychiatry, 74,* 1587–1589.

Williams, M.L. & Payne, S. (June 2003). A qualitative study of clinical nurse specialists' views on depression in palliative care patients. *Palliative Medicine, 17*(4), 334–338.

Wulsin, L.R. & Singal, B.M. (2003). Do depressive symptoms increase the risk for the onset of coronary disease? A systematic quantitative review. *Psychosomatic Medicine, 65,* 201–210.

Zhang, X., Norris, S.L. & Gregg, E.W. (2005). Depressive symptoms and mortality among persons with and without diabetes. *American Journal of Epidemiology, 161,* 652–660.

Zigmund, A. & Snaith, R.P. (1983). The Hospital Anxiety and Depression Scale. *Acta Psychiatrica Scandinavica, 67,* 361–370.

Chapter 6

Depression in later life

Introduction

This chapter discusses the impact of depression and bereavement in late life. It is acknowledged that most people will be bereaved at some time throughout the life cycle; however, the impact upon the older person can be very significant. The chapter initially reviews causes of depression in later life, the management and treatment of depression in older people and also the perceptions of care workers caring for older people. Different types of treatments are discussed as well as the important aspects of adherence, compliance and concordance with treatment regimes when treating depression.

The importance of respecting the dignity of older people has become a main focus as highlighted by recent government reports and by the Commission for Health Audit and Inspection (2007). Dignity and respect are important issues to consider when caring for older vulnerable people who may also be depressed and unable to verbalize their needs. Depression may ultimately influence behaviour and ability to respond to treatment and self-care. Concordance and compliance are explored highlighting how carers and health professionals can support older people when adapting their treatment options. Many issues are explored throughout the chapter including the importance of recognizing depression in older people and the need to undertake risk assessments when assessing suicidal risk in this potentially vulnerable group of people. The Geriatric Depression Scale is one of the tools used to assess for suicidal risk in the older person. There have been a variety of policies and reports published by the Department of Health and Audit Commission, and the National Service Framework (NSF) for Older People (DH, 2001) aims to support underpinning knowledge and practice throughout the chapter.

The second part of this chapter discusses aspects of the grieving process and different models of grief. It highlights that bereavement and the grieving process is a normal aspect of coping with the loss of a loved one. However, it also briefly discusses abnormal grief and the importance of seeking help and support ensuring appropriate interventions are sought.

Ethnicity as well as cultural aspects of grief in old age are explored. Support and perceived support are important for bereaved people and can provide a lifeline when helping older depressed people come to terms with their loss. The chapter concludes with discussion about bereavement in adult life.

Causes and incidence of depression in late life

Livingston *et al.* (1990) recognized that depression affected approximately 15% of people over the age of 65 years and was the most common mental disorder in later life. The DH (1997) anticipated that over the next 20 years, the number of UK residents aged over 65 years would increase to approximately 14.5 million.

It is evident from this number of older people, surviving into old age, that these demographic changes have become a reality for the UK. An increase in the older population has an impact upon mental health as many older people with long-term physical conditions may also suffer with mental health problems, both having a knock on effect upon the other.

Katona and Katona (1996) undertook a consensus on depression in old age and identified that some older people would definitely suffer from depression. Psychiatric epidemiological studies undertaken by Copeland *et al.* (1991) and Evans and Katona (1993) demonstrated that older people were more likely to suffer from mental health problems particularly depression and dementia.

More recently, the Audit Commission (2000) undertook a report into mental health services for older people. It was named 'forget-me-not' as it aimed to highlight the specific mental health needs of older people. It highlighted a variety of reasons why older people become depressed which included:

- Disability
- Poverty
- Poor physical health
- Lack of social support
  (Audit Commission, 2000).

Other factors that must also be considered are dementia, alcohol abuse and anorexia as they may also be associated with depression in old age.

Depression and dementia

Depression impacts upon cognitive functioning. People with dementia may also suffer from depression but it may not be recognized or diagnosed as the person's mental state and functioning may have deteriorated to such a state that assessment for depression is difficult to achieve. Jorm (2000) recognized that depression in early life could become a risk factor for dementia and cognitive decline in old age.

After undertaking a meta-analysis, Jorm (2000) found that depression was associated with dementia, and also recognized that further research needed to be undertaken. Lam *et al.* (2004) undertook research into depression in dementia. They compared the accuracy of four depression scales in an older Chinese population with varying degrees of dementia. The scales used were the Geriatric Depression Scale (GDS), Even Briefer Assessment Scale for depression (EBAS DEP) and Single Question and the Cornell Scale for Depression in Dementia (Cornell). The dementia was categorized into mild and moderate to severe. The study concluded that administering the Single Question followed by the Cornell Scale was the most efficient way of detecting depression in dementia.

However, all scales highlighted the difficulty in detecting depression in people with more severe dementia. Other behaviours such as alcohol abuse can also affect older people and may either be the cause of depression or used as a means to cope with depression.

Alcohol misuse in old age

The Royal College of Psychiatrists (RCPsych, 2007) estimated that 9 out of 10 people in the UK drank alcohol. They estimated that 1 in 4 men and 1 in 7 women were drinking enough alcohol to cause some medical damage. The more alcohol one drank the greater the tolerance level, thus more is required to achieve the same effect. Alcohol can become addictive causing both physical and psychological effects upon the body. The RCPsych (2007) highlighted how alcohol addiction causes memory loss and can cause dementia, psychotic behaviour and dependence. There is also an increased chance of suicide where alcohol abuse is associated with depression. They stated that as alcohol changes the brain chemistry, it causes depression. Johnson (2000) predicted that there would be an increase in alcohol addiction in older people during the next century. This has major implications for carers and service providers as they will be treating a group of people that are not expected to abuse alcohol. Along with that come the issues of mental decline, cognitive impairment and also other chronic illnesses and diseases.

It is also evident that older people's tolerance level to alcohol may be affected due to poor absorption, metabolism and inability to excrete waste products due to liver, kidney or blood pressure complications. Thus, treating older depressed people with alcohol addiction will become a complex matter. Khan *et al.* (2002) highlighted how drinking patterns in older people were often hidden and misdiagnosed as screening was often focused around younger people. As the ageing population increases, screening and diagnostic criteria will need to be adapted to ensure that the health needs of the older population are met.

The National Institute on Alcohol Abuse and Alcoholism (2003) has recognized a trend where many adults as well as younger people have increased their alcohol intake with devastating effects to both themselves and their families. As a consequence of drinking, some people also neglect themselves and suffer from nutrient deficiencies and may also suffer from anorexia.

Anorexia in old age

Poor nutrition in older people has been a focus of media attention and television programmes in the UK. It is apparent that this has become a global problem as identified by Chapman (2007) in Australia and Donini *et al.* (2003) in Italy.

They highlighted that much of the published research has focused upon hospital inpatients and older people in residential homes and nursing home settings. Chapman (2007) stated that this reduction in food intake in older people has become known as 'the anorexia of ageing'. Many older people lack the motivation to eat which can occur as a result of inability to access the shops, due to financial reasons, inability to cook for themselves, living alone, being socially isolated, physically ill or as a result of depression. Health promotion and public policy determines and promotes healthy lifestyles for older people by encouraging them to eat less and eat more healthily. However, Donini *et al.* (2003) argued that many older people eat less anyway and as a result may be predisposed to anorexia or chronic physical conditions, particularly if protein is reduced in their diet. Some of these concepts are also influenced by older people's beliefs about the causation of illness.

Beliefs about depression

Older people's beliefs about the causes of depression influence their conceptualization of the condition. Lawrence *et al.* (2006) undertook a study in the UK to explore how older adults with depression and the general older population conceptualized depression. This was a multicultural study incorporating White British, Black Caribbean and South Asian older adults.

Many of the participants perceived depression as a consequence of personal or social occurrences prevalent to old age. There appeared to be some differences in responses between the different ethnic groups; however, most participants responded to questions about their mood. It was apparent that health care professionals needed to consider the different interpretations used by older people from ethnic groups when considering their perceptions of causes of depression.

A variety of studies have been undertaken to predict depression in old age. Stek *et al.*'s (2006) study which was undertaken in Holland identified the incidence, course and predictors of depression in the general population of the oldest old. It was a prospective population study of 500 people between the ages of 85 and 89 years. Depression was assessed using the GDS. The study findings showed that poor daily functioning and institutionalization were strongly associated with depression in this age group and that amongst the oldest old depression was frequent and persistent.

Thus, health care professionals need to understand the importance of maintaining older people's independence when caring for them in longer-term care settings. Walker *et al.* (1998) found that depression was common in up to 40% of older people living in nursing homes, residential homes or sheltered accommodation. Rosswurm (1983) stated that a move from their own home into a care environment can be very traumatic for older people. This is not surprising, as they may already have experienced a variety of losses which may include: loss of a partner, loss of independence, disability and poor health. On top of these, they now face losing their home.

Carers need to understand that depression in older people may not be recognized when the focus is upon physical illnesses, confusion or dementia which may mask the symptoms of depression.

A variety of causes of depression in older people have been explored by Lawrence *et al.* (2006). Lawrence *et al.*'s (2006) study recognized that loss was strongly associated with depression in older people. This could be loss of health, loss of loved ones, loss of freedom or loss of independence.

Bagley (2000) highlighted that carers needed to be aware of this to prevent them believing that depressive symptoms were understandable reactions to loss and life changes. This may be one reason why depression is underreported in older people. Ruggles (1998) suggested that although life events such as bereavement can trigger depression, it is likely to be caused by a combination of factors and life stresses. This could include loss of a partner, loss of home and a move into a care home. This demonstrates a variety of loss and change in a short space of time for an older person. Thus, it is not surprising that some older people become depressed.

Lawrence *et al.* (2006) acknowledged that retirement was also a time when depression was evident for some older people who try to adapt to their new role without paid employment. For many people, retirement is a time of excitement and an opportunity to achieve their lifelong ambitions. However, this is not always fulfilled due to financial implications, disability or long-term illness. For some, this may lead to marital breakdown which may add to the severity of the depression.

Some White older people from Lawrence *et al.*'s (2006) study believed that depression was genetically determined and that people with weaker personalities were more likely to be affected. They also identified social circumstances such as lack of finances to be a cause of depression.

However, there appears to be a cultural difference in interpreting the causes of depression in old age. Many of these perceived causes will be experienced by people of all ages during their lifespan; however, the older people are more vulnerable in relation to loss due to timely events in their life.

Thus, it is important that appropriate assessments are used to detect depression in older people. The GDS is the most frequently used scale to assess for depression in older people.

The Geriatric Depression Scale-15

Appropriate assessment for depression is essential to ensure that older people get the right treatment and services they require. As already stated, many older people are vulnerable and often socially isolated. They may receive care from a variety of health and social care professionals as well as carers and family members.

Nurses can play a key role in the assessment of depression by using screening tools to aid them to recognize and report causes and symptoms of depression in older people. Bagley (2000) and Teresi *et al.* (2001) both advocate early assessment and observation to help detect depression. One of the most appropriate assessment scales used by most professionals for older people is the GDS-15. It has been so frequently used that Keiffer and Reese (2002) found 338 published articles which cited the use of the scale. Montorio and Izal (1996) suggested that its use was less accurate when assessing for mild to moderate depression in older people; however, Beck (1991) and Anderson (2001) advocated its use by the British Geriatric Society and also the Royal College of General Practitioners. The scale is relatively easy to use and score and is suitable for both health and social care professionals. Brink *et al.* (1982) suggested that a score of 11 or above out of the 30 possible scores was a strong indicator of depression. Sheikh and Yesavage (1986) highlighted the development of the shorter version of the GDS scale which had 15 items instead of 30, suggesting that this was equally as effective when assessing for depression in older people. Having assessed for depression, it is then important to manage the condition appropriately.

Management of depression in old age

To ensure that depression in older people is managed appropriately, a correct diagnosis as well as the appropriate treatment is needed. Carson and Margolin (2005) highlighted the causes and management of depression in older people with neurological illness and also the importance of addressing their physical and psychological needs.

Marks *et al.* (1979) highlighted concern about the ability of general practitioners (GPs) to detect psychiatric illness. They recognized that GPs were more likely to diagnose and treat physical illness than mental illness. The National Institute of Mental Health (NIMH) (2001) highlighted that by focusing on physical symptoms rather than on how the person was feeling gave an altered presentation. Lawrence *et al.*'s (2006) study suggested that clinicians needed to ask older people about life events and recent loss when assessing for depression. It was also important for health professionals to have an understanding of cultural and language differences when asking questions about depression.

As a consequence of these factors, it is not surprising that many older people do not receive the correct treatment. This was highlighted by Blanchard *et al.* (1994)

who recognized that only 15% of older people received appropriate treatment for depression from both primary and secondary services.

Because of the limited amount of research undertaken at that time, Watts *et al.* (2002) undertook a survey to determine the mental health needs of older people in Salford in Manchester. The findings showed a large number of older people using primary care services requiring treatment. In this study, anxiety was the main mental health condition identified.

It did not highlight a large number of older people purely with depression due to the use of different methodologies to gather the research. This survey considered mental needs as a whole and not just specifically depression in older people. However, it was evident that when a diagnosis of depression had been made the older person could then be helped to seek appropriate treatment.

Baldwin and Wild (2004) suggested that physical, psychological and social factors must be considered when managing depression in older people. This supports a holistic approach to care. However, to provide this care, a variety of professionals must work together ensuring a multidisciplinary approach. There has been literature published on multidisciplinary approaches to care (BMA, 2003; Unutzer *et al.*, 2002) and also for interdisciplinary working (Burns and Lloyd, 2004). There is evidence to support how collaborative working helps to reduce depressive symptoms and improve response rates to treatment. Hunkeler *et al.* (2006) undertook a randomized control study which was followed up after 2 years. They concluded that collaborative primary care management was more effective than the usual care provided for older people with depression. This was supported by Gensichen *et al.* (2006) who had undertaken a systematic review into how case management improved major depression in primary health care.

Organizations need to consider how this will be achieved and what needs to be put into place to make it happen. Gilbody *et al.* (2004) considered both educational and organizational interventions to improve the management of depression in primary care.

In addition to considering physical and psychological factors, social aspects of depression are also important. Thus, illness and disability need to be considered when establishing an older person's ability to socialize. Other social factors highlighted by Baldwin and Wild (2004) which help to alleviate depression include improved access to transport and crime reduction. Not surprisingly, many older people live in fear and are afraid to go out because of these social factors. Having considered these important issues, health care professionals need to ensure that older people are offered appropriate treatment for depression.

Treatment

It is important for health professionals to consider all treatment options prior to treating depression in later life. Baldwin and Wild (2004) advocated using a combination of both antidepressant treatments and psychological treatments to maintain well-being. They also suggested that improved collaboration was needed between both specialist and primary care services in order to promote appropriate case management and monitor interventions.

Baldwin *et al.* (2002) expressed concern that despite the availability of a variety of treatments, depression was not very well managed. The types of treatments available to treat depression include antidepressants, psychosocial and psychological inventions.

As already established, it may be appropriate for some people to have a combination of these treatments. Each person needs to be assessed, diagnosed and treated accordingly. Medication such as antidepressants may be prescribed. However, a variety of factors need to be considered before prescribing.

Baldwin and Wild (2004) suggested the following factors needed to be considered when prescribing medication for older people:

- Has the older person got any physical condition which may affect the way medication is metabolized, particularly in relation to impaired renal or hepatic function.
- Do they have increased susceptibility to side effects?
- Do they have a poor physical condition such as pressure areas, dehydration or weight loss?

Raj (2004) suggested that the anticholinergic effects of some drug treatments were particularly troublesome for older people and this needed to be considered when prescribing for older people. Raj (2004) advocated that SSRIs (selective serotonin reuptake inhibitors) were an effective drug treatment for depression in older people due to their efficiency and overall safety. However, it was important to select medication that was compatible with other medication they may be taking, thus reducing potential side effects and contraindications.

Adherence, compliance and concordance

Other important factors to consider when prescribing medication for older people are non-adherence and non-compliance. Non-adherence to medication results in negative outcomes for patients which can have devastating consequences for older people.

However, Hughes (2004) suggested that many older people make a conscious decision not to adhere to medication. This is often referred to as intentional non-adherence and occurs due to concerns about the side effects of medication. Health professionals must ensure that they inform all patients about side effects of medication, however, being informed allows patients to make decisions and choices about their health and treatment. Their *decision* not to take medication needs to be weighed against the *risk* of not taking medication. If the person has low mood and depressive symptoms they could become suicidal and attempt or actually commit suicide as a result of their depressed mood.

The risk of overdose is also another factor to be considered and will determine the type of medication prescribed.

SCIE (2005) provided a variety of key messages when helping older people take prescribed medication at home. It highlighted that 45% of medication prescribed in the UK was for older people aged 65 years and over. It also suggested that many older people living at home failed to comply with prescribed medication regimes.

Various articles and literature have been published on concordance with medication as shown by Chen (1999), Bending (2002), Bissell (2003), Banning (2004) and Ryan-Woolley and Rees (2005). Compliance of the patient along with the type of information given by the health professional are key aspects in relation to concordance as shown by Hughes (2004) who argued that concordance relied upon an alliance between the patient and the health care professional. Concordance is one way of allowing people to voice their concerns about their medication. This is achieved by the patient discussing the medication with the prescriber and agreeing with the treatment and quantity to be taken.

It must be acknowledged that it is not only doctors who prescribe medication for people. With new approaches to care delivery and advanced roles, supplementary and independent prescribing have become a reality for pharmacists and nurses from a variety of specialities including health visiting, district nursing, community mental health nursing, nurse practitioners and specialist nurses in hospitals and are key individuals prescribing treatment for patients. Some nurse consultants and specialist nurses running nurse-led clinics are also nurse prescribers and are in prime positions to offer support to patients and give advice regarding their medication.

SCIE (2005) suggested that concordance was a way of dealing with intentional non-compliance. Published work in relation to patients with mental health problems are illustrated by Day (2003) who used examples of concordance in mental health to illustrate problems that occurred when carrying out research in the area of compliance.

Ryan-Woolley and Rees (2005) discussed concordance in relation to prescribing *with* rather than prescribing *for* frail older patients with the help of a medicine organizer. Their study included sheltered housing residents and concluded that a pharmacy-prepared medicines organizer provided a visual way of reminding patients to take their medication. This approach improved communication by reminding the older people to take their medication and also reduced wastage.

SCIE (2005) supported this approach by suggesting that reminders, compliance aids and supervision were the most appropriate ways of improving compliance in older people.

Types of treatment available

Medication

A Cochrane Review was undertaken by Wilson *et al.* (2001) which showed that antidepressants were an appropriate treatment for older people with major depression. However, it recommended that more research needed to be undertaken when using low-dosage antidepressants to treat depressive episodes in primary care. Katona and Livingston (2002) advocated the use of SSRIs and Venlafaxine as they had fewer reported side effects in older people.

Some of the severe side effects of antidepressants in older people include postural hypotension and cardiac arrhythmias, and potential gastrointestinal haemorrhage. These side effects must be considered and balanced against the risks of not taking the medication. Thus, prescribers have an important role to play in deciding which medication is appropriate for individual patients.

Baldwin and Wild (2004) suggested that in addition to being more prone to side effects, older people with depression may be more likely to suffer from dehydration and weight loss. They also highlighted that care needed to be undertaken when discontinuing antidepressant treatment especially after taking them for more than 8 weeks. Raj (2004) acknowledged that older people needed to be informed that some medication may take up to 6 or 12 weeks to reach its optimum effect and that patience and compliance were important factors to be considered. Raj (2004) also suggested that poor responses to antidepressants occurred as a result of not allowing the drug to reach its therapeutic dose which was the fault of doctors not adjusting the dose range. For some patients, medication can be combined with psychological interventions and approaches such as cognitive behavioural therapy (CBT).

Psychological interventions

CBT is the most frequently used psychological approach to treat depression.

Thompson *et al.* (2001) undertook a study comparing the use of the antidepressant desipramine with CBT with a group of older outpatients diagnosed with mild to moderate depression. The findings demonstrated that CBT was a very effective treatment in older people. Baldwin and Wild (2004) suggested that further research was needed into the effectiveness of CBT with physically frail older people; however, Thompson *et al.* (2001) advocated that it was more effective to use a combination of both antidepressants and CBT when treating people with major depression than using either treatment approach on its own. This combined approach also helped prevent relapse which is an important factor to be considered.

McEvoy and Barnes (2007) found that even though effective medication and psychological treatments were available, the outcome for depressed older adults with physical conditions was poor. They developed a systematic approach to care by using a chronic care model with the aim of effectively supporting depressed people. This model has been supported by previous research studies including a trial highlighted by McEvoy and Barnes (2007) regarding the prevention of suicide in the older person in primary care. Many older people have multiple pathology, thus it is not just isolated conditions that are being treated. This highlights the importance of considering all appropriate treatments in relation to older people with depression.

Electroconvulsive therapy

Electroconvulsive therapy (ECT) is used to treat depression that has not responded well to antidepressants. Tew *et al.* (1999) considered its use in old age, finding it applicable for those older people who may be suicidal or when the depression is so severe that the person is at risk of nutritional deficiency and dehydration. These are potential life-threatening situations where the person requires quick and effective interventions. However, Baldwin and Wild (2004) highlighted that ECT is not without side effects and should be used with caution in older people with cardiac problems or hypertension. These risks to health must be balanced against undertaking ECT treatment. It is evident that older people with depression need to be treated appropriately. It is also clear that older people must be treated equally effectively as any other age group as they may also attempt or actually commit suicide.

Suicide and older people

Gallo *et al.* (1994) suggested that attempted suicide tended to be less common in older people. However, Conwell *et al.* (1998) argued that suicidal intent in older people needed to be taken very seriously as it was undertaken with determination and forward planning and was often associated with physical illness and loss including bereavement.

This view is supported by a report entitled Older People and Suicide (2007) which was written following a study undertaken at the Centre for Ageing and Mental Health at Staffordshire University. The report suggested that older people were more likely to commit suicide than any other age group. It highlighted that for every 200 suicide attempts by 16- to 25-year olds, only one would be successful; however, one in every two suicide attempts was successful in older people aged 80 years and older.

This has major implications for older people and also for both their formal and informal carers. It identifies and reinforces the need to recognize potential causes of depression in older people and to take these symptoms very seriously and not just assume that these feelings are part of the normal ageing process. Retirement, dementia and physical illness have an impact upon older people and should be considered important factors when assessing for depression. Harwood *et al.* (2000) found that older men were more likely to hang themselves and that older women were more likely to take drug overdoses. This was particularly evident in the UK; however, in America McIntosh (2002) suggested that men were more likely to shoot themselves with a firearm. This demonstrates that access to the means enables a person to choose a different mode of suicide. Within America, the gun laws are different to the UK and it is more likely that they would have access to firearms and guns.

This highlights that from a cultural perspective health care professionals must be aware of the means of and access to both attempted and actual suicide.

Because of the demographic changes with an increasing older population living to a great old age, the WHO (2003) predicted that there will be over one billion people over the age of 60 years by the year 2020. Many older people live alone where there is potential for them to become depressed, thus suicide prevention for older people should become a key focus for health and social policy across the globe, particularly when reporting morbidity and mortality in older people.

Morbidity and mortality

Morbidity is linked to causes of a particular condition or illness, whilst mortality refers to death rates from a particular condition or illness. Thus, causes of depression are associated with morbidity and suicide as a consequence of depression would be associated with mortality.

This is supported by Penninx et al. (2000) who found that depressive illness had a negative effect on the quality of a person's life and was associated with suicide in later life. Further evidence by Cuijpers and Smit (2002) who undertook a meta-analysis of community studies found that depression was a predictor of mortality. Penninx et al. (1999) had undertaken a previous study in the Netherlands to determine the risk of death in older people from minor and major depression. It included 3056 men and women and was undertaken over a 4-year period.

After considering a variety of variables such as health status, socio-demographics and health behaviour, the study concluded that minor depression in older men and major depression in both older men and women increased their risk of dying. Even though this was not a very large study, the findings need to be considered carefully.

Baldwin and Wild (2004) stated that the prevalence of depression in older patients in care homes and hospitals was double that of older people in their own homes. The rationale was that depression and disability were closely associated. This is supported by Tuma (2000) who suggested that mortality was high in depressed older people as many of them also had long-term physical conditions.

These studies focused upon hospital-based patients; however, many older people are being cared for in their own homes and this highlights the need for more research into depression and older people in their own homes. Wherever depressed older people are being cared for there is a need to ensure that the people caring for them understand both the condition and how to help them to access the correct services.

Perceptions of care workers caring for older depressed adults

Older people are cared for by a variety of health and social care agencies as well as by the voluntary sector and friends and family members. Carers whether professionally qualified or unqualified play an essential role. These individuals need to understand that their own perceptions of the people they care for will influence the care they provide. Thus, it is important that all carers have a sense of self-awareness.

McCrae *et al.* (2005) undertook a qualitative study of social care workers who were caring for depressed older people. The study considered the care workers' perceptions of the older person's condition. It was a very small study consisting of only 20 social care practitioners in South London; however, the findings showed that depression was very common amongst the old people they cared for and that social isolation was the main perceived cause of depression. The social care workers believed generally that primary care services did not consider depression in older people to be a priority whilst the mental health services provided a better service. This highlights the differences in perception not only from the care workers but also the perceived perception of the service providers.

The findings of this study recommended improvements in the provision of both social and psychological interventions for older depressed people. This study recognized the importance of primary care provision and that with the right interventions older depressed people could be supported in their local community to live a much better quality of life. Thus, it is important that both local and national health and social policies address equality of care and access to services across the nation.

National Service Framework for older people

The NSF for Mental Health was published by the DH (1999). However, older people appeared to have been neglected until the publication of the NSF for Older People in March 2001 (DH, 2001) and incorporated eight fundamental standards of care for older people. The most relevant standard to older people and mental health was standard seven. Standard seven focused upon the importance of multi-agency team working through specialist mental heath teams. The focus was on dementia services and patients with depression. Development of protocols for both dementia and depression were recommended within primary care. This demonstrates that there has been an attempt at a national level to address the mental health needs of older people, however, more focus is needed as to how these services will be resourced and delivered to the population during the latter years of their lifespan.

The second part of this chapter discusses bereavement in relation to the grieving process and highlights issues associated with abnormal grief.

Bereavement and grief

Bereavement is experienced by individuals of all ages across the lifespan; however, the bereavement experience can cause major life changes for adults depending on when these life events occur and the support networks they are able to access.

It is important to recognize the symptoms of normal grief and distinguish them from abnormal grief reactions. Kubler Ross is a famous author who constructed a theoretical model around the dying process. This model was developed to help people understand the mental, emotional and psychological feelings experienced by the dying person. Kubler Ross (1969) wrote the book *On Death and Dying* after talking to dying patients and bereaved people. Stages within the theoretical model were developed which she believed to be universal; however, she also recognized that individuals who were dying would experience the stages at different times and not necessarily in the same order.

Kubler Ross stages of dying

- Denial and isolation
- Anger
- Bargaining
- Depression
- Acceptance
        (Kubler Ross, 1969).

There is little evidence to show that all dying people will go through these exact stages or experience all of these emotions; however, this process does help other people to put the dying persons' feelings and emotions into some perspective. The stages of grief experienced by the dying person can also be experienced by the bereaved as they try to come to terms with their loss. Having experienced this loss and void in their lives, the bereaved and their family and close friends need to recognize the difference between sadness and grief and depression. This can be difficult due to the experience of similar emotions and feelings.

It can also be a time when depression is not initially recognized as it is accepted that bereaved people should feel and act in a certain way. Lawrence *et al.*'s (2006) study found that older people were able to distinguish between depression and sadness and grief. They recognized that sadness and grief were reactions to life events or circumstances and would pass, whereas depression was something that if left untreated could go on forever.

However, it must be recognized that there may be cultural differences. Lawrence *et al.* (2006) found that Black Caribbean older people associated grief and depression as being much more strongly linked than older people from White cultures. However, Lawrence *et al.*'s (2006) study found that White older people believed that bereavement caused depression, particularly loss of a spouse. There may also be gender differences when looking at illness causation and lay peoples' perspectives. Culture, beliefs and past experience are issues that have been explored in earlier chapters. Ethnicity and depression must also be considered by health care services.

Ethnicity and depression

Depression affects many people from different cultures and communities. This is supported by Bhui *et al.* (2001) who recognized that there were high levels of depression amongst older people from South Asian and Black Caribbean communities. Research undertaken by Boneham *et al.* (1997) highlighted the unmet needs of older ethnic minorities and barriers to accessing mental health services in Liverpool. They found that access to services for older people was very low. This may be due to a variety of factors including language barriers, cultural differences and perceptions of illness.

Goldberg and Huxley (1980) recognized that these individual beliefs about illness were important as they determined whether individuals sought help or accessed appropriate services. One example identified by Bhuga (1996) were South Asian women who understood the psychological aspects of depression, however, were not familiar with traditional medical models of health.

Stigma associated with mental health may also prevent ethnic minorities from accessing care and treatment. Comino *et al.* (2001) found that Asian and Black Caribbean people were less likely to be diagnosed with depression than White people. An immediate reaction would be to think that this is unfair treatment and inequitable provision of services. However, health care professionals need to understand potential reasons as to why this occurs. These may include cultural differences in the way that ethnic minorities respond to questions about their health. Some examples highlighted by Abas (1996), Baker *et al.* (1995) and Mallet *et al.* (1994) suggested that many older Caribbean people used different terms and phrases which would then lead health care professionals to consider whether they were depressed.

Some examples included feeling low-spirited. When assessing patients, White professionals were more likely to ask if the patient was feeling sad or unhappy. These terms were not used by Black Caribbeans and the diagnosis of depression could be missed.

Thus, cultural sensitivity and understanding must be considered when developing new assessments and rating scales or when using current assessment rating scales and assessment tools for people from a variety of different backgrounds and cultures. Theories have been developed to help individuals understand stages and experiences undertaken throughout the lifespan.

Lifespan developmental theories

Back in 1950, Erikson proposed a theory of lifespan development which was based upon eight stages experienced by people in their lifetime. These stages included: birth, childhood, adolescence, leaving home, marriage, having a baby, retirement and loss of a partner. It is recognized that not all people will fulfil these life events at these recognized points in their lifespan, however, for many short term. These would include normal grief reactions following death of a loved one, loss of a job or relationship breakdown. It is the inability to function normally for that individual which will determine if the depression requires intervention over a longer period of time. It is the number of symptoms experienced over a longer period of time that is a key indicator of depression. The cause of these symptoms is also an important factor to consider as there are different types of depression. Also, there are issues about compliance with treatment regimes which can affect the severity of the illness and also choice of treatment options.

Different types of depression

Thompson and Mathias (2000) suggest that depression is often categorized as a mood or affective disorder; however, there are a variety of types and varying degrees of depression.

The *ICD-10 Classification of Mental and Behavioural Disorders* (WHO, 1997) reviews the categories of mild, moderate and severe depression when diagnosing an initial depressive episode. Further depressive episodes are classified under categories of recurrent depressive disorder.

Scott (1988) suggested that chronic depression is defined when the symptoms occur for 2 or more years. Scott (1988) highlighted many factors which predicted the chronicity of major depression. It is more likely to affect females with neurotic personality traits who have high familial commitments. Other important factors to consider are the length of time the person has had the illness prior to getting treatment and the appropriateness of the treatment given.

Major depression

Major depression is also called clinical depression or unipolar depression. These symptoms are based upon the *ICD-10 Classification of Mental and Behavioural Disorders* (WHO, 1997).

Typical symptoms

- Depressed mood
- Loss of interest and enjoyment
- Reduced energy

Common symptoms

- Reduced concentration and attention
- Reduced self-esteem and self-confidence
- Ideas of guilt and unworthiness
- Bleak and pessimistic view of the future

- Ideas or acts of self-harm or suicide
- Disturbed sleep
- Diminished appetite

The *ICD-10 Classification of Mental and Behavioural Disorders* (WHO, 1997).

The severity is based upon the number of symptoms and the effect this has upon the individual's daily living. These symptoms will have been experienced for a period of at least 2 weeks.

Dysthymia

Dysthymia is a more chronic but milder depressive order than major depression. It is more prevalent in women than in men and also is more likely to occur in the older person.

Common symptoms

- Depressed mood for most of the day for at least 2 years
- Presence of at least two of the following:
  Poor appetite
  Insomnia
  Low energy or fatigue
  Poor concentration and difficulty in making decisions
  Feelings of hopelessness
- Absence of mania

These symptoms affect the ability to function socially and occupationally. These symptoms are taken from the *DSM IV* criteria. The criteria is a well-used classification system within the UK which views mental disorders as comprising specific symptoms.

Manic depression or bipolar disorder

Manic depression is also known as bipolar disorder where a person has high- and low-mood swings. Bipolar disorder or manic depression causes major depressive episodes and is shown when the person displays extreme alternations in mood between mania and deep depression.

Bland (1997) estimated that about 1% of the population will experience bipolar disorder and that it is during the late teens or early adulthood that symptoms appear. The National Institute of Mental Health Genetics Workgroup (1998) identified that there is a genetic link and that research with twins demonstrates individuals these life events occur, albeit in a different order. During many of these stages, conflict and life crisis occur. This lifespan approach is relevant in relation to bereavement and dying particularly if the death is timely or untimely. As a result, it may be easier for the bereaved to accept the death of an older person who had a terminal illness or severe disability as the death is seen as timely and is perceived to be at an appropriate crisis point in their life rather than a young adult or child. The lifespan stage of the bereaved is also an important factor to consider in relation to timely events.

For many older people, there may be susceptibility between illness and life events. This was explored by Totman (1979) who highlighted that social support was a protective influence upon health. If there is a supportive family or close network of friends, the person is more likely to maintain improved health than individuals who are socially isolated. Totman (1979) also recognized that there was an increased likelihood of mortality following bereavement, residential moves and retirement, which were stages also identified by Erikson (1950). This highlights the importance of recognizing multiple losses in people and how social support helps to maintain better health. This is also recognized by Bowlby (1980) who studied attachment and loss. Much of his work focused around children and mothers in relation to being separated from their mother at a very young age. However, it is also evident that adults also experience similar feelings when they have been bereaved. This was pursued by Murray Parkes (1972) who suggested that the grieving process was a necessary adaptation to enable individuals to function appropriately after experiencing loss. Cultural belonging and religious rituals can also help the bereaved to cope with loss.

This is shown in people who believe that there is life after death or that the person lives on in another being. Funerals are also a means of offering support to the bereaved and offer a right of passage for the dead. These rituals also help to finalize and create an ending for what may have been a long process of illness and stress. This is where health care professionals need to be sensitive to different faiths and beliefs and to recognize that people from different cultures may demonstrate a variety of behaviours when grieving and adapting to their loss. Even though they may not appear normal reactions in one culture, they may well be normal behaviours and experiences in another culture, thus it is important to acknowledge normal grief reactions.

Normal grief reactions

There are a variety of feelings and emotions experienced by the bereaved. Most of these feelings are normal grief reactions which help individuals to adapt to their situation and changes ahead. Zerbe and Steinberg (2000) discussed how coming to terms with grief and loss were important aspects of the grieving process.

Grieving incorporates physical, emotional, behavioural and cognitive experiences which are shown below:

- Numbness
- Disbelief and denial
- Lamentation
- Searching and yearning
- Anger
- Anxiety
- Physical distress
- Guilt
- Pining
- Mourning
- Depression and despair
- Apathy
- Lack of interest
      Adapted from Murray Parkes (1972).

Similar to these identified grief reactions, Worden (1986) developed tasks of mourning which he believed the bereaved needed to experience in order to enable them to move on in their lives. He argued that this was a process of emotional work that the bereaved needed to accomplish as part of the grieving process:

- Task 1: The person needs to accept the reality of the loss.
- Task 2: The person needs to experience the pain of grief.
- Task 3: The person needs to adjust to an environment where the deceased is missing.
- Task 4: The person needs to withdraw emotional energy and reinvest it in another relationship.

      Adapted from Worden (1986).

This process can help the bereaved person to cope, adapt to new circumstances and take control over their own life. Bereavement counselling may be used to help the person with their grief. However, for some individuals their grief may be more complicated due to delayed or prolonged grief caused by anger, resentment and disappointment. This can occur in individuals if the death was not timely, i.e. due to suicide, murder, missing person or the person being blown up by a bomb resulting in there being no body to bury. Death caused by these situations may not elicit closure as grief remains an ongoing process. The importance of rituals such as attending the funeral can help the bereaved person to conclude the death experience. Also, seeing the dead person and being able to say goodbye prior to the funeral can help the grieving process. When this is not possible, the bereaved may experience complicated grief.

Abnormal or complicated grief

With abnormal or complicated grief, individuals may experience problems during the grieving process. Some examples would include the person with a depressive illness or suffering from posttraumatic stress disorder. Worden (1986) suggested that a variety of factors needed to be considered when assessing for complicated grief. These include the timing of the death which could be delayed or prolonged. This could be as a result of a missing person, suicide or due to chronic illness.

How the death occurred may also have an impact upon the bereaved as it may have been sudden, traumatic and untimely. As a result, the person may experience extreme symptoms and behaviour which are out of keeping with their culture and society. The bereaved person may also have an underlying mental illness or mental disorder which complicates the grieving process.

Worden (1986) also suggested that multiple recent losses may affect the normal grieving process. This could be an accumulation of the death of a parent, death of a child, another child leaving home and then the spouse deciding to end the marriage. Before the person has had a chance to get over one loss, others closely follow resulting in complicated grief.

Bereavement therapy is undertaken by trained therapists from a variety of professional backgrounds with the aim of supporting the bereaved person to make sense of their feelings, explore their grief and to adapt to their circumstances without their loved ones.

Conclusion

This chapter has been divided into two parts and provides an overview of key issues and factors affecting older people with depression. The first part of the chapter has discussed aspects including dementia, alcohol misuse and anorexia. Older people's beliefs about depression have been explored from a cultural and individual perspective. The importance of risk assessment has been discussed and the use of the GDS which is supported by the British Geriatric Society and the Royal College of General Practitioners. The chapter has highlighted the importance of the nurse's role in assessing the risk of attempted and actual suicide. From a management perspective, a correct diagnosis of depression must be given for depressed older people. This age group may also suffer from multiple pathology and as a consequence the diagnosis of depression can potentially be missed. The role of the GP in primary care is essential when asking about life events leading up to this encounter. Some evidence has shown that it is easy to focus entirely upon the physical causes and symptoms rather than psychological experiences and feelings.

Treatment options are discussed incorporating medication, CBT, psychological therapies and ECT. Adherence, compliance and concordance are very important aspects when considering older people's choice and decisions not to adhere to treatment which have to be weighed against the risk of not taking treatment. Expanding and changing roles of nurses are briefly discussed in relation to independent and supplementary nurse prescribing and the relevance of this in supporting older depressed people when taking medication. Medication taking has relevance to attempted and actual suicide as many older women commit suicide by overdosing. It is also important to consider the perceptions of the care workers as well as the older person. Their perception of causes of depression can influence what services the depressed older person accesses. This chapter has been supported with evidence from international research studies, DH guidance documents and national policy.

The second part of this chapter focuses upon bereavement and grief in older people. It explores the symptoms of normal grief and distinguishes them from abnormal grief supported by Kubler Ross (1969) stages of dying. The chapter also explores the perspectives of grief experienced by different cultures and ethnicity.

Life events are explored through lifespan developmental theories and the impact this has upon timely versus untimely loss. Some examples include suicide, murder, missing people and the impact this has upon the bereaved person. Rituals are explored in relation to the funeral, saying goodbye and seeing the dead person and rights of passage. These all help the bereaved person to cope with their loss and accept the death of their loved ones. This part of the chapter concludes by discussing normal grief which is supported by Murray Parkes (1998) accepted grief reactions and also Worden's (1986) tasks of mourning. Overall, this chapter has provided the reader with a very comprehensive view of depression in older people supported by national policies and international research studies.

Reflection and discussion

What factors influence depression in late life?

- *Disability*
- *Poverty*
- *Poor physical health*
- *Lack of social support*
- *Alcohol abuse*
- *Anorexia*
- *Dementia*
- *Loss*

It is also important to highlight that the older person may have had depression prior to old age.

There is also a need to recognize depression in older people with dementia. Depression in early life can become a risk factor for dementia and cognitive decline in old age.

Discuss adherence, compliance and concordance of treatment in relation to older people with depression

- *Many older people make a conscious decision not to adhere to medication.*
- *This is often referred to as intentional non-adherence and occurs due to concerns about the side effects of medication.*
- *Health professionals must ensure that they inform all patients about side effects of medication, however, being informed allows patients to make decisions and choices about their health and treatment.*
- *Their decision not to take medication needs to be weighed against the risk of not taking medication.*
- *If the person has low mood and depressive symptoms they could become suicidal and attempt or actually commit suicide as a result of their depressed mood.*
- *The risk of overdose is also another factor to be considered and will determine the type of medication prescribed.*
- *Compliance of the patient along with the type of information given by the health professional is important in relation to concordance.*
- *Concordance is one way of allowing people to voice their concerns about their medication by discussing medication with the prescriber and agreeing with the treatment and quantity to be taken.*

Discuss the impact of suicide in older people

- *Suicidal intent in older people must be taken very seriously as it is often undertaken with determination and forward planning.*
- *Suicide in older people may be associated with physical illness and loss including bereavement.*
- *Older people are more likely to successfully commit suicide than any other age group.*

Discuss the importance of the grieving process and the difference between normal and abnormal grieving

- *It is important to recognize the symptoms of normal grief and distinguish them from abnormal grief reactions.*
- *The bereaved and their family need to recognize the difference between sadness and grief and depression.*
- *This can be difficult due to the experience of similar emotions and feelings.*
- *With abnormal or complicated grief, individuals may experience problems during the grieving process.*
- *Some examples would include the person with a depressive illness or suffering from posttraumatic stress disorder.*
- *Factors to be considered are the timing of the death, which may have been delayed or prolonged.*

- *This could be as a result of a missing person, suicide or due to chronic illness.*
- *How the death occurred may also have an impact upon the bereaved as it may have been sudden, traumatic and untimely.*
- *As a result, the person may experience extreme symptoms and behaviour which are out of keeping with their culture and society.*
- *The bereaved person may also have an underlying mental illness or mental disorder which complicates the grieving process.*
- *Multiple recent losses may affect the normal grieving process. This could be an accumulation of the death of a parent, death of a child, another child leaving home and then the spouse deciding to end the marriage.*
- *Before the person has had a chance to get over one loss, others closely follow resulting in complicated grief.*

References

Abas, M.A. (1996). Depression and anxiety among older Caribbean people in the UK: Screening, unmet need, and the provision of appropriate services. *International Journal of Geriatric Psychiatry, 11*, 377–382.

Anderson, D.N. (2001). Treating depression in old age: The reasons to be positive. *Age and Ageing, 30*, 13–17.

Audit Commission (2000). *Forget-Me-Not: Mental Health Services for Older People.* London: Audit Commission.

Bagley, H. (2000). Recognition of depression by staff in nursing and residential homes. *Journal of Clinical Nursing, 9*(3), 445–450.

Baker, F.M., Parker, D.A., Wiley, C., Velli, S.A. & Johnson, J.T. (1995). Depressive symptoms in African American medical patients. *International Journal of Geriatric Psychiatry, 10*, 9–14.

Baldwin, R.C., Chiu, E. & Katona, C. (2002). *Guidelines on Depression in Older People: Practicing the Evidence.* London: Martin Dunitz.

Baldwin, R. & Wild, R. (2004). Management of depression in later life. *Advances in Psychiatric Treatment, 10*, 131–139.

Banning, M. (2004). Enhancing older people's concordance with taking their medication. *British Journal of Nursing, 13*(11), 669–674.

Beck, J.C. (1991). *Geriatric Review Syllabus: A Core Curriculum in Geriatric Medicine.* New York: American Geriatrics Society.

Bending, A. (2002). Just how do you make sure the medication goes down? *Nursing in Practice, 4*, 26–28.

Bhuga, D. (1996). Depression across cultures. *Primary Care Psychiatry, 2*, 155–165.

Bhui, K., Bhuga, D., Goldberg, D., Dunn, G. & Desai, M. (2001). Cultural influences on the prevalence of common mental disorder: General practitioners assessments' and help seeking among Punjabi and English people visiting their general practitioner. *Psychological Medicine, 31*, 815–825.

Bissell, P. (2003). Compliance, concordance and respect for the patient's agenda. *The Pharmaceutical Journal, 271*, 498–500.

Blanchard, M., Waterreus, A. & Mann, A.H. (1994). The nature of depression in older people in Inner London, and the contact with primary care. *British Journal of Psychiatry, 164*, 396–402.

BMA (2003). National enhanced service – specialized care of patients with depression. Report funded by Lundbeck. Impact of depression. A multidisciplinary comment on treating depression (1995). Available at http://www.bma.org.uk. Accessed 17 December 2007.

Boneham, M.A., Williams, K.E., Copeland, J.R.M., McKibbin, P., Wilson, K. & Scott, A. (1997). Elderly people from ethnic minorities in Liverpool: Mental illness, unmet need, and barriers to service use. *Health and Social Care in the Community*, 5, 473–483.

Bowlby, J. (1980). *Attachment and Loss: Loss, Sadness and Depression*. New York: Basic Books.

Brink, T., Yesavage, J.A., Lum, B., Heersma, P. & Adey, M. (1982). Depressive symptoms and depressive diagnosis in a community population. *Archives of General Psychiatry*, 45, 1078–1084.

Burns, T. & Lloyd, H. (July 2004). Is a team approach based on staff meetings cost-effective in the delivery of mental healthcare? *Current Opinion in Psychiatry*, 17(4), 311–314.

Carson, A. & Margolin, R. (October 2005). Depression in older adults with neurologic illness: Causes, recognition and management. *Cleve Clinical Journal of Medicine*, 72(Suppl 3), 52–64.

Chapman, I.P. (November 2007). The anorexia of ageing. *Clinics in Geriatric Medicine*, 23(4), 735–756.

Chen, J. (1999). Medication concordance is best helped by improving consultation skills. *BMJ*, 318(7184), 670.

Comino, E.J., Silove, D., Manicavasagar, V., Harris, E. & Harris, M.F. (2001). Agreement in symptoms of anxiety and depression between patients and GPs: The influence of ethnicity. *Family Practice*, 18, 71–77.

Commission for Healthcare Audit and Inspection (2007). *Caring for Dignity. A National Report on Dignity in Care for Older People while in Hospital*. London: Healthcare Commission.

Conwell, Y., Duberstein, P.R., Cox, C., Herrmann, J., Forbes, N. & Caine, E.D. (1998). Age differences in behaviors leading to completed suicide. *American Journal of Geriatric Psychiatry*, 6, 122–126.

Copeland, J.R.M., Dewey, M.E. & Saunders, P. (April 1991). The epidemiology of dementia: GMS-AGECAT studies of prevalence and incidence, including studies in progress. *European Archives of Psychiatry and Clinical Neuroscience*, 240, 4–5.

Cuijpers, P. & Smit, F. (2002). Excess mortality in depression: A meta-analysis of community studies. *Journal of Affective Disorders*, 72, 227–236.

Day, J. (2003). How reflections on concordance in mental health can affect research and clinical practice in adherence. *The Pharmaceutical Journal*, 271, 505–507.

Department of Health (1997). *A Handbook on the Mental Health of Older People*. London: The Stationary Office.

Department of Health (September 1999). *National Service Framework for Mental Health: Modern standards and Service models*. London: DH.

Department of Health (2001). *National Service Framework for Older People*. London: The Stationary Office.

Donini, L.M., Savina, C. & Cannella, C. (2003). Eating habits and appetite control in the elderly: The anorexia of ageing. *International Psychogeriatrics*, 15, 73–87.

Erikson, E.H. (1950). *Childhood and Society*. New York: Norton.

Evans, S. & Katona, C. (1993). Epidemiology of depressive symptoms in elderly primary care attenders. *Dementia and Geriatric Cognitive Disorders*, 4(6), 327–333.

Gallo, J.J., Anthony, J.C. & Muthen, B.O. (1994). Age differences in the symptoms of depression: A late trait analysis. *Journal of Gerontology*, 49, 251–264.

Gensichen, J., Beyer, M. & Muth, C. (2006). Case management to improve major depression in primary health care: A systematic review. *Psychological Medicine, 36,* 7–14.

Gilbody, S., Whitty, P. & Grimshaw, J. (2004). Educational and organizational interventions to improve the management of depression in primary care: A systematic review. *JAMA, 329,* 602–605.

Goldberg, D. & Huxley, P. (1980). *Mental Illness in the Community: The Pathway to Psychiatric Care.* London: Tavistock.

Harwood, D.M., Hawton, K., Hope, T. & Jacoby, R. (2000). Suicide in older people: Mode of death, demographic factors and medical contact before death. *International Journal of Geriatric Psychiatry, 15,* 736–743.

Hughes, C.M. (2004). Medication non-adherence in the elderly. How big is the problem? *Drugs and Ageing, 2*(12), 793–811.

Hunkeler, E.M., Katon, W. & Tanq, L.Q. (2006). Long term outcomes from the IMPACT randomized trial for depressed elderly patients in primary care. *BMJ, 332,* 259–262.

Johnson, I. (2000). Alcohol problems in old age: A review of recent epidemiological research. *International Journal of Geriatric Psychiatry, 15*(7), 575–581.

Jorm, A.F. (2000). Is depression a risk factor for dementia or cognitive decline? A Review. *Gerontology, 46*(4), 219–227.

Katona, P. & Katona, C. (1996). A consensus on depression in old age. *Geriatric Medicine, 26*(1), 45–48.

Katona, C. & Livingston, G. (2002). How well do antidepressants work in older people? A systematic review of number needed to treat. *Journal of Affective Disorders, 69,* 47–52.

Keiffer, K.M. & Reese, R.J. (2002). A reliability generalization study of the geriatric depression scale. *Educational and Psychological Measurement, 62,* 969–994.

Khan, N., Davis, P., Wilkinson, T.J., Selman, J.D. & Graham, P. (2002). Drinking patterns among older people hidden from medical attention. *New Zealand Medical Journal, 115,* 72–75.

Kubler Ross, E. (1969). *On Death and Dying.* London: Tavistock. Cited in Kubler Ross (1977).

Lam, C.K., Lim, P.P.J., Low, B.L., Li Ling, N.G., Chiam, P.C. & Sahadevan, S. (2004). Depression in dementia: A comparative and validation study of four brief scales in the elderly Chinese. *International Journal of Geriatric Psychiatry, 19*(5), 422–428. Available at http://www3.interscience.wiley.com/cgi-bin/abstract. Accessed 10 January 2008.

Lawrence, V., Murray, J., Banerjee, S., Turner, S., Sangka, K., Byng, R., Bhugra, D., Huxley, P., Tylee, A. & Macdonald, A. (2006). Concepts and causation of depression: A cross cultural study of beliefs of older adults. *The Gerontologist, 46,* 23–32.

Livingston, G., Hawkins, A., Graham, N., Blizard, B. & Mann, A. (1990). The Gospel Oak study: Prevalence rates of dementia, depression and activity limitation among elderly residents in inner London. *Psychological Medicine, 20,* 137–146.

Mallet, R., Bhugra, D. & Leff, J. (April 1994). *African-Caribbean Perspectives on Depression.* Paper presented to the Royal College of Psychiatrists Defeat Depression consensus meeting. London, England.

Marks, J.N., Goldberg, D.P. & Hillier, V.F. (1979). Determinants of the ability of general practitioners to detect a psychiatric illness. *Psychological Medicine, 9*(2), 337–353.

McCrae, N., Murray, J., Banergee, S., Huxley, P., Bhugra, D., Tylee, A. & Macdonald, A. (2005). 'They're all depressed aren't they? A qualitative study of social care workers and depression in older adults. *Ageing and Mental Health, 9*(6), 508–516.

McEvoy, P. & Barnes, P. (2007). Using the chronic care model to tackle depression among older adults who have long term physical conditions. *Journal of Psychiatric and Mental Health Nursing*, 14, 233–238.

McIntosh, J.L. (2002). USA Suicide 1999 Official Statistics. NCHS/CDC. Available at http:/www.iusb.edu/jmcintos/SuicideStats.html. Accessed June 25 2005.

Montorio, I. & Izal, M. (1996). Geriatric Depression Scale: A review of its development and utility. *International Psychogeriatrics*, 8, 103–112.

Murray Parkes, C. (1972). *Bereavement: Studies of Grief in Adult Life.* London: Tavistock.

Murray Parkes, C. (March 1998). Coping with loss. Bereavement in adult life. *BMJ*, 316(7134), 856–859.

National Institute on Alcohol Abuse and Alcoholism (2003). Alcohol Alert No. 40. Bethesda. Available at www.niaaa.nih.gov/publications/aa40.htm. Accessed 9 September 2003.

National Institute of Mental Health (2001). *Older Adults: Depression and Suicide Facts* (NIH Publication No. 01-4593). Bethesda, MD: NIMH.

Older People and Suicide (March 2007). Report. Available at www.staffs.ac.uk. Accessed 10 September 2008.

Penninx, B.W., Deeg, D.J. & van Eijk, J.T. (2000). Changes in depression and physical decline in older adults: A longitudinal perspective. *Journal of Affective Disorders*, 61, 1–12.

Penninx, B.W.J.H., Geerlings, S.W., Deeg, D.J.H., Van Eijk, J.T.M., Van Tilburg, W. & Beekman, A.T.F. (1999). Minor and major depression and the risk of death in older persons. *Archives of General Psychiatry*, 56, 889–895.

Raj, A. (June 2004). Depression in the elderly. Tailoring medical therapy to their special needs. *Postgraduate Medicine*, 115(6), 26–42. Available at http://www.postgradmed.com/issues. Accessed 5 October 2006.

Rosswurm, M. (December 1983). Relocation and the elderly. *Journal of Gerontological Nursing*, 12, 632–637.

Royal College of Psychiatrists (2007). Accessed www.rcpsych.ac.uk. Accessed 10 January 2008.

Ruggles, D.J. (1998). Pearls for practice. Depression in the elderly: A review. *Journal of the Academy of Nurse Practitioners*, 10(11), 503–507.

Ryan-Woolley, B.M. & Rees, J.A. (2005). Initializing concordance in frail elderly patients via a medicines organizer. *The Annals of Pharmacotherapy*, 39(5), 834–839.

SCIE (2005). Research briefing 15: Helping older people to take prescribed medication in their own home: What works? Available at www.scie.org.uk/publications/briefings/briefing15/alpha.asp. Accessed 7 December 2007.

Sheikh, J.I. & Yesavage, J.A. (1986). Geriatric Depression Scale (GDS): Recent evidence and development of a shorter version. In: Brink, T.L. (ed) *Clinical Gerontology: A Guide to Assessment and Intervention.* New York: Harworth Press, pp. 165–173.

Stek, M.L., Vinkers, D.J., Gussekloo, J., Van Der Mast, R.C., Beekman, A.T.F. & Westendorp, R.G.J. (2006). Natural history of depression in the oldest old. *The British Journal of Psychiatry*, 188, 65–69.

Teresi, J., Abrams, R., Holmes, D., Ramirez, M. & Eimicke, J. (2001). Prevalence of depression and depression recognition in nursing homes. *Social Psychiatry and Psychiatric Epidemiology*, 36(12), 613–620.

Tew, J.D., Mulsant, B.H., Haskett, R.F., Prudic, J., Thase, M.E., Crowe, R.R., Dolata, D., Begley, A.E., Reynolds, C.E. & Sackheim, H. (1999). Acute efficacy of ECT in the treatment of major depression in the oldest old. *American Journal of Psychiatry*, *156*(2), 1865–1870.

Thompson, L.W., Coon, D.W. & Gallagher Thompson, D. (2001). Comparison of desipramine and cognitive/behavioral therapy in the treatment of elderly outpatients with mild to moderate depression. *American Journal of Geriatric Psychiatry*, *9*, 225–240.

Totman, R. (1979). *Life Events and Illness*. London: Souvenir Press.

Tuma, T.A. (2000). Outcome of hospital-treated depression at 4.5 years. An elderly and a younger adult cohort compared. *British Journal of Psychiatry*, *176*, 224–228.

Unutzer, J., Katon, W. & Callahan, C.M. (2002). Collaborative care management of late-life depression in the primary care setting: A randomized controlled trial. *JAMA*, *288*(22), 2836–2845.

Walker, M., Orrell, M., Manela, M., Livingston, G. & Katona, C. (1998). Do health and use of services differ in residents of sheltered accommodation. A pilot study. *International Journal of Geriatric Psychiatry*, *13*(9), 617–624.

Watts, S.C., Bhutani, G.E., Stout, I.H., Ducker, G.M., Claetor, P.J., McGarry, J., Day, M. (2002). Mental health in older adult recipients of primary care services: Is depression the key issue? Identification, treatment, and the general practitioner. *International Journal of Geriatric Psychology*, *17*(5), 427–437.

WHO (2003). *Population Ageing – A Public Health Challenge*. Available at http://www.who.int/inf-fs/en/fact135.html. Accessed 22 October 2003.

Wilson, K., Mottram, P. & Sivanranthan, A. (2001). *Antidepressant versus Placebo for Depressed Elderly*. Cochrane Library, Issue 4. Oxford: Update Software.

Worden, J.W. (1986). *Grief Counseling and Grief Therapy*. London: Tavistock.

Zerbe, K.J. & Steinberg, D.L. (November 2000). Coming to terms with grief and loss. *Postgraduate Medicine*, *108*(6), 97–106. Available at www.postgradmed.com.issues/2000/11/00. Accessed 4 October 2006.

Useful website resources

www.ipa-online.org – International Psycho-geriatric Association which aims to support the mental health of older people through education, research, practice development, advocacy, health promotion and with the development of services.

www.niaaa.nih.gov – National Institute on Alcohol Abuse and Alcoholism.

www.psych.org – American Psychiatric Association is a worldwide medical speciality. It aims to support doctors to provide humane, effective care and treatment for all people with mental disorder, retardation and substance-related disorders.

www.rcpsych.ac.uk – Royal College of psychiatrists are professional psychiatrists in the United Kingdom and Republic of Ireland providing mental health information.

Chapter 7

Suicide and self-harm

Introduction

This chapter highlights the importance of mental health policy in relation to preventing suicide and self-harm. The WHO (2006a) launched an initiative highlighting depression and the implications for public health. The WHO (2006a) stated that in the year 2000, approximately one million people died from suicide, accounting for about one death every 40 seconds.

This chapter begins by providing background information on suicide, information on rates and statistics and reasons why there has been a reported reduction in suicide rates in England. Strategies, guidelines and recommendations for suicide prevention are also discussed. The role of the general practitioner (GP) in preventing suicide and the importance of GPs having relevant up-to-date training on depression and suicide and risk assessment is highlighted. Socio-economic factors are explored in relation to suicidal behaviour. These include stressful life events, unemployment, previous suicide attempts and social isolation.

The role of the community psychiatric nurse (CPN), discharge liaison and the care programme approach (CPA) are also addressed. Suicidal behaviour is explored and the reasons why some individuals are more likely to commit suicide than others is discussed. High-risk individuals and groups most likely to be associated with suicidal activity are mentioned throughout the chapter. These high-risk individuals include children and young people, prisoners, older people, people with mental illness, those individuals who abuse alcohol and drugs and those with HIV/AIDS.

Risk assessment is highlighted and the importance of assessing risk when detecting potential and actual suicidal activity is addressed. Risk assessments including Beck's Depression Inventory are discussed in relation to identifying patients at risk of suicide and self-harm. Self-harm in young people is reviewed and the association between self-harm and suicide is discussed. Suicide prevention strategies are highlighted focusing upon the role of professionals caring for patients. These include the role of the doctor and the increasing role of nurses in preventing suicide and self-harm. Good practice guidelines, management and referral to specialist care are advocated and supported by relevant literature. This is advocated by the WHO (2000a) action plan focusing upon suicide risk and assessment. Reference is also made to recent health policy regarding suicide prevention strategies.

Background on suicide

The WHO (2006a) established that over the past 45 years, suicide rates had increased by 60% worldwide and that suicide was the third most common cause of death for both men and women between the ages of 15 and 44 years demonstrating a change from earlier figures where older people were the most likely group to commit suicide. There are a variety of reasons why someone may attempt or actually commit suicide. The WHO (2006a) stated that depression and substance misuse accounted for approximately 90% of all cases of suicide, whilst other socio-economic factors such as loss of a loved one, loss of job or relationship breakdown could also lead to a person committing suicide. For many individuals, it may be an accumulation of these factors which ultimately leads to them to take their own life. However, the National Institute for Mental Health in England (2007) produced their fourth annual report on progress in implementing the National Suicide Prevention Strategy for England in 2006. This report found that the suicide rate for 2005, which was the most up-to-date record of suicides recorded, was lower than in 2004. This provides some encouraging news for England, however, within certain areas and age groups in South Wales, suicide appears to be on the increase. This had led the Welsh Assembly Government (WAG) to develop guidance and a much-needed National Suicide Prevention Strategy for Wales.

Suicide prevention strategies in both England and Scotland have demonstrated positive efforts in helping to reduce suicide rates in these countries in the UK.

Suicide rates and statistics

To help reduce the rates of suicide some areas identified national targets. Health policy in Wales promoted the development of targets. Suicide mortality at a national level was put into a health gain target aiming to reduce suicide in all ages by 10% by the year 2010. Targets may be helpful when identifying issues of concern but what is not always clear is the process as to how these targets will be met. More research is required to establish evidence as to what is effective in identifying and reducing suicide rates.

As a result of this, the National Public Health Service for Wales (NPHSW, 2007) produced an evidence-based review of best practice for the WAG in 2007.

This review identified effective interventions which had a positive influence upon the reduction of suicide rates in Wales.

Supporting evidence taken from the National Confidential Inquiry into Suicide and Homicide by People with Mental Illness (2001) also suggested that suicide rates of psychiatric inpatients had decreased.

This study was undertaken over a 7-year period from 1997 to 2003 and included all patients admitted to NHS inpatient psychiatric care in England during that period. The study showed that the rates fell for both men and women and that the highest reduction in suicide was in the 15–44 years age group. Kapur *et al.* (2001) have published their findings on the National Confidential Inquiry website.

Potential reasons for reduction in reported suicide rates in England

There are a variety of reasons for this reduction in reported suicide rates. It is likely that more professionals are aware of guidance and the National Suicide prevention Strategy for England (2003) which highlighted the importance of risk assessment. It also identified the type of mix of patients to be cared for in the same inpatient environment. This also highlighted that by assessing the patient's condition and risk assessing them adequately, access to different types of methods of suicide could be reduced. What needs to be considered is that some patients will have been discharged home and that some of the risk may be more evident in the community than as an inpatient. What also needs to be evaluated are the suicide rates at the person's home or in other environments than inpatient facilities. Other factors to be considered are that these reductions in suicide rates from the National Confidential Inquiry study are predominantly for inpatients in England.

This demonstrates the need for national Suicide reduction strategies in all four countries across the UK. It also shows that there is inequity of provision of services across the four countries of the UK when addressing the needs of suicidal people.

National strategies to reduce suicide

There have been developments and initiatives undertaken from a national UK perspective which include the National Confidential Inquiry into Suicide and Homicide by People with Mental Illness, which is a national research project funded by the National Patient Safety Agency (NPSA). The purpose is to collect detailed clinical information on all suicides and homicides in mental health services in England, Wales, Northern Ireland and Scotland. From a strategic perspective, information is centrally gathered and prevention strategies can be developed across the whole of the nation to support the reduction of suicide. There have also been international attempts by the WHO (2006b) to improve awareness of depression across communities.

The WHO (2006b) developed initiatives to reduce the impact of depression by developing specific objectives:

- To educate patients, family members, providers and policy makers about depression.
- To reduce the stigma associated with depression.
- To train primary care personnel in the diagnosis of and management of depression.
- To improve the capacity of countries to create policies supportive of improving care for depression and to provide effective management of depression in primary care.

(WHO, 2006b).

The WHO (2006b) identified a variety of ways of achieving these objectives including raising awareness of depression from a regional, national and global perspective. This can be achieved through workshops, accessing website information and sharing resources.

They acknowledged that one of the most important ways of improving services for depression in primary care was by undertaking multisite intervention studies and to discuss how suicide could be prevented.

The role of the GP in the prevention of suicide

The WHO (2000a) developed a resource guide for GPs on suicide prevention which identified that suicide was a significant risk in unrecognized and untreated depression. Gunnell and Frankel (1999) identified that between 40 and 60% of people who committed suicide had seen a GP rather than a psychiatrist in the month prior to committing suicide. This highlights the importance of GPs being able to detect, refer, manage and treat depressed people appropriately.

However, it must also be acknowledged that there are a large number of people who commit suicide who have not seen any health professional in the events leading to their suicide. The WHO (2000a) stated that depression was highly prevalent in the general population and approximately 30% of people seen by a GP were suffering from undiagnosed depression. One of the challenges for GPs is that many patients present with physical problems masking the symptoms of depression. GPs may be familiar with physical illness and disease but may need to collaborate with psychiatrists and other mental health professionals to ensure that depressed patients are managed appropriately.

Many people with ideas of committing suicide are seen by doctors in their surgeries or as outpatients. Thus, the role of the GP is essential in determining the element of risk when determining whether the person should remain at home or require immediate active intervention which may result in the patient being admitted to inpatient psychiatric services. Different organizations have different referral systems and there may also be opportunities to refer to nurse-led clinics or other therapists or specialists in the mental health field. Improving knowledge and understanding of suicide through training is important for primary care professionals. Rutz *et al.* (1992) reviewed the impact of an educational programme for GPs in Sweden when identifying and treating depression. Evidence showed that this approach helped to reduce suicide rates in Sweden significantly. As part of this training primary care professionals needed to be aware of the wide range of socio-economic factors which could cause individuals to become a high suicidal risk.

Socio-economic factors associated with suicidal behaviour

Gunnell and Frankel (1999) highlighted evidence that both stressful life events and social factors determined high suicidal risk. They identified the following risk factors:

- Mental illness (particularly depression, alcoholism and personality disorders).
- Physical illness (particularly terminal illness, pain, debilitation and AIDS).
- Previous attempted suicide.
- Family history of suicide, alcohol abuse, psychiatric illness.
- Divorced, widowed, living alone.
- Social isolation.
- Unemployed or retired.
- Bereavement in childhood.

Adapted from Gunnell and Frankel (1999).

Primary care professionals need to be aware that there is increased risk of suicide if the person has:

- A mental illness
- Recently been discharged from hospital
- Made previous suicide attempts

This highlights the importance of effective discharge and follow-up care.

Discharge liaison, the role of the community psychiatric nurse and the care programme approach

The above factors highlight the importance of appropriate discharge and liaison services when dealing with suicidal behaviour. The role of the CPN is important ensuring appropriate visits and interventions through the Care Programme Approach (CPA). The CPA is a framework underpinning mental health care for all service users. The CPA was introduced by the DH (1990) to ensure that an appropriate assessment was made of an individual's health and social care needs. The NHS Executive and Social Services Inspectorate (1999) revised the CPA to form a single care co-ordinated approach for adults of working age with mental health needs. This enabled an individual's needs to be assessed, planned and reviewed in all environments whether as an inpatient or an outpatient. The document Back on Track Briefing 29 (SCMH, 2005) was developed by the Sainsbury Centre for Mental Health to support the CPA for people who were detained under the Mental Health Act (DH and Welsh Office, 1993). This occurred as a result of Mental Health Act Commissioners' visits to inpatients detained under the Mental Health Act. They identified that special care was needed in discharge planning, follow-up and aftercare. As already highlighted, there is a risk of suicide for some patients who have been discharged from inpatient services to their communities, so this approach is crucial in preventing suicide for these individuals.

There are two tiers of care provision in the CPA which include standard and enhanced provision of care:

■ Standard care would include low-level support by one agency where the persons would be a lower risk to themselves or others and would be able to self-manage their care.
■ Whilst enhanced care would be provided for a person who is considered to be a high risk of harming themselves or others and would require frequent, intensive interventions from a variety of members of the interdisciplinary team.
■ Thus, enhanced care would be required for depressed patients who were considered a high suicidal risk

(DH, 2008).

Qin and Nordentoft (2005) research, in Denmark, highlighted that suicidal risk increased during psychiatric hospitalization especially for women but peaked in the first week of psychiatric hospitalization and during the first week post-discharge. Despite this evidence Links and Hoffman (2005) highlighted that very little intervention research had been undertaken with recently discharged patients. Thus, it is important to have guidelines and policies in place.

Potential guidelines and recommendations on suicide prevention prior to discharge

■ Ensure there are suicide prevention policies and guidelines in every hospital-based inpatient psychiatric unit.
■ Undertake a risk assessment of each inpatient with a history of suicidal behaviour 12–24 hours prior to discharge to alleviate the immediate risk of suicide.

- Observe all inpatients for potential self-harm or attempted suicide behaviour.
- Listen to and report any cues that the patient may attempt suicide.
- Community follow-up by a named practitioner for each discharged patient with severe mental illness or risk of self-harm or suicide.
- Community practitioner to visit within 3 days of hospital discharge.
- Only give 1-week supply of medication on discharge to high-risk patients.
- Ensure the patients can obtain their medication on discharge.
- Named community practitioner to monitor compliance with medication following discharge.
- Individual action plan agreed with patient and recommendations made to intervene if patient is non-compliant or is considered an increased risk of suicide.
- Named practitioner to monitor non-attendance at outpatient appointments.
- Named practitioner to ensure regular contact with the patient and report concerns.
- Regular reviews undertaken, records kept and regular communication with family and other professionals providing support and care for the patient.

These guidelines have been adapted from guidance given by Links and Hoffman (2005).

Suicidal behaviour

It is important to establish when the suicidal behaviour started and reasons why it occurred. This would be considered as part of the assessment process.

Melhem et al. (2007) undertook a prospective study to identify the likelihood of suicidal behaviour in children of parents with a history of mood disorder and suicidal behaviour. The findings of the study showed that children of parents with mood disorders were more likely to commit suicide if they also had mood disorders, had aggressive impulsive tendencies, a history of suicidal attempt had experienced sexual abuse and self-reported depression. They concluded that targeting these known factors could reduce morbidity of suicidal behaviour in high-risk young people.

There is evidence to show that substance abuse and suicidal behaviour are strongly linked. Jenkins (2002) reported that after depression, substance abuse was the second most frequent factor that led individuals to attempt suicide. Jenkins (2002) believed that suffering from both depression and substance abuse formed a lethal combination. She advocated prompt treatment for co-morbid depression in helping to prevent suicide in substance abusers. Alcohol abuse has been strongly linked with suicide. An important survey undertaken by Coulthard et al. (2002) demonstrated that high stress and low social support in both alcohol and drug abusers was evident. Thus, it is not surprising that these factors increase the chance of suicide. Hawton et al. (1993) concluded that substance abuse was a predictor of eventual suicide.

Murphy and Weltzel (1990) suggested that the risk of suicide doubled in countries such as Sweden, Austria and Germany resulting in relatively high suicide rates compared to countries with lower suicide rates. This was demonstrated also by Rossow and Amundson (1995) in their prospective study on alcohol abuse and suicide.

Gunnell *et al.* (2004) recognized that even though suicidal thoughts may lead to suicide, fewer than 1:200 people who experienced suicidal thoughts actually committed suicide. Gunnell *et al.*'s (2004) study aimed to determine the factors associated with the development of and recovery from suicidal thoughts in the British population.

They undertook an 18-month follow-up survey of 2404 adults who had been part of the second National Psychiatric Morbidity Survey. This had also been identified by Kessler *et al.* (1999). Gunnell *et al.*'s (2004) study found that the incidence of suicidal thoughts were more common in women and people between the ages of 16 and 24 years. Other important factors that influenced this were the absence of a stable relationship, unemployment and poor social support.

This demonstrates that health and social care professionals need to have a greater understanding of factors that influence social, psychological and treatment issues. This was highlighted by the DH (2002) when developing the National Suicide Prevention Strategy for England.

It is important to be aware that there are certain individuals or groups of people who may be more likely to attempt suicide than others.

People associated with higher incidence of suicide

Young people

There are many reasons why young people may commit suicide. One cause is family breakdown which can occur as a result of separation, divorce or death of parents. This can have a big impact upon a young person who may be experiencing hormonal changes and personal challenges both physically and emotionally during this stage of their lifespan. Within the family, there may also have been a history of psychiatric illness or suicidal behaviour or previous self-harm. Fox and Hawton (2004) have explored deliberate self-harm in young people. The young person may also have experimented with drugs and alcohol and be abusing either or both of these substances. Moscicki (1997) highlighted that antisocial behaviour and aggression were common amongst young people who committed suicide. Gould *et al.* (2003) reviewed the previous 10 years of youth suicide and considered preventative interventions. Within the United States of America, Gilatto and Rai (1999) found that suicide rates amongst young people had more than doubled in recent years leading to Satcher (1999) undertaking a call to action to prevent suicide.

There has been a high incidence of teenagers taking their own lives in Ireland in 2007 and South Wales in 2008 highlighted by the media. Madeline Moon,

Member of Parliament for Bridgend in South Wales (2008) held a debate in Westminster raising concerns that the rate of suicide was 35% higher in Wales than in England. There are ongoing investigations into the causes of these suicides; however, there has been speculation about suicide pacts where young people agree to commit suicide together. There have also been views about the role of computer websites having an influence on younger people as this is one of the main means of communication for many young people.

Member of Parliament, Madeline Moon (2008) stated that there needed to be a National Strategy for Suicide Prevention in Wales as there had been 14 suspected teenage suicides in her constituency in the past year.

This highlights the role of the family, teachers, college lecturers and employers of young people in recognizing symptoms of depression and potential causes of self-harm and suicide. The BBC News (2008a) reported the need to train teachers in suicide awareness which was supported by the Mental Health charity Mind who stated that suicide was the highest cause of death in young men in Wales. The media also reported an increase in self-harm in Scotland. A national strategy has already been developed in Scotland to prevent suicide.

In September 2007, findings from a study undertaken by Dr Roy O'Connor into self-harm amongst teenagers were reported by the BBC (BBC News, 2007a, 2007b). Dr O'Connor found that out of the 2000 teenagers between the ages of 15 and 16 years studied those 1:5 girls and 7% of the boys had self-harmed. Findings from this study showed that there were a variety of causes of self-harm including being bullied, suffering from physical abuse or drug abuse and concerns over sexual orientation. An organization named Choose Life set up a website on prevention, local action plans and training issues relevant to reducing suicide rates in Scotland. Choose Life (2008) reported that in 2006 there were 765 recorded suicides in Scotland which equates to approximately 2 suicides per day. Even though Scotland has the highest number of reported suicides compared to other countries in the UK, since 2002 the rates appear to be falling. Suicide is the leading cause of death in the under 35 age groups and has almost doubled in the most deprived parts of Scotland.

From an international perspective Fergusson et al. (2000) undertook a longitudinal study in New Zealand over a 21-year period. The study examined links between childhood circumstances, adolescent mental health and life events. This was considered in relation to suicidal behaviour in young people between the ages of 15 and 20 years.

Fergusson et al. (2000) reported relevant factors highlighting children most likely to consider committing suicide:

- Poor social economic environment
- Marital disruption
- Poor child–parent relationships
- Sexual abuse
- Attention-seeking behaviour
  (Fergusson et al., 2000).

Family breakdown, diversity of family life, poor communication, poor self-esteem and lack of interest in teenagers within some families can lead to them relying on the internet sites for sources of friendship.

The impact of suicide on both the family and society is immeasurable and was highlighted by the WHO (1992) suggesting that on average a single suicide affects six other people. However, if the suicide affects a school or workplace it will have an impact upon hundreds of people. This is an area that requires further research as this will potentially influence the mental health of many other people. It may well be that this is what has influenced the young people in Ireland and South Wales to take their own lives. Crowley (2005) highlighted in a letter to the *BMJ* that there were many gaps in the research regarding prevention of suicide in young people and recognized the importance of this subject area from a public health perspective.

A group of people often not considered as a risk of suicide are young people with learning disabilities. However, there is some evidence to show that these young people are more likely to suffer from depression.

Suicide and depression in young people with learning disabilities

Bender *et al.* (1999) suggested that young people with learning disabilities were more likely to suffer from depression. They were also more likely to be impulsive and have poor social skills. As a result of these factors they were considered to be an increased risk of suicide. Bender *et al.* (1999) also suggested that depression was more common in young people with non-verbal learning disability and those with poor academic ability. Many of these young people will be cared for at home by family and carers and will attend special schools. Thus, it is not just trained professionals who need to have knowledge of the symptoms of depression and causes of self-harm and suicide. This raises an important issue when strategies and guidelines are developed. Guidance also needs to be developed from a carer's perspective to enable family and carers to assess for risk of suicidal behaviour in their loved ones.

It is not just teenagers who are vulnerable, other groups of people may also be likely to attempt or actually commit suicide.

Prisoners

A BBC News report (2008b) identified that prison overcrowding had caused many problems including inability to address the mental health needs of some prisoners. As a consequence this had potentially led to an increase in the number of suicides within the prison population.

Anne Owens, HM Inspector of Prisons, reported to the BBC News (2008b) that she was shocked at the increase in the number of suicides in prisons.

Seventeen inmates committed suicide whilst in prisons across London during 2007 demonstrating the highest number in 1 year for a decade.

It is important to address the health needs of the prison population, which is achieved by undertaking mental health needs assessments. There needs to be more of a focus on gathering data regarding the health needs of prisoners, which may help to detect not only their access to physical health care but also their access to mental health services whilst in prison.

If depression in prisoners is highlighted, risk assessments and observation can be instigated at an early stage and appropriate intervention strategies implemented. The BBC (2008b) reported that prisoners on remand were potentially more at risk of committing suicide. Thus, the mental health needs of prisoners on remand are of equal importance as the mental health needs of long-term prisoners. Having recently undertaken some research to establish the health needs of prisoners in Wales it is evident that this area needs to be continually reviewed. Whilst in the prison environment, it was evident that the clergy have an important role in supporting prisoners. However, some clergy themselves may be at risk of depression and suicide.

Clergy

There are many professional groups which need to be aware of suicide and self-harm. After speaking to religious leaders and members of the church, it is also evident that some clergy have committed suicide whilst undertaking their training. This may question the individual's reason for entering religion as a career. It may be that these individuals have chosen this path to help them to come to terms with their own issues or complicated lives rather than to help others with their lives. As for many careers maybe interview panels need to consider the true reasons why individuals wish to enter certain professions. This highlights the need to raise awareness amongst people from all walks of life about depression and the potential implications of choosing certain career options. As highlighted by the WHO (2006b) depression and suicide can affect people from all social classes, cultures and backgrounds and is a regional, national and global concern.

Alcohol abuse

The WHO (2000a) identified that people who abused alcohol and those who were alcohol-dependent were more likely to commit suicide.

They identified that it was particularly prevalent in younger people. It is not surprising that with the extended opening hours for many clubs and pubs there is more opportunity for people to drink alcohol. Alcohol is also more readily available in supermarkets and off-licences and is relatively cheap compared to some non-alcoholic drinks.

Even though there has been a focus on asking young people for identification, there are still opportunities for them to obtain alcohol.

The factors that link alcohol abuse and suicide are shown below:

■ Early onset of alcoholism
■ Long history of drinking
■ High level of dependence
■ Depressed mood
■ Poor physical health
■ Poor work performance
■ Family history of alcohol abuse
■ Poor or loss of interpersonal relationships
(WHO, 2000a).

The Royal College Psychiatrists (2004) highlighted the link between alcohol and suicide. They stated that 40% of men who attempted suicide had a long-standing alcohol problem and 70% of people who successfully committed suicide had drunk alcohol prior to taking their own life. The Royal College Psychiatrists (2004) also identified that depression and alcohol abuse were strongly associated. This was evident where alcohol changed the chemistry in the brain increasing the risk of depression. Alcohol abuse and depression create a two-way process where depression can lead to increased drinking and increased drinking can lead to increased symptoms of depression. Initially, feelings of well-being may help to deal with the depression but as the alcohol takes effect tiredness, hangovers, arguments and relationship breakdown occur.

Some individuals who abuse alcohol may also have mental health problems resulting in them having a dual diagnosis.

Psychiatric illness associated with suicide

There is a prevalence of psychiatric illness associated with suicide. However, this does not mean that all people with mental health problems will be suicidal.

Beautrais *et al.* (1996) undertook a case control study where they established that depression and bipolar disorders were more likely to be associated with suicide. Substance abuse was also a key factor associated with suicide.

Hamilton (2000) suggested that people suffering from psychosis were less likely to commit suicide than those with depression; however, if they suffered with hallucinations which encouraged them to take their own life, then they were usually successful. Walsh (2007) discussed the different types of hallucinations experienced by people with mental illness highlighting that auditory and visual hallucinations were often experienced by people with psychosis. Florid hallucinations are frequently associated with taking hallucinogenic drugs and the person may attempt or commit suicide as a result of the hallucinogenic experience.

Moscicki (1997) and Beautrais *et al.* (1996) both provided evidence that most suicides or serious suicide attempts were committed by people with more than one psychiatric disorder. There was also a strong association with substance abuse demonstrating that people with dual diagnosis may have a higher risk of suicide. People who have previously attempted suicide are the most likely people to successfully commit suicide.

Gupta *et al.* (1998) recognized that there was a high risk of suicide amongst people suffering from schizophrenia.

They identified the following risk factors:

- Young unemployed male
- Recurrent relapses
- Fear of deterioration
- Suspiciousness and delusions
- Depressive symptoms

Gupta *et al.* (1998) also identified that the person with schizophrenia was more likely to commit suicide during the early stages of the illness, during early relapse and after early recovery. This is very relevant as it can help practitioners to implement preventative strategies during these crucial times. It may highlight the need for increased supervision and observation status for vulnerable inpatients. Early recovery is also a time when the person may request to be discharged home so the element of risk needs to be assessed. Assessment of risk also needs to be considered when allowing patients to have weekend leave or time allowed home prior to discharge.

As already highlighted, depression is the most common diagnosis in people who have committed suicide and the combination of depression and alcohol abuse increases the risk of suicide.

Appropriate strategies need to be implemented to prevent suicide as the WHO (2000a) stated depression is treatable and suicide is preventable. There are other high-risk individuals who may commit suicide. These include people diagnosed with HIV/AIDS.

HIV and AIDS

The WHO (2000a) highlighted that diagnosis of HIV or AIDS is a crucial time for individuals, particularly young people and is a time when the risk of suicide is increased. If the person is an intravenous drug user the incidence is higher. This also reflects the access to the means of suicide. In this situation, the drug abuser may decide to overdose on potentially lethal drugs. It must also be acknowledged that some individuals may accidentally overdose or use drugs as a means of attempted suicide when seeking help.

This can result in accidental death if the person is not found in time or has taken drugs which were mixed with other products or are pure substances. It has to be acknowledged that not all people who are diagnosed with HIV/AIDS are drug abusers. Some of them may have acquired the infection through infected blood via blood transfusions, during birth or through sharing infected items. This highlights that the stigma of HIV/AIDS infection may influence the person resulting in them attempting or actually committing suicide. Another factor may be the actual illness itself, which may cause the person to become depressed and want to take his or her own life.

If the person is a drug abuser he or she may also unintentionally commit suicide by overdosing on drugs. This highlights the importance of assessing risk in vulnerable people.

Older people are also vulnerable and at certain times in their life may attempt or commit suicide.

Older people

A report undertaken by Beeston (2007) at Staffordshire University entitled Older People and Suicide found that older people were more likely to succeed in committing suicide than any other age group. The report stated that for every 200 suicide attempts amongst 16- to 25-year olds, only one would be successful. However, for suicide attempts in the over 80-year age group, one in every two would be successful. The study concluded that dementia, retirement and disease led to depression in older people. Health care professionals associated this with part of the normal ageing process. This is of concern as demonstrated by an increasing older population over the age of 80 years.

If health care professionals are not taking older peoples' symptoms and feelings seriously and are not treating their needs with equal importance to younger age groups, then it is no wonder that the suicide rate in the older population is increasing and will continue to do so. This highlights the need for primary care practitioners to be vigilant as these findings demonstrate that in this study people over the age of 65 years were more successful in taking their own lives. With improved intervention these rates of suicide could potentially be reduced in older people.

For any group or individual considering suicide, it is important for health professionals and family members to help identify the risk of harm. By making individuals aware of the potential risks through information and education maybe more lives can be saved.

There have been some risks of suicide associated with antidepressants.

Antidepressants and the risk of suicidal behaviour

Jick et al. (1995) undertook a study to estimate the rate and means of suicide amongst young people taking at least one of the 10 most commonly prescribed antidepressants prescribed by GPs in the UK between January 1988 and February 1993.

These antidepressants included dothiepin, amitryptyline, clonmipramine, imipramine, flupenthixol, lofedapine, mianserin, fluoxetine, doxepin and trazodone. It identified that males were more likely to commit suicide than females. The study concluded that people who took higher doses of antidepressants and who were prescribed medication in the 30 days prior to the suicide were a higher risk than those people on lower doses who had their prescriptions for more than 30 days prior to the suicide. They suggested that overdose using the antidepressants accounted for only 14% of the suicides. More recently, Jick *et al.* (2004) undertook another study to estimate the risk of non-fatal suicide behaviour with people commenced on antidepressants. They concluded that the risk of suicidal behaviour increased in the first month particularly between days 1 and 9 after commencing antidepressants. This is very relevant information and should influence GPs prescribing practice. It is also important that family members and carers are alerted to this information so they can observe for any changes in the depressed person's behaviour and seek appropriate help if required.

Thus, risk assessment is an essential part of managing the suicidal patient.

The importance of managing suicidal risk

Risk assessment

Risk assessment is an important aspect of managing risk as it is about minimizing harm and preventing further harm. Assessing the risk of suicidal intent needs to be undertaken in collaboration with the suicidal person. Assessment of risk needs to consider physical, psychological, social and spiritual aspects. The WHO (2000a) developed an action plan which identified suicide risk, symptoms, assessment and actions to enable GPs to make decisions about the risk of suicide. It is easy to criticise decisions made in practice; however, primary care practitioners may only be with a patient for a few minutes and within those few minutes they have to make a decision about the element of risk during a very short consultation. The GP may not be aware of all the facts particularly if the patient is unknown to them. So, it is important that they ask the right questions with regard to intent to commit suicide and methods considered and also observe the patient's behaviour. The WHO (2000a) enables the GP to undertake a quick review of the patient and enable them to make decisions about immediate actions.

As already established, it can be difficult to predict suicidal intent in depressed patients. Van Gaskell *et al.* (1997) studied 338 adult depressed psychiatric inpatients. They assessed them using the Hamilton Depression Rating Scale (HDRS), Beck Depression Inventory (BDI), Zung Self Rating Depression and Anxiety Scales (SDS and SAS). They found that suicidal ideation was significantly related to severity of depression.

The following were strongly associated with suicidal ideation:

- Hopelessness
- Depressed mood
- Feelings of guilt
- Loss of interest
- Low self-esteem

Suicide risk identification, assessment and action plan

Suicide risk	Symptom	Assessment	Action
0	No distress	—	—
1	Emotionally disturbed	Enquire about suicidal thoughts	Listen with empathy
2	Vague ideas about death	Enquire about suicidal thoughts	Listen with empathy
3	Vague suicidal thoughts	Assess the intent (plan and method)	Explore possibilities Identify support
4	Suicidal ideas **but no** Psychiatric disorder	Assess the intent (plan and method)	Explore possibilities Identify support
5	Suicidal ideas **and** Psychiatric disorder **or** Severe life stresses	Assess the intent (plan and method) Make a contract	Refer to psychiatrist
6	Suicidal ideas **and** Psychiatric disorder **or** Severe life stressors **or** Agitation **and** Previous attempt	Stay with the patient to prevent access to means	Hospitalise

WHO (2000) Preventing suicide. A resource for General Physicians.

Van Gaskell *et al.* (1997) also concluded that personality disorder and depression were associated with suicide. Depressed patients with personality disorders were more likely to attempt suicide and have suicidal thoughts than depressed patients without personality disorder.

It is important to listen to what depressed patients are saying and not to just appear to be ticking the box when asking them how they feel. Jones (2000) researched psychiatric inpatient's experience of nursing observation by suggesting that engagement and social support were important aspects of patient care.

This is achieved by active listening and involving the patient when planning care. If the nurse does not show empathy and demonstrate active listening skills, then the information given by the patient may be inappropriately responded to and incorrect assumptions made. Many people who have contemplated suicide will actually have told someone of their intention prior to committing suicide. It may have been at this stage that family or health care professionals could have sought intervention to prevent them taking their own life. This can lead family members to feel guilt and remorse after the person has died. The WHO (1992) stated that the impact of suicide upon the family and society is immeasurable and that one suicide will affect at least six other individuals. If the person was a young person at school, the impact could be upon hundreds of other people.

There have been conflicting views about the effectiveness of no-suicide contracts as a means of assessing suicidal risk in depressed patients.

No-suicide contracts

Kroll (2007) suggested that no-suicide contracts could be established with depressed people who are of high risk. The importance of this contract in suicide prevention is that it is based upon the strength of the relationship between a patient and a clinician. The element of risk can be determined by whether there is an agreed contract or not. However, Drye et al. (1973) argued that if a person will not enter into this agreement then there is a higher risk of the person committing suicide.

However, it could also be perceived that by not agreeing to the contract the person is crying out for help and this is a sign that intervention is required. Thus, no-suicide contracts may not be an ideal predictor of risk. Drew (2001) provided some evidence that inpatients with no-suicide contracts were more likely to self-harm rather than commit suicide. There appears little evidence that no-suicide contracts reduce the risk of suicide. Rudd et al. (2006) advocated that it was more beneficial for the patient to agree and make a commitment to have treatment. The most important aspect of risk assessment is documentation of the risk and sharing the information with relevant members of the multidisciplinary team. Thus, risk assessment needs to be managed in a planned way involving the individuals at risk and also other members of the multidisciplinary team. The DH (2007) developed principles and guidance on best practice in managing risk to self and others in mental health services.

Review of risk assessment scales

There are a variety of risk assessment scales used to predict suicidal intent and self-harm. These include the Hospital Anxiety and Depression Scale (HADS), BDI, Hopelessness Scale and the General Health Questionnaire (GHQ).

Bjelland et al. (2002) undertook a literature review to review the validity of the HADS. They reviewed 747 papers which had used the HADS scale. They concluded that HADS performed well in assessing symptom severity of both anxiety disorders and depression in both somatic, psychiatry and primary care patients as well as in the general population. Other scales have also been equally researched for effectiveness such as Beck's Depression Inventory.

BDI is used to assess levels of depression and as Hagen (2007) suggested the assessment criteria can help professionals to determine the effectiveness of antidepressant treatment and electroconvulsive therapy.

Beck *et al.* (1961) developed the original BDI as a 21-point inventory to measure the severity of depressive symptoms. The inventory was based upon Beck's observation of depressed peoples' attitudes and symptoms. Because of the concerns regarding the validity of the criteria, Beck *et al.* (1996) revised the inventory in line with the American Psychiatric Association (1994) DSM-IV diagnostic criteria for depression. Thus the BDI-II was developed.

Using the BDI (1961), Beck *et al.* (1985) reviewed 207 inpatients with suicidal ideation on admission to hospital. These patients had not attempted suicide prior to hospitalization. A 10-year prospective follow-up study was undertaken which showed that 14 of these patients actually committed suicide. The assessment scales undertaken on admission predicted that these suicides were the Hopeless Scale and the Beck Depression Inventory. Beck *et al.* (1985) showed that a score of 10 or more on the Hopeless Scale correctly identified 91% of these suicides. This study demonstrated as previous studies that there was a link between hopelessness and suicidal intent. This study concluded that the degree of hopelessness was the key indicator of long-term suicidal risk in depressed inpatients.

Hagen (2007) argued that despite the BDI demonstrating reliability and validity, ease of use and being widely used there are some limitations that need to be considered by professionals who use it when assessing risk and depression. Dozois and Covin (2004) argued that it does not address the needs of people from other countries and other cultures. This view is supported by Falicov (2003), who suggested that the different cultural factors which influence how depression is experienced by different ethnic and cultural groups are not included in the assessment. There were also concerns expressed by Barroso and Sandelowski (2001) that women scored higher than men and that gender may be an issue to consider when asking questions about crying as this may hold different meanings for men as opposed to women.

Hamilton (2000) suggested that the most important questions to ask patients with psychological distress during assessment are:

Have things gotten so bad you have considered taking your own life?
Do you have a plan to harm yourself?

Following these responses the doctor should explore the patient's intent and means of suicide, i.e. medication, drugs, hanging, firearms, poison etc. Some patients may have read about it or accessed websites on ways of committing suicide.

This should raise concern and heighten the element of risk as it is likely that these people have planned both intent and the means to commit suicide. Hamilton (2000) reinforces the importance of holding these discussions in private as the patient is more likely to be honest and answer the questions truthfully. Cochrane-Brink (2000) acknowledged that a thorough psychiatric mental health assessment by the practitioner is the best approach. They identified that risk assessment scales used in isolation were not as effective as a combination of the above.

Martin and Hamilton (2005) suggested that many of these scales rely on recording verbal responses from the patient during consultations. Practitioners undertaking the risk assessment need to also observe for non-verbal communication. This is supported by Patterson (1996) who advocated that non-verbal communication was more relevant than verbal communication during interactions between clients and professionals. Martin and Hamilton (2005) advocate the importance of recording the observed non-verbal behaviour as well as the verbal responses given. To ensure a holistic approach, both verbal and non-verbal communication are essential when assessing for suicidal intent.

Hawton and Fagg (1988) highlighted the link between self-harm and suicide indicating that 1% of self-harmers went on to commit suicide in the following 12 months. Thus, knowledge of the factors leading to self-harming behaviour is very important for health and social care providers.

Self-harm

The Mental Health Foundation (2006) reported on the National Inquiry into Self-Harm Among Young People. They highlighted that rates of self-harm amongst young people in the UK were the highest in Europe. This raises concerns and recognizes the need to focus on the mental health needs of young people. As well as considering the health promotion needs of young people, the relatively high number of these young people attending casualty units should also be considered from an economic perspective. The National Institute for Clinical Excellence (2004a) reported that self-harm constituted the top five causes of medical admissions. Allen (2007) recognized a variety of definitions of self-harm and concluded that it is not surprising that information is difficult to understand as different authors use different terminology often for the same thing.

Reasons why young people self-harm

Some of the most common reasons why young people self-harm need to be highlighted to teachers in schools and lecturers in colleges and universities. This information is also important for family members and organizers of clubs and facilities that young people access such as youth clubs, sports groups and after school clubs. The more the people are aware of these potential causes of self-harm, the earlier the problems can be identified and the appropriate help sought. Hawton *et al.* (2003) studied the characteristics and trends of young people who deliberately self-harmed in Oxford between 1999 and 2000. They found a variety of motives and reasons why young people may self-harm. These included the following:

- The wish to die
- To escape from a situation
- To demonstrate how desperate they feel
- To seek help
- To gain relief from tension
- To make other people feel guilty
- Alcohol and/or drug abuse
- Low self-esteem
- Disputes with peers
- Being bullied
- Family disputes
- Relationship breakdown
- Inability to do school work
- Awareness of self-harm by peers or from the internet
- Physical illness
- Sexual problems

(Hawton *et al.*, 2003).

Hawton *et al.* (2002) were concerned about the number of young people who had self-harmed. Depression in young people may initially be difficult to diagnose due to the emotional and psychological changes occurring during and after puberty. However, this is one of the reasons why teachers, family members and close friends need to understand that self-harm can also lead to suicidal intent and suicide. There are specific factors that are associated with self-harmers which make them a high suicidal risk. Some of these factors were identified by Hawton *et al.* (2002) in their self-report survey in schools in England. Hawton *et al.* (1997) also highlighted the association between deliberate self-harm with alcohol abuse and substance abuse. This was also recognized by Murphy (2000) who considered psychiatric aspects of suicidal behaviour in relation to substance misuse.

Self-harm and high suicidal risk

The National Institute for Clinical Excellence (NICE, 2004b) developed Clinical Guideline 16 on the management and prevention of self-harm in primary and secondary care.

NICE (2004b) developed eight key priorities which are listed below:

- Respect, understanding and choice
- Staff training
- Activated charcoal

- Triage
- Treatment
- Assessment needs
- Assessment of risk
- Psychological, psychosocial and pharmacological interventions

It was acknowledged that self-harmers must be treated with respect and that professionals must be mindful of the distress experienced by these individuals. Staff caring for self-harmers also needed specific training to prepare them for their role and staff treating poisoning needed to have access to activated charcoal. The guidelines also highlighted the importance of assessing the person after self-harming to determine their mental capacity in a non-stressful environment.

Some professionals may make judgments about the person who has self-harmed or perceive them as time wasters and not worthy of help, particularly if self-harm has been undertaken on previous occasions. Professionals caring for self-harmers need to try to develop a non-judgmental approach and become more self-aware of their own attitudes and approaches to these individuals.

This highlights the need for education, training and raising awareness of mental health issues and the importance of mental health promotion. This is particularly relevant when offering treatment in busy casualty departments. Nurses and other professionals will need to gain consent for treatment. Self-harmers may also require pain relief and it is important that care provided is given in a non-judgmental way. Undertaking a risk assessment is very important in relation to the patient's physical and mental state as they may have access to various means of self-harm. A thorough psychiatric, psychological and social assessment needs to be undertaken as part of the risk assessment. The person may plan to self-harm during times when others are not likely to find them or do it because others are unaware that they are actually self-harming.

This suggests that there is an element of planning by the person, as the act of committing self-harm is often undertaken when he or she is alone.

This is similar to the planning under-taken by people who commit suicide. People who commit suicide may have discussed their intentions with someone and may have left a suicide note or left instructions for after their death. Thus, any person who mentions concerns about taking his or her own life or has considered different means of suicide needs to be taken seriously. This discussion may have been undertaken with friends, colleagues or family members. Often, it is only after the event that people realize how desperate the person had been and how serious the intent to commit suicide. NICE (2004b) highlighted specific considerations to be addressed when dealing with children and young people under 16 years of age who have self-harmed. These young people need to be assessed by properly trained paediatric staff and issues of consent may need to be addressed after discussion with parents or guardians. There will also need to be involvement with child and adolescent mental health service practitioners (CAMHS).

It is not just young people who self-harm. NICE (2004b) stated that older people who have self-harmed are considered at much higher risk of committing suicide than younger people and need to be assessed by practitioners who are experienced in assessing older people with suicidal intent.

There is a large responsibility for professionals to assess the element of risk and intent to commit suicide as well as access to the means. If the serious attempt to commit suicide is not successful, then this leads to considerations about future risk. Discussion around the reasons for and events leading up to it need to be discussed with the person. What is also important is that the person may become an even higher risk as they feel that they are a potential failure after an unsuccessful attempt to take their own life. It is also important to review events and relationships within the family and also whether there is a history of mental illness within the family. Individual or family therapy may be offered to resolve any issues.

The professional's role in suicide prevention

The doctor's role

Mann *et al.* (2005) undertook a systematic review of the effectiveness of specific suicide prevention interventions in studies undertaken between 1966 and 2005. They concluded that educating doctors about the symptoms of depression and appropriate treatments and restricting access to method of suicide were key features in reducing suicide rates. Hamilton (2000) recognized the important role of GPs in primary care in preventing suicide. He advocated that they needed to understand and recognize the risk factors and also become more familiar with medication in patients with suicidal intent. Gilatto and Rai (1999) supported this view and stated that doctors needed to ask patients about their suicidal thoughts and feelings. This is evident in many of the assessments used to determine suicidal risk (Beck *et al.*, 1961). If they are not asked, depressed suicidal patients may not volunteer this information to professionals who are in a position to offer support, treatment and appropriate management. As described by Hamilton (2000) appropriate early assessment and treatment can often save the person's life. Some professionals may be concerned that by raising issues about the patients' thoughts about suicide and the means of committing suicide that this will actually encourage them to take their own lives. It has to be acknowledged, however, that some individuals will actually commit suicide after discussion with health professionals as this may have helped them to put their thoughts and plans into motion. However, if professionals do not ask key questions then it is difficult to assess the true element of the risk of suicide. As discussed earlier in this chapter, it is about reducing the element of risk, however some people will still decide to take their own lives despite support, intervention and treatment.

The nurse's role

Nurses play a key role in preventing suicide and there is evidence that nurse-led projects can help to reduce suicides. Duffin (2007) highlighted that nurses had provided support to people who had self-harmed and nurses had also advised GPs regarding the use of antidepressants for depressed people. Louis Appleby, National Director for mental health, stated that these nurse-led projects had helped to reduce the number of deaths from suicide by 8.5 per 100 000 of the population between 2003 and 2005. Primary care liaison nurses working alongside GPs in London had supported them with safer prescribing for both antidepressants and analgesics. Duffin (2007) highlights other nurse-led initiatives which included liaison nurses in Emergency Department units who provided training to general nurses in recognizing patients who self-harm and who are at risk of suicide. Patients who self-harmed were encouraged to write down on a card that they were a self-harmer so that they did not have to say it in front of a crowded waiting room.

There have also been multidisciplinary initiatives where school nurses and practice nurses attend suicide prevention master classes with other professionals. Non-specialist nurses should not work with suicidal patients in isolation. They need to understand the importance of referring the patient to the mental health team to ensure appropriate assessment, care and treatment are provided.

Conclusion

It is evident from the literature reviewed and discussions within this chapter that suicide is a key cause of concern from a global perspective. The NIMHE (2007) identified a suicide prevention target to reduce the death rate from suicide and injury of undetermined intent by at least a fifth by the year 2010. Despite concerns, this latest report suggested that suicide amongst the general population was at the lowest rate on record. However, this report only focused upon England and does not include Wales, Scotland and Ireland. It is of concern that there is evidence of higher incidences of suicide amongst teenagers in both Ireland and South Wales after this timeframe. So, despite documents reporting a downward trend in suicide rates it must be acknowledged that this evidence was based on information gathered between 2003 and 2005. The NIMHE (2007) also reported a reduction in self-inflicted deaths in prisons and the 20% reduction target in the strategy had been met. However, on 29 January 2008, BBC News reported grave concerns about prison overcrowding and the concern about the mental health of inmates. It also highlighted that as a consequence of this overcrowding and lack of mental health provision the incidence of suicide in prisons was increasing. The NIMHE (2007) had reported a reduction in suicides amongst mental health inpatients. What is not mentioned is whether the number of patients with mental illness who had been discharged home had increased. It could be that the risk of suicide has been shifted to the post-discharge period. However, Louis Appleby, Director of the National Confidential Inquiry argued that the reduction of inpatient suicides is due to better quality of care and improved physical environments of inpatient facilities. This has to be a positive for those people with mental illness and those caring for them. Suicide prevention is everyone's business and it is important that a multisector approach is undertaken which includes the police, teachers, health and social care professionals, religious members and politicians.

It is only by working together that these agencies can help a variety of vulnerable individuals from all walks of life at different times in their lives during times of crisis.

Reflection and discussion

Case scenarios and key observations

Scenario 1

An older lady named Sally aged 70 years has recently been widowed. Her whole life evolved around her husband whom she had been married to for 50 years. They had a long and happy life together and she misses him dreadfully. Sally has had depression in the past and now wants to end her life. She sees no future without her husband and is not eating or sleeping very well. She is starting to become socially isolated and has withdrawn from her normal social activities. She has stopped going to the shops and attending the local club. During a routine visit to the GP, she tells him she does not want to live without him.

Key issues

- *Older person*
- *Recently widowed*
- *Suffered with depression in the past*
- *Wants to end her life*
- *Not eating*
- *Not sleeping*
- *Socially isolated and withdrawn*
- *Tells GP, she does not want to live*

Scenario 2

Jayne is a 21-year-old student at university. She has struggled academically and has been drinking heavily. Her parents have recently separated and told her they are going to sell the family home. She is an only child and has been self-harming for 6 months and has attempted suicide by overdosing on tablets on two previous occasions. Her relationship with her boyfriend has broken down due to her drinking to excess. She feels isolated and depressed.

Key issues

- *Young person*
- *Drinking heavily*

- *Parents recently separated*
- *Selling family home*
- *Previous attempted suicide attempts*
- *Access to means, i.e. tablets*
- *Relationship breakdown*
- *Feeling isolated and depressed*

Reflect on the two case scenarios and discuss your actions with colleagues

Actions

- *What will you do with this information?*
- *How will you assess the risk of suicide in this person?*
- *Who will you inform?*
- *What care might this person require?*

References

Allen, S. (2007). Self-harm and words that bind: A critique of common perspectives. *Journal of Psychiatric and Mental Health Nursing, 14*, 172–178.

American Psychiatric Association (1994). *Diagnostic and Statistical Manual of Mental Disorders*, 4th edn. Washington, DC: APA.

Barroso, J. & Sandelowski, M. (2001). In the field with the Beck Depression Inventory. *Qualitative Health Research, 11*(4), 491–504.

BBC News (2007a). *Suicide Training Call for Schools*. Monday 28th January 2008. Available at http://www.bbc.co.uk/1/hi/wales/7231617.stm. Accessed 7 February 2008.

BBC News (2007b). *Teenage Girls Self-Harm Warning*. Tuesday 25th September 2007. Available at http://news.bbc.co.uk/1/hi/scotland/tayside_and_central/7102233.stm. Accessed 7 February 2008.

BBC News (2008a). *Call for Action on Young Suicides*. Thursday 7th February 2008. Available at http://www.bbc.co.uk/1/hi/wales/7231617.stm. Accessed 7 February 2008.

BBC News (2008b). *Rise in London Prisoner Suicides*. Tuesday 29th January 2008. Available at http://www.bbc.co.uk. Accessed 7 February 2008.

Beautrais, A.L., Joyce, P.R., Mulder, R.T., Fergusson, D.M., Deavoll, B.J. & Nightingale, S.K. (1996). Prevalence and co-morbidity of mental disorders in persons making serious suicide attempts: A case control study. *American Journal of Psychiatry, 153*(8), 1009–1014.

Beck, A.T., Steer, R.A. & Brown, G.K. (1996). *Beck Depression Inventory Manual*, 2nd edn. San Antonio, TX: Psychological Corporation.

Beck, A.T., Steer, R.A., Kovacs, M. & Garrison, B. (May 1985). Hopelessness and eventual suicide: A 10 year prospective study of patients hospitalized with suicidal ideation. *American Journal of Psychiatry, 142*(5), 559–563.

Beck, A.T., Ward, C.H., Mendleson, M.J., Mock, J. & Erbaugh, J. (1961). An inventory for measuring depression. *Archives of General Psychiatry, 4*, 561–571.

Beeston, D. (2007). *Older People and Suicide*. Available at www.staffs.ac.uk. Accessed 28 March 2008.

Bender, W.N., Rosenkrans, C.B. & Crane, M.K. (Spring 1999). Depression and suicide among patients with learning disabilities: Assessing the risk. *Learning Disability Quarterly, 22*(2), 143–156.

Bjelland, I., Dhal, A.A., Haug, T.T. & Neckelmann, D. (January 2002). The validity of the Hospital Anxiety and Depression Scale. An updated literature review. *Journal of Psychosomatic Research, 52*(2), 69–77.

Choose Life (2008). *A National Strategy and Action Plan to Prevent Suicide in Scotland.* Available at www.choselife.net/ststistics/statistics.asp. Accessed 7 February 2008.

Cochrane-Brink, K.A. (2000). Clinical rating scales in suicide risk assessment. *General Hospital Psychiatry, 22,* 445–451.

Coulthard, M., Farrell, M., Singleton, N. & Meltzer, H. (2002). *Tobacco, Alcohol and Drug Use and Mental Health.* London: Stationery Office.

Crowley, P.A. (May 2005). Evidence on youth suicide prevention highlights research gaps [Letter]. *BMJ, 330,* 1210.

DH (1990). *Caring for People.* The CPA for people with a mental illness referred to specialist mental health services. Joint Health/ Social Services Circular. C (90)23/LASSL(90) 11.

DH (2002). *National Suicide Prevention Strategy for England.* London: DH.

DH (2007). *Best Practice in Managing Risk: Principles and Guidance for Best Practice in the Assessment and Management of Risk to Self and Others in Mental Health Services.* London: DH.

DH (March 2008). *Refocusing the Care Programme Approach. Policy and Practice Guidelines.* London: DH.

DH and Welsh Office (1993). *Mental Health Act (1983) Code of Practice.* London: TSO.

Dozois, D.J.A. & Covin, R. (2004). The Beck Depression Inventory II (BDI-II), Beck Hopelessness Scale (BHS) and Beck Scale for suicide ideation. In: Herson, M. (Series ed.), Segal, D.L. & Hilsenroth, M. (Volume eds). *Comprehensive Handbook of Psychological Assessment. Vol. 2: Personality Assessment and Psychopathology.* New York: Wiley, pp. 50–69.

Drew, B.L. (2001). Self harm behavior and no-suicide contracting in psychiatric inpatient settings. *Archives of Psychiatric Nursing, 15,* 99–106.

Drye, R.C., Goulding, R.L. & Goulding, M.E. (1973). No-suicide decisions: Patient monitoring of suicidal risk. *American Journal of Psychiatry, 130,* 171–174.

Duffin, C. (2007). Nurse led projects help reduce suicides. *Nursing Standard.* Available at http://www.nursing- standard.co.uk/thisweek/news2.asp. Accessed 23 April 2007.

Falicov, C.J. (2003). Culture, society and gender in depression. *Journal of Family Therapy, 25,* 371–387.

Fergusson, D.M., Woodward, L.J. & Horwood, L.J. (2000). Risk factors and life processes associated with the onset of suicidal behavior during adolescence and early adulthood. *Psychological Medicine, 30,* 23–39.

Fox, C. & Hawton, K. (2004). *Deliberate Self Harm in Adolescence.* London: Jessica Kingsley.

Gilatto, M.F. & Rai, A.K. (1999). Evaluation and treatment of patients with suicidal ideation. *American Family Physician, 59*(6), 1500–1506.

Gould, M., Greenberg, T., Velting, D.M. & Shaffer, D. (2003). Youth suicide risk and preventative interventions: A review of the past ten years. *Journal of the American Academy of Child and Adolescent Psychiatry, 42,* 386–405.

Gunnell, D. & Frankel, S. (1999). Prevention of suicide: Aspirations and evidences. *BMJ, 308,* 1227–1233.

Gunnell, D., Harbord, R., Singleton, N., Jenkins, R. & Lewis, G. (2004). Factors influencing the development and amelioration of suicidal thoughts in the general population. *British Journal of Psychiatry*, *185*, 385–393.

Gupta, S., Black, D.W., Arnat, S., Hubbard, W.C. & Andreasen, C. (1998). Factors associated with suicide attempts among patients with schizophrenia. *Psychiatric Services*, *49*(10), 1353–1355.

Hagen, B. (2007). Measuring melancholy: A critique of the Beck Depression Inventory and its use in mental health nursing. *International Journal of Mental Health Nursing*, *16*, 108–115.

Hamilton, N.G. (2000). Suicide prevention in primary care. *Postgraduate Medicine*, *108*(6). Available at www.postgradmed.com/issues/2000. Accessed 5 October 2006.

Hawton, K. & Fagg, J. (1988). Suicide and other causes of death following attempted suicide. *British Journal of Psychiatry*, *152*(3), 359–366.

Hawton, K., Fagg, J., Platt, S. & Hawkins, M. (1993). Factors associated with suicide after Para suicide in young people. *BMJ*, *306*, 1641–1644.

Hawton, K., Hall, S., Simkin, S., Bale, L., Bond, A., Codd, S. & Stewart, A. (2003). Deliberate self-harm in adolescents: A study of characteristics and trends in Oxford, 1999–2000. *Journal of Child Psychology and Psychiatry*, *203*(44), 1191–1198.

Hawton, K., Rodham, K., Evans, E. & Weatherall, R. (2002). Deliberate self-harm in adolescents: Self report survey in schools in England. *BMJ*, *325*, 1207–1211.

Hawton, K., Sinton, S. & Fagg, J. (1997). Deliberate self harm in alcohol and substance misuse: Patient characteristics and patterns of clinical care. *Drug Alcohol Review*, *16*, 123–129.

Jenkins, R. (2002). Addressing suicide as a public health problem. *Lancet*, *359*, 813–814.

Jick, H., Kaye, J.A. & Jick, S.S. (January 1995). Antidepressants and suicide. *BMJ*, *310*(6974), 215–218.

Jick, H., Kaye, J.A. & Jick, S.S. (July 2004). Antidepressants and the risk of suicidal behaviors. *JAMA*, *292*(3), 338–343.

Jones, J. (2000). Psychiatric inpatients' experience of nursing observation. *Journal of Psychosocial Nursing*, *38*(12), 10–20.

Kapur, N., Hunt, I.M., Shaw, J. & Appleby, L. (2001). Available on line at www.national-confidential-inquiry.ac.uk. Accessed 30 January 2008.

Kessler, R.C., Borges, G. & Walters, E.E. (1999). Prevalence of and risk factors for lifetime suicidal attempts in the National Co morbidity survey. *Archives of General Psychiatry*, *56*, 617–626.

Kroll, J. (July 2007). No-suicide contracts as a suicide prevention strategy. *Psychiatric Times24*, 8.

Links, P.S. & Hoffman, B. (2005). Preventing suicidal behavior in a general hospital psychiatric service: Priorities for programming. *Canadian Journal of Psychiatry*, *50*, 490–296.

Mann, J.J., Apter, A., Bertolote, J., Beutrais, A., Curruer, D., Haas, A., Hegem, U., Lonnquist, J., Malone, K., Marusic, L., Patton, G., Phillips, M., Rutz, W., Rihmer, Z., Schmidtke, A., Shaffer, D., Silverman, M., Takahashi, Y., Varnik, A., Wasserman, D., Yip, P. & Hendin, H. (October 2005). Suicide prevention strategies: A systematic review. *JAMA*, *294*(16), 2064–2074.

Martin, D. & Hamilton, S. (2005). How to use non-verbal signs in assessments of suicide risk. *Nursing Times*, *102*(2), 36. Available on line at http://www.nursingtimes.net/nav. Accessed 4 July 2006.

Melhem, N.M., Brent, D.A., Ziegler, M., Iyenger, S., Kolko, D., Oquendo, M., Birmaher, B., Burke, A., Zelansey, J., Stanley, B. & Mann, J.J. (2007). Familial pathways to early onset suicidal behavior: Familial and individual antecedents of suicidal behavior. *American Journal of Psychiatry, 164*, 1364–1370.

Mental Health Foundation (2006). *Truth Hurts: Report of the National Inquiry into Self-Harm Among Young People.* London: Mental Health Foundation.

Moon, M. (2008). Available at http://www.bbc.co.uk/1/hi/wales/7231617.stm. Accessed 7 February 2008.

Moscicki, E.K. (1997). Identification of suicide risk factors using epidemiological studies. *Psychiatric Clinics of North America, 20*(3), 499–517.

Murphy, G.E. (2000). Psychiatric aspects of suicidal behavior: Substance abuse. In: Hawton, K. & Van Heerington, K. (eds) *The International Handbook of Suicide and Attempted Suicide.* Chichester: Wiley.

Murphy, G.E. & Weltzel, R.D. (1990). The lifetime risk of suicide in alcoholism. *Archives of General Psychiatry, 47*, 383–392.

National Confidential Inquiry into Suicide and Homicide by People with Mental Illness (2001). Available at www.natonal-confidential-inquiry.ac.uk.

National Institute for Clinical Excellence (2004a). *Self-Harm Scope.* Final version 3. London: NICE.

National Institute for Clinical Excellence (NICE) (2004b). *Self Harm. The Short-Term Physical and Psychological Management and Secondary Prevention of Self-Harm in Primary and Secondary Care.* Clinical Guideline 16. London: NICE.

National Institute for Mental Health in England (NIMHE) (April 2007). *Fourth Annual Report on Progress in Implementing the National Suicide Prevention Strategy for England 2006.* Crown: NIHME.

National Public Health Service for Wales (NPHSW) (2007). Available at www.wales.nhs.uk/sites3/page.cfm?org1d=719&pid=23582. Accessed 15 November 2007.

NHS Executive and Social Services Inspectorate (1999). *Effective Care Co-Ordination in Mental Health Services.* Modernizing the CPA. A Policy Booklet. London: NHSE and SSI.

Patterson, C.H. (1996). *The Theory and Practice of Counseling and Psychotherapy.* New York: Harper Collins.

Qin, P. & Nordentoft, M. (2005). Suicide risk in relation to psychiatric hospitalization: Evidence based on longitudinal registers. *Archives of General Psychiatry, 62*, 427–432.

Rossow, I. & Amundson, A. (1995). Alcohol abuse and suicide: A 40 year prospective study of Norwegian conscripts. *Addiction, 195*(90), 685–691.

Royal College Psychiatrists (2004). *Alcohol and Depression Leaflet.* Available at www.rcpsych.ac.uk/mentalhealthinformation/mentalhealthproblems/alcohol. Accessed 4 July 2006.

Rudd, M.D., Mandrusiak, M. & Joiner, T.E., Jr. (2006). The case against no-suicide contracts: The commitment to treatment statement as a practice alternative. *Journal of Clinical Psychology, 62*, 243–251.

Rutz, W., von Knorring, L. & Walinder, J. (1992). Long term effects of an education programme for general practitioners given by the Swedish Committee for Prevention and Treatment of Depression. *Acta Psychiatrica Scandinavica, 85*, 83–88.

Satcher, D. (1999). *The Surgeon Generals Call to Action to Prevent Suicide.* Washington, DC: US Public Health Service. Available at http://www.surgeongenral.gov/library/calltoaction. Accessed 22 August 2000.

The Sainsbury Centre for Mental Health (2005). *The Care Programme Approach – Back on Track*. Briefing 29. London: SCMH. Available at www.scmh.org.uk.

Van Gaskell, A., Schotte, C. & Maes, M. (October 1997). The prediction of suicidal intent in depressed patients. *Acta Psychiatrica Scandinavica*, *96*(4), 254–259.

Walsh, L. (May 2007). Caring for patients who experience hallucinations. *Nursing Times*, *103*(21), 28–29.

WHO (1992). *International Statistical Classification of Diseases and Related Health Problems*, Vol. 1, 10th revision. Geneva: WHO.

WHO (2000a). *Preventing Suicide: A Resource for General Physicians*. Department of Mental Health. Geneva: WHO.

WHO (2000b). *Preventing Suicide: A Resource for Primary Healthcare Workers*. Department of Mental Health. Geneva: WHO.

WHO (2006a). *Suicide Prevention (SUPRE)*. Available at www.who.int/mental_health/ prevention/suicide/suicideprevention /en/index.html. Accessed 9 October 2006.

WHO (2006b). *WHO Initiative on Depression in Public Health*. Available at http://who.int/ mental_health/management/depression/depressioninph/print.ht. Accessed 9 October 2006.

Chapter 8

Treatment for depression

Introduction

This chapter discusses some of the treatments available for depression. These treatments include antidepressant medication, psychological treatments including cognitive behaviour therapy (CBT) and counselling, electroconvulsive therapy (ECT) and the NICE guidelines on electromagnetic stimulation. Exercise and dance therapy are also considered therapeutic for some people with depression.

Compliance with treatment is an important factor to consider when deciding on the most appropriate treatment for individual people. This is very important as untreated symptoms of psychiatric illness can worsen psychiatric outcome. The nurse's role in the treatment of depression is highlighted as well as the implications of nurse prescribing for people with mental illness. The chapter concludes by discussing case management in primary care, variations in prescribing and equity of treatment and the importance of crisis resolution services.

The Office National Statistics (ONS, 2006) undertook surveys of psychiatric morbidity among adults in Great Britain. They determined that 1:6 adults would have a neurotic disorder which included anxiety and depression. They also highlighted that 1:7 people had considered suicide at some point in their lives. As already established in previous chapters, psychiatric disorders and suicidal attempts are more likely to occur in people with unskilled jobs, the unemployed, those with no formal qualifications, those living alone, socially isolated and living in rented local authority accommodation. These factors are very important when considering the number of people who receive treatment for mental health disorders.

The ONS (2006) demonstrated that the rates of psychiatric disorder were similar in 1993 and 2000. However, the number of people receiving treatment increased by 10%. Evidence from the statistics showed that 14% of people were having treatment in 1993, whilst by the year 2000 the number of people receiving treatment had increased to 24%. There may be a number of reasons for this increase. It may be that services have improved, people with mental illness are diagnosed and treated more efficiently or that more people with mental illness are taking their prescribed medication due to prescriptions and compliance being monitored more effectively. It could also be as a result of mental health user groups lobbying commissioners and care providers enabling the needs of people with mental illness to be addressed more effectively resulting in improved interventions and treatments.

It was evident from the ONS (2006) data that the number of people having prescribed medication had almost doubled, yet the number of people having psychological therapies had remained constant. However, there have been some new developments which may well help to address this balance of opportunity for treatment.

The DH (2008) promoted psychological therapies by developing guidance for health and social care professionals. The aim was to improve access to psychological therapies for people with depression and anxiety. They also developed a commissioning toolkit to help primary care trusts implement the NICE guidelines for people suffering from depression and anxiety disorders. This has also been supported by the National Institute for Mental Health in England (NIMHE, 2008) through their Care Services Improvement Partnership (CSIP) on their website. The NIMHE (2008) mission is to relieve misery and transform lives.

Their approach to improving access to psychological therapies has the following aims:

■ Help people with depression and anxiety disorders
■ Give people a choice of treatments for the first time
■ Promote evidence-based therapies
■ Measure people's recovery

(NIMHE, 2008).

However, despite the recent focus on psychological therapies, antidepressants remain the initial treatment prescribed for many patients with depression. The treatment prescriber will need to weigh up many options and discuss the treatment options with the patient. It is important for those prescribing antidepressants to understand how they work and also their potential side effects. For some patients, the side effects may be worse than the actual symptoms of depression. Thus, as Blenkiron (1998) advocated any treatment needs to be discussed with the patient to ensure optimal compliance and effectiveness. Medinfo (2004) stated that antidepressants work by allowing the body to make better use of its own depleted neurotransmitters which are essential chemicals in the brain. Patients need to be aware that antidepressants do not work immediately and that they need to take them for a while before having any effect. Antidepressants need to build up in the system to reach a therapeutic level for individual patients, so initially the patient may feel worse for a few days before feeling better. Many antidepressants like any other type of medication may incur side effects. These must be monitored closely and reported to health professionals.

Some antidepressants need to be gradually reduced rather than stopped immediately as the original symptoms of depression may reappear or different symptoms may be experienced.

MIND (2007) acknowledged the National Institute Clinical Excellence (NICE, 2004) guidelines on the treatment of depression. The recommendations suggest that for mild depression, guided self-help, CBT and exercise programmes were the most beneficial. For more severe depression they advocate the use of antidepressants such as selective serotonin reuptake inhibitors (SSRIs) which have fewer side effects than other antidepressants. One recommendation is to combine both antidepressants and psychological therapies.

Antidepressants

MIND (2007) stated that antidepressants work by alleviating the symptoms of depression by raising the level of mood. There are a variety of antidepressants including SSRIs, tricyclic antidepressants and monoamine oxidase inhibitors (MAOIs) available as treatment options for depression.

Types of antidepressants

- *Selective serotonin reuptake inhibitors*
  Example: *fluoxetine, fluoxamine, paroxetine, citalopram, escitalopram, sertraline*
- *Tricyclics*
  Example: *amitryptyline, imipramine, lofepramine*
- *Monoamine oxidase inhibitors*
  Example: *phenelzine, isocarboxaid, tranylcypromine*
- *Other types of antidepressants*
  Example: *venflaxine, tryptophan, flupenthixol*

Selective serotonin reuptake inhibitors

The SSRIs are newer drugs and are often prescribed initially due to having fewer side effects. However, all drugs need to be used with caution and there have been concerns that young children and young people who were prescribed SSRIs were more likely to commit suicide.

Risk of self-harm and suicide whilst taking antidepressants

Olfson *et al.* (2006) undertook a case–control study to estimate the relative risk of suicide attempt and suicide death in severely depressed children and adults. They compared those treated with antidepressant drugs with those not treated with antidepressant drugs.

These concerns occurred following of the Food and Drug Administration in America issuing a boxed warning regarding the evidence of increased suicidal ideation and behaviour in those children and young people who were taking antidepressant drugs. The outcomes used were suicide attempts and suicide deaths. Olfson *et al.* (2006) study concluded that there was some evidence to show that between the ages of 6 and 18 years, suicidal attempts were significantly linked with those individuals taking antidepressant drugs.

Geler (2006) commented on Olfson *et al.*'s (2006) study stating that there was no apparent link between suicide attempts or suicide deaths in the adults studied but that suicide attempts were increased amongst White children and young people taking any antidepressants. Suicide attempts were more associated with taking sertraline, tricyclic antidepressants and venlafaxine, whilst suicide deaths were more associated with any antidepressant and particularly SSRIs. These are important findings and need to be considered when prescribing treatment for young people. More research studies need to be undertaken to validate these findings especially if there are increases in suicide attempts and deaths in young people.

The United Kingdom Committee on Safety of Medicines (2003) highlighted concerns about the risk of suicide following reports about self-harm and suicidal behaviour in young people treated with paroxetine.

Whittington *et al.* (2004) were aware of concerns in the UK about the safety of using SSRIs to treat depression in children. As a result of these concerns, they undertook a systematic review of published versus unpublished data on the use of SSRIs as a treatment for childhood depression. They concluded that most evidence was based upon published research findings which indicated that the benefits outweighed the risks when using antidepressants to treat young people. However, some unpublished findings contradicted these findings suggesting that with the exception of fluoxetine, using antidepressant treatments in young people actually increased the risk of suicide. This highlights the importance of research into this sensitive area to ensure that young people are given the right treatment options at the right time.

Jick *et al.* (2004) researched general practices in the UK to determine the risk of suicide attempt and actual suicide after commencing antidepressants. The risks were higher in the early stages of taking the antidepressants particularly up to 9 days. This may be because the drugs had not reached the required level to have any effect and it is at this time when the depression may be most severe. Prescribers need to determine the benefits and risks when prescribing antidepressants.

Gunnell and Ashby (2004) considered benefits and harm in relation to antidepressant use and suicide. They highlighted that in the UK, there was no strong evidence to support the view that increased antidepressant prescribing reduced the rates of suicide. However, they suggested that there was evidence from paediatric trials to demonstrate that SSRIs were linked with increased suicidal behaviour and appeared to be less effective in treating depression in children.

They highlighted that more trials needed to be undertaken over a longer period of time as much of the evidence and data collected was only over a few weeks. However, it was also suggested that due to SSRIs having low toxicity in overdose, it is likely that this would have prevented suicide in some people.

Apt *et al.*'s (2006) study evaluated suicidal thoughts and behaviours in children and young people taking paroxetine. Out of 1191 children in the study, 642 were prescribed paroxetine and 549 were prescribed a placebo. Suicide behaviour was more frequent in the young people taking paroxetine who had a major depressive disorder. However, they concluded that it was difficult to identify a single cause for suicide in this patient group. One reason may be that major depressive illness is more likely to be treated with antidepressants as opposed to minor depression and anxiety. Thus, these young people would have been more likely to consider suicide due to their depressed state. There may have been a vested interest in the researchers finding no apparent link with the drug paroxetine as the company were supporting this study.

Gibbons *et al.* (2005) reported that about 3000 people died in America as a result of suicide annually. Many of them died as a result of untreated depression. Gibbons *et al.* (2005) wanted to establish if there was an association between antidepressants and suicide rates across America, so they studied data on people who had committed suicide in America between 1996 and 1998. They established links between people taking tricyclic antidepressants and suicide, particularly those living in rural areas who were on low incomes. This is interesting as much of the recent literature cites the relationship between SSRIs and suicidal links.

An American study cited in the *American Journal Psychiatry* (2006) argued that children who were prescribed SSRIs were less likely to commit suicide. Prescription rates for SSRIs were compared amongst 5- to 14-year olds. The research found that over a 2-year period there were 933 suicides and that suicide rates were higher in countries which did not prescribe SSRIs compared with those that did. What is of interest is that one of the American researchers had previously received pharmaceutical industry funding. This raises concerns about whether his views were biased towards the pharmaceutical company that had funded his research.

Trial data in 2003 which demonstrated evidence of links between suicidal ideation and actual suicide was suppressed by the pharmaceutical companies. As a result of this SSRIs are rarely prescribed for children in the UK. However in adults, there are advantages in prescribing SSRIs compared to other antidepressants. The BMA/RPSG (2003) stated that SSRIs were generally better tolerated by patients due to them having a less sedative effect and if there was a risk of self-harm or suicide, patients were less likely to have cardiotoxicity following overdose.

There have been controversial reports in the media regarding the effectiveness of antidepressants. Ford (2008) news editor for the *Nursing Times* reported that over 31 million prescriptions were given out in England in 2006 for antidepressants. It was also reported in the media that antidepressants had little effect as a treatment for minor depression and were only beneficial to treat severe depression. This was supported by Kirsch (2008) who suggested that the overall effect of the newer antidepressants were below expectations when reporting any clinical significance. These reports raised concern amongst psychiatrists in case people stopped taking their medication with immediate effect. This would potentially cause more harm and increase the risk of other symptoms for some depressed people. For most people taking antidepressants they need to reduce the dosage gradually over a period of time as stopping the antidepressant immediately could cause potential harm.

Staines (2008) reported that government watchdogs were putting tighter regulations on reporting clinical trials. This occurred over concerns that a drug manufacturer did not report concerns about links between Seroxat and suicidal ideation in children.

One example is research to examine the effect of antidepressants in dementia. The National Institute for Health Research Technology Assessment Programme is funding the study and will consider the clinical impact and cost-effectiveness of antidepressant medication in dementia sufferers. Many people with dementia are denied effective treatment for depression and this study will provide findings as to whether antidepressants will be able to help dementia sufferers.

Monoamine oxidase inhibitors

The BMA/RPSG (2003) highlighted that MAOIs needed to be used with caution due to the side effects of hypertension when interacting with other drugs or with certain foods containing high tyramine contents. These foods include broad beans, marmite and cheese. Despite this occurrence there have been new approaches developed to administer MAOIs.

Tobin (2007) discussed the use of Selegiline which is an MAOI available in America as a dermal patch. Patka *et al.* (2006) identified the treatment as Selegiline transdermal system (STS). They stated that it is the only triple action antidepressant inhibiting the breakdown of dopamine, serotonin and norepinephrine which can be administered transdermally at therapeutic doses without dietary tyramine restrictions. Similar to administering any oral treatment, administering Selegiline via the transdermal route can take up to 4 weeks to reach any effect. As with any medication, the effect needs to be monitored and dosage changes need to be considered within recommended therapeutic guidelines. Tobin (2007) highlighted that even though STS is administered transdermally, consideration should be given in patients who are suicidal to prevent overdose. Patient education is important for individuals taking MAOIs and they also need to be informed about the importance of informing other relevant health care practitioners in their care. Wristbands are available for patients to wear to inform health care practitioners in case emergency care is required.

Overview of antidepressants

Moreno *et al.* (2007) found that antidepressants were generally effective when used to treat depression in adults. They reviewed the use of tricyclic antidepressants in children finding that the drugs were not very effective. They found that SSRIs were more effective in treating adults than children. They also identified a lack of accuracy in data reports which made it difficult to determine the true effectiveness and safety of using antidepressants as opposed to placebos.

It is evident that antidepressants do have an important role to play in treating depression, particularly severe depression. However, treatments can be combined to maintain optimum health. This is demonstrated by Reynolds *et al.* (2006) who reviewed treatment for older people with depression. Older people are particularly likely to have other physical illnesses, disabilities and are more likely to suffer from recurrent depression. They concluded that maintenance therapy was a key factor in the over 70-year age group who had major depression. They found that monthly psychotherapy alone did not prevent recurrent depression, however, when combined with paroxetine for a period of 2 years then this helped to prevent recurrent depression.

Paykel (2007) highlighted that despite antidepressants being an effective acute treatment for depression there were high rates of relapse and recurrence demonstrating a much longer-term problem. This was supported by earlier studies undertaken by Keller *et al.* (1984) and Kiloh *et al.* (1998).

There were also concerns about adherence to medication so Ramana *et al.* (1999) undertook a study focusing upon the aftercare patients received in the 18 months following discharge from hospital. This study demonstrated that both adherence and prescribing levels of antidepressants were good. However, further research by Paykel *et al.* (1998) found that antidepressants were more effective in inducing remission and recovery than in preventing further episodes of depression. Thus, it is also important to consider other treatments for depression. There are a variety of psychological therapies available to treat people with depression.

Psychological therapies

Psychological therapies encompass a variety of therapies including problem solving, CBT, guided self-help and interpersonal therapy (IPT) which focus upon relationships or counselling and have been widely recognized by the WHO (2000).

The DH (2004) highlighted that psychological therapies were fundamental treatments when maintaining mental health.

Problem-solving therapy

Problem-solving therapy helps the person to make their problems more manageable and helps them to develop coping strategies. This is a very effective way of helping someone to take both responsibility and ownership of their problems. This can be achieved by identifying solutions to their own problems. This may require a number of sessions to help build on previous skills (MIND, 2007).

Counselling

Counselling provides a means of talking to a counsellor in a safe environment where issues can be discussed in a confidential manner. It allows the individual to express their feelings to someone who will listen to them and will support them in making their own choices and decisions. Counselling is not about making choices for the person, it is about helping them to change behaviour and to cope with things that affect their daily lives. Counselling is undertaken on a regular basis at agreed times and an agreed place. It is important that ground rules are established at the beginning so that both the counsellor and client are aware of what will be discussed and what expectations will be met and also that this will be a professional relationship. This is important if the counsellor is already known to the client or has known them in a different role. Through counselling a person is encouraged to express their feelings and helped to establish solutions to their problems. This is best undertaken with a trained counsellor.

The counsellor and the client may formalize the counselling arrangement by agreeing ground rules and timescales and structure of the sessions at the beginning of the counselling arrangement. This is beneficial to the client as well as the counsellor as there may need to be time when the sessions are no longer beneficial for the client.

Counselling can be undertaken in a directive manner where the counsellor takes the lead in suggesting exercises or homework to be undertaken by the client in between the formalized counselling sessions or it can be non-directive. Non-directive counselling is much more client-focused where they decide how the sessions will go and what will be discussed.

Counselling takes many forms and includes the following:

- Psychodynamic counselling
- Client-centred or person-centred counselling
- Transpersonal counselling
- Transactional analysis
- Existential counselling
- Gestalt counselling
- Rational emotive behavioural counselling
- Cognitive behavioural counselling

Some counsellors practice as private consultants where the client pays privately for their treatment. Counselling can also be provided by professionals employed in the NHS.

One of the most appropriate psychological treatments for depression is CBT.

Cognitive behaviour therapy

CBT is a treatment that helps people to identify negative thoughts and feelings. By helping them to understand these emotions the therapy helps them to understand their behaviour. It was initially developed by Beck *et al.* (1979) and is a treatment that helps to empower people to learn important new skills. Williams and Garland (2002) suggested that CBT helps people to understand how past events have affected them and also how it currently affects them. They can learn how to deal with distressing events and cope with them in a positive manner. It is important that by making themselves aware of negative feelings and thoughts they can begin to challenge them. It is evident that negative thoughts can deepen the depression and lower the mood, thus challenging negative thoughts provides a productive step forward.

By understanding why they feel this way, the person can be helped to look at alternatives and develop new coping strategies. This also helps them to take responsibility for their own mental health. As part of the therapy the person is encouraged to keep a diary of events and complete tasks which are agreed with the therapist. It is important that the client/therapist work together and as Beck (1976) stated, it needs to be a joint effort where the therapist works with the client to support them with the problem. Thus, they become partners in the problem-solving process.

The DH (2007b) supported ten CBT pilot sites for treating anxiety and depression. This followed on from previous studies undertaken in Doncaster and Newham. The view being that if depressed people access therapy quickly then they will be able to function better and maintain their employment, thus improving their general health and well-being. The implications of being unable to work can lead to financial and relationship problems making the depression worse.

Blenkiron (1998) found that CBT was effective in treating mild to moderate depression and combined with antidepressants was effective in treating more chronic depression and was also effective in preventing relapse. Butler *et al.* (2006) undertook a meta-analysis of the effect of CBT.

They found that in a large number of cases CBT was very effective in treating unipolar depression, generalized anxiety disorders, panic attacks, social phobias, posttraumatic stress disorders (PTSD) and depression and anxiety in children. A moderate effect was achieved for marital disorders, anger, chronic pain and childhood somatic disorders.

The meta-analysis showed that CBT was very effective in the treatment of adult depression. CBT could also be used to help people who have lost someone through suicide. Many family members or friends may blame themselves for the death of their loved one and this may influence their own feelings, emotions and behaviour. Thus, by using CBT the person can be helped to come to terms with their negative feelings.

An innovative interactive e-learning service has been established by the Oxfordshire and Buckingham Mental Health partnership NHS Trust for nurses who are interested in CBT (www.octc.co.uk). Trainee therapists are enabled to have interactive video tutorials and caseload discussion online. This demonstrates the importance of keeping skills updated and also recognizes that due to time, travel and working commitments professionals can maintain their competence and confidence when using CBT as a treatment for depressed people.

Similar approaches have been supported by DH (2007a) in their document Improving Access to Psychological Therapies (IAPT) programme. They have advocated a computerized CBT implementation guide. In February 2006, NICE produced a technology appraisal on the use of computerized delivery of CBT. They supported the use of computerized CBT for mild to moderate depression and also for managing phobias and panic disorders. The DH (2007a) stated that computerized CBT is an alternative to CBT delivered by a therapist and can be accessed through a computer, via the internet or through telephone interactive voice response. These sessions can be facilitated by health or social care services. The costs were reviewed after having used this approach across Primary Care Trusts in England and it was found that the estimated costs saved using computerized CBT as opposed to therapist face-to-face CBT were estimated at £116–£136 million pounds in England.

Parker and Fletcher (2007) undertook a critique of the use of evidence-based psychotherapies to treat depression. They recognized that CBT and IPT were popular treatments for depression. However, they suggested that even though their use is valid in universal circumstances, their use needs to be treated with caution on a universal basis. They advocated researchers moving away from testing treatments from a universal perspective and encouraging researchers to be more critical when interpreting evidence. This is important as the clinical implication of overselling these as superior psychological treatments can impact upon both patients and practitioners.

Despite these concerns there is evidence in the literature that both therapies are effective treatments for depression. Dobson (1989) stated that CBT was superior to other forms of psychotherapy when treating depression. This was also supported by the American Psychiatric Association (2000), which stated that CBT and IPT have the best-documented evidence for treating major depressive disorders, and by Kennedy et al. (2003), who stated that CBT and IPT were recommended as the first-line treatment for mild to moderate depression and were just as effective as antidepressants in the treatment of depression.

Cuijpers et al. (2007) recognized that depression had a major impact upon a person's quality of life. This was also identified previously by Cuijpers et al. (2004) and Preisig et al. (2001). Due to limited studies undertaken into sub-threshold depression, Cuijpers et al. (2007) undertook a meta-analytic review to review the impact of psychological treatments in depression. They examined the effects on depressive symptoms and the preventative effects on the incidence of major depression.

They reviewed seven high-quality randomized controlled studies with 700 subjects. Sub-threshold depression has been defined in a variety of ways.

Initially Kessler et al. (1997) suggested that depressive symptoms were on a continuum going from no symptoms to sub-threshold depression in the middle to major depression. Fechner-Bates *et al.* (1994) suggested that sub-threshold depression had unique characteristics which distinguished it from other forms of depression, which is shown in the DSM-IV and ICD-10 Diagnostic Classifications. Sub-threshold depression is also considered to be the prodromal stage before major depression. Thus, it is very important that it is diagnosed and relevant treatment interventions commenced. Psychological treatment aims to reduce the symptoms of depression and improve the person's quality of life. It was evident from reviewing these studies that a person with sub-threshold depression had a greater risk of having major depression.

Cuijpers *et al.*'s (2007) study demonstrated that psychological therapies were effective treatments for sub-threshold depression. This is very important as Wagner *et al.* (2000) highlighted how sub-threshold depression resulted in increased use of medical services and increased mortality rates.

Thus, if psychological therapies are effective they can help to reduce inpatient admissions and promote primary care interventions. This will be achieved where depressed people are cared for in their own homes supported by health and social care professionals.

Paykel (2007) was concerned about potential relapse and recurrence in people with depression whilst taking medication for severe depression. Thus, alternative treatments can be provided to support people with depression. A variety of treatments have been discussed throughout this chapter and CBT has been valued as an effective treatment for milder depression but there has been little evidence regarding its effectiveness for more severe depression. Generally, CBT is considered more expensive compared with antidepressants due to the therapist's time for multiple sessions as shown by Scott *et al.* (2003). Paykel (2007) advocated that studies needed to be undertaken that specifically tested the relapse reduction rate in patients having CBT.

After reviewing studies by Fava *et al.* (1994, 1996), Paykel *et al.* (1999, 2005), Teasdale *et al.* (2000), Jarrett *et al.* (2001), Ma and Teasdale (2004) and Bocking *et al.* (2005), Paykel (2007) suggests that CBT does help to reduce relapse and recurrence rates of depression by providing a coping framework for people whose depressive symptoms return or deteriorate.

CBT enables the person to have some control over their emotions, feelings and behaviour and helps them to make decisions as opposed to taking medication as it takes control away from the person.

However, people should not stop their medication without seeking medical advice as this could be counterproductive to their physical and mental health.

Paykel (2007) concluded that CBT was particularly effective if there was a history of relapse or recurrence of depression. This is important for many people with depression. CBT can also be provided to support people who are already taking antidepressants and also it can be commenced when the person is starting to feel better from the symptoms of depression. Thus, CBT should be undertaken when the person is still experiencing negative thoughts and experiencing negative emotions.

Guided self-help

Guided self-help supports a person to take responsibility for their own mental health. This may initially be undertaken with the guidance of a health care professional. This can be achieved in a short space of time from 6 to 8 weeks but will depend upon the motivation of the person. For someone with severe depression this approach may not be helpful (MIND, 2007).

Group work

Donoghue *et al.* (2007) advocated using group work with a group of people with bipolar disorder. The purpose of the group was to help people to recognize relapse symptoms. Donoghue *et al.* (2007) intends to use an inpatient group as a feeder group for a study on community relapse prevention for bipolar disorder. It will be interesting to evaluate the effectiveness of this approach with people with bipolar disorder and the findings may be helpful in comparing the findings from a previous randomized control study undertaken by Colom *et al.* (2003) highlighting that group intervention was helpful in preventing both manic and depressive mood swings.

Interpersonal psychotherapy

MIND (2007) suggested that IPT focused upon helping the person to deal with relationships. Depending on the severity of the problem, this may need to continue for up to a year.

Individual psychotherapy involves intensive one-to-one counselling which may involve discussing childhood experiences and relationships. This may benefit people who have experienced childhood abuse or difficult relationships during their lives. This approach may be helpful in some patients who attempt suicide.

It is important to understand that many people may attempt or actually commit suicide whilst in their own communities when commencing treatment for depression.

A study was undertaken by Simon and Savarino (2007) which compared the time patterns of suicide attempts amongst outpatients who were starting medication or psychotherapy treatment. They found that the incidence of suicidal attempts was highest amongst those patients who had been prescribed antidepressants by a psychiatrist. The rates were lower in those patients commencing psychotherapy and lowest of all in those patients who were prescribed antidepressants in primary care. This is relevant and there are reasons as to why this may occur. It may be due to a different type of referral system or more likely that the patients with the most severe depression were prescribed antidepressants from the psychiatrist. The severity of the depression is more likely to be associated with attempted or actual suicide. It is also evident that those people with more severe depression are more likely to have had previous connections with mental health services.

Other treatments are available for people with severe depression who have not responded to antidepressants or other treatments. These people may require electroconvulsive therapy known as ECT.

Electroconvulsive therapy

Electroconvulsive therapy is often referred to as ECT and is given when other treatments have not been very effective. ECT is given to treat more severe depression. The depressed person is given a general anaesthetic and a muscle relaxant and an electric current is passed through the brain inducing a convulsion.

Some patients are treated very effectively with ECT whilst others have side effects including memory loss. Thus, it is important that the patient is assessed appropriately and the decision to give ECT made on an individual basis.

The medical practitioner may have to balance the risk of giving ECT as a treatment from both a physical and psychological perspective. ECT may not be desirable in the frail older person who is too frail physically and has heart problems or other physical implications. However, ECT maybe given when the risk of the patient committing suicide is high or the person has become so depressed that they cannot feed or take care of themselves. ECT remains a controversial treatment as little is known about its true implications upon the brain; however, for some patients ECT as a last resort has provided the only effective treatment.

There are other types of therapies which have become beneficial for depressed people. One therapy that is often underestimated for mild to moderate depression is exercise.

Exercise and dance

The Mental Health Foundation (2005) supported the use of exercise in treating mild to moderate depression. Generally, exercise is inexpensive compared to medication and benefits individuals as it encourages feelings of well-being. Biddle *et al.* (2000) advocated the importance of undertaking physical activity to promote psychological well-being.

The Mental Health Foundation (2005) suggested that exercise gives people a sense of power over their recovery.

This is important because people who make decisions about healthy choices will take responsibility for their health and will become empowered to take control of their lifestyles.

This is supported by NICE (2003) guidelines on depression by advocating that structured and supervised exercise can have a clinically significant impact on depressive symptoms. The Mental Health Foundation (2005) supported the use of exercise referral schemes by GPs for people with depression. It is evident that exercise has been prescribed by GPs for obesity, diabetes and heart disease; however, they found little evidence that it was prescribed on a regular basis for patients with depression and anxiety. However, due to depression being such a leading cause of disability requiring almost double the amount of prescriptions between 1990 and 1995 (Clinical Standards Advisory Group, 2000), there needs to be alternative ways of treating people with depression.

Exercise therapy can help individuals in a variety of ways. Daley (2002) suggested that it had physical benefits due to the release of endorphins and feelings of well-being. It also enables people to socialize by attending a structured event and to get out and meet new friends. Exercise can also help people to achieve new skills and master new goals. Finally, it can create a diversion of thoughts from feelings of gloom and doom and despair as the mind is activated into other activities.

After studying patients undertaking short-term aerobic exercise over a 10-day period, Dimeo *et al.* (2001) found that depression scores on the patients studied had greatly reduced. These findings were similar to an earlier study undertaken by Blumenthal *et al.* (1999) who suggested that exercise was as effective as anti-depressants in the treatment of depression. However, they did recognize that out of the patients they studied those taking medication alone had the best recovery rates.

The severity of the depression may be a factor as most studies have highlighted that mild to moderate depression rather than severe depression is more likely to be treated with exercise therapy.

What also needs to be considered is the methodology used to undertake studies, which needs to be robust as highlighted by Lawlor and Hopker (2001) and Moore and Blumenthal (1998). As well as exercise, dance can be effective for depressed people.

Salsa dancing has become popular in the UK as a form of exercise, enjoyment and socialization. When reviewing the impact of dance therapy undertaken by people with depression, it must be acknowledged that it may actually be the social aspect that makes the person feel better rather than the exercise itself. If this is the case then this needs to be considered as a variable when undertaking research studies. Birks (2007) undertook a small study of 24 people who had been diagnosed with depression using Beck's Depression Inventory (1961).

Birks (2007) highlighted that physical exercise was beneficial to people with depression and that dance classes needed to be explored further. Halliwell (2005) stated that only 5% of GPs prescribed exercise as a treatment for mild to moderate depression; however, 42% of them had access to exercise referral schemes. This highlights that GPs may be reluctant to refer to exercise as a treatment for depression as there needs further evidence to demonstrate its effectiveness. There are also many other factors to consider such as patient compliance which can be influenced by where the patient lives and how they can access the exercise facilities. Thus, larger studies need to be undertaken over a longer period of time, maybe longitudinal studies need to be undertaken which may help to provide more evidence.

Electromagnetic stimulation

NICE (2007) Guideline 242 provides information for people who have been recommended to have electromagnetic stimulation of the brain to treat severe depression. The medical term for this procedure is transcranial magnetic stimulation (TMS). The person is not anaesthetized and does not require hospital admission as it can be undertaken as an outpatient.

The procedure involves placing an electromagnet on the scalp and stimulating areas of the brain through an electromagnet current over a 30-minute session.

These sessions usually last over a 2- to 4-week period depending on the severity of the depression and individual patient need. This treatment is given to patients after having gained their consent and is currently provided as part of a research study.

Some of the key aspects of this treatment are establishing the most effective dose, the number of electrical impulses required to ensure maximum effect and the length of time that they should be given.

The main side effects of this treatment reported by patients are headache, earache, migraine, seizure, nausea, memory problems and mood disorder in the form of mania.

These side effects need to be considered as with all other treatments the benefits should outweigh the disadvantages of the treatment. However, very few treatments are without any side effects at all. Thus, these studies need to be continually evaluated to determine the effectiveness of this treatment for severe depression. NICE Guidelines (2007) stated that there are currently no major safety concerns with TMS; however, there was some uncertainty about the efficacy of the procedure in relation to intensity, duration and application. Further results will be concluded in due course.

Compliance with treatment

Non-concordance and non-compliance with treatment occurs when patients do not always take the advice of practitioners. This is particularly relevant in relation to medication.

Compliance with treatment is important and is often associated in the literature with the Health Belief Model (HBM) where people's own perceptions of health influence their decisions. Often patients who perceive their condition as serious will be more compliant with their medication. This is supported by Babiker (1986) who also suggested that people respond by deriving their susceptibility to the illness and also the benefits of them adhering to medication regimes.

Cohen *et al.* (2000) reviewed literature into predictors of non-compliance in patients with unipolar depression and bipolar disorder using the Health Belief Model. They found that social influences and treatment alliance were important factors to consider when complying with medication. This is important as practitioners may be influenced and make judgements about patients who are non-compliant seeing them as deviant. This can ultimately affect their relationship if the practitioner is not able to see things from the patient's perspective. What needs to be considered is that many patients are very well informed, actively seeking out information about their condition and treatment options. They also may fear being addicted to medication or experience a variety of side effects which prevent them from taking the medication. Side effects are important aspects to consider and the type of medication prescribed needs to be weighed against the effectiveness of the medication.

Studies undertaken by Wieden *et al.* (1986) and Renton *et al.* (1963) both highlighted that side effects of medication had a major impact upon compliance.

If health care professionals are to work in partnership with patients then there has to be a middle ground where agreements are made about medication adherence. Carers and family members have an important role to play in supporting patients to take medication. McEovy *et al.* (1989) suggested that compliance was better in patients whose medication was supervised by family members. What is evident is that patients who have insight into their condition and who believe that medication is doing them good are more likely to take their medication.

Adherence suggests that there is some aspect of negotiation and that the patient does have some control over their decision making with regard to treatment whereas the term *compliance* is more associated with the practitioner controlling the decisions of the patient.

Other factors such as case management are also important when adhering to treatment. It is important to support people to manage their depression when back home in the primary care setting. Gensichen *et al.* (2006) undertook a systematic review to determine whether provision of case management in the community improved symptoms and medication adherence in people with depression.

Thirteen randomized control trials met the inclusion criteria and after 6–12 months it was evident that compared with standardized care, case management reduced the severity of symptoms of depression. The systematic review highlighted that within primary care case management helped to reduce symptom severity, improved clinical responses and remission rates and also helped depressed people to adhere to their medication. It would have also been interesting to evaluate whether depressed patients were more likely to adhere to CBT or other psychological approaches using a case management approach. This may provide opportunity for future research studies and reviews into alternative treatments for depression.

Accessing treatment

It is important to ensure equity of treatment for people with depression. Goyder *et al.* (2006) demonstrated that there have been variations in mental health prescribing within the United Kingdom population. As a result of these variations, Goyder *et al.* (2006) undertook a study to determine whether variation in prescribing in deprived communities in England were associated with access to primary care. They studied 39 deprived neighbourhoods and considered cultural and social differences in prescribing.

Prescribing rates for depression and anxiety amongst the deprived areas were predicted by the proportion of the population with English as a first language and also by the number of GPs per 10 000 of the population. Some factors influencing this could have been poor health, maternal deprivation or ethnicity as identified in previous studies undertaken by Hull *et al.* (2001) and Hull *et al.* (2005) who had highlighted some of these issues when discussing variations in antidepressant prescribing.

One of the main findings in Goyder *et al.*'s (2006) study was the differences in accessing primary care for those people with mental health-related symptoms. This was evident when considering ability to access the services as well as the actual services available. Some interesting conclusions were made from this study. It highlighted that lower prescribing rates may not reflect better health but may in fact determine poorer access to mental health care. Also, increased prescribing rates could be a reflection of good access to care rather than poor health.

This highlights the importance of undertaking good quality research and also appropriate interpretation of results and findings. It also determines the importance of appropriate analytical ability of research data and findings.

A recent study undertaken by Moussavi *et al.* (2007) highlighted that depression has a greater effect upon a person's health than any of the reported long-term conditions such as angina, diabetes, asthma or arthritis. This study was based upon figures on the basis of the World Health Organization's data covering 245 404 adults aged 18 years and over from 60 different countries. Moussavi *et al.* (2007) recognized the importance of early diagnosis and appropriate treatment for depression.

Kisely *et al.* (2006) found that inadequate treatment led to increased symptoms and that having to wait a long time to get the correct diagnosis and treatment had an impact upon overall outcome and the overall experience of the illness.

Nurse prescribing

It is not just doctors who prescribe medication for patients. The role of nurse prescribing and supplementary nurse prescribing is now a reality in nursing specialities across the United Kingdom. However, some mental health nurses have been reluctant to undertake this role. Nolan *et al.* (2001) undertook a study to determine mental health nurse's perceptions of the advantages and disadvantages of nurse prescribing. They also identified the educational needs of mental health nurses in relation to prescribing.

A questionnaire was given to 73 mental health nurses in clinical practice, 14 nurses working in outpatient's services and 59 mental health nurses working in the community. The findings of the study showed that mental heath nurses believed that mental health nurse prescribing would improve patient's access to medication, improve compliance, prevent relapse and was cost-effective.

Their main concerns were that they lacked the skills and knowledge required to undertake nurse prescribing. This was not surprising as they would need to understand pharmacology in a much greater depth than was usually expected. To enable this to take place mental health nurses would require training, supervision and collaboration with doctors to ensure that patients received the service they required. It is essential that mental health nurses have the skills to deliver the right service at the right time in a confident and competent manner.

It appears that mental health nurse prescribing is still not as popular as nurse prescribing within general nursing specialities. Bradley *et al.* (2008) undertook a focus group study to consider how mental health nurses prescribe in practice. Despite the introduction of supplementary nurse prescribing which aimed to break down interdisciplinary barriers and speed up the process of patients receiving their medication, the number of mental health nurses prescribing medication was relatively low.

It appeared from the study findings that organizations needed to be very clear about the role specifications and support provided for nurse prescribing roles as it generated more debate about their prescribing ability. This was in contrast to the purpose of training nurses to prescribe which was to make them more confident and competent at prescribing. May be there needs to be more evidence regarding the evaluation of the benefits of nurse prescribing for the patient, the nursing profession and the organization.

Crisis resolution services

Crisis resolution services provide intensive treatment and support for people at home who are going through acute mental health crisis. For this service to be effective, teams need to be available to support people with acute mental health issues on a 24-hour basis, 7 days a week. This requires intensive resources and appropriate funding and support for the practitioners providing this service. These practitioners need to be very skilled as they will determine what risks and interventions are required. They will also need to support the person if they need to go into hospital and promote early discharge back to the person's own home if possible. This service is appropriate for depressed people and for those experiencing psychiatric crisis.

Conclusions

This chapter has considered a variety of treatments in relation to depression. Comparisons have been made between a variety of different antidepressants and psychological therapies. Suicide risk has been discussed where recent media reports linked SSRI antidepressants with increased likelihood of suicide attempts. This needs to be considered when weighing up both the benefits against the potential harm as depression has a major impact upon a person's quality of life. Other therapies and approaches have been discussed including the benefits of exercise therapy and dance therapy for minor depression and new therapies currently being researched such as electromagnetic stimulation for severe depression.

The most popular psychological treatment for anxiety and depression is CBT. This has been acknowledged in relation to treating minor depression and is advocated by DH and NICE guidelines as an effective approach for treating depression.

Compliance with treatment is an important aspect to consider in relation to patient choice and decision making. It is clear that patients need to be considered as partners for both care and treatment options when ensuring optimum benefits for people with depression.

Reflection and discussion

Case study scenarios

Case study 1

Mary is a 35-year-old lady who lives with her two sons who are 18 years old and 12 years old. She has been depressed for 6 months following the sudden death of her husband in a car accident. She is finding it difficult to cope and has been to see her GP who has prescribed antidepressants. She does not like taking them because she feels drowsy and not in control of her life. She also has lost interest in the boys and she cannot talk to them any more and they appear to be doing their own thing. However, Tom the 18-year-old has asked if she can have different treatment as the tablets are not doing her any good.

Key issues

- *35-year-old lady*
- *Two teenage sons*
- *Grieving for husband*
- *Coping with a sudden death*
- *Feels she is coping alone*
- *Diagnosis of depression*
- *Prescribed antidepressants*
- *She states she cannot cope*
- *Side effects of medication, feeling drowsy*
- *Does not feel in control of her life*
- *Patient's confidentiality*

Reflect on the case study and discuss your actions with colleagues

Actions

- *What will you do with this information?*
- *Who is monitoring the side effects of the medication?*
- *What other treatment options are available?*
- *What other treatment options might be suitable?*
- *Who will you inform?*
- *Who else may be able to help?*

Case study 2

A man of 50 years has been diagnosed with depression. He was recently made redundant and his wife left him due to financial worries as their relationship deteriorated. He has always found it difficult to make friends and feels he cannot invest in a new relationship due to his experience of poor relationships in the past. He is feeling low and has lots of negative thoughts and keeps dwelling on past events. He has been referred to you as the nurse therapist who will be commencing CBT in the next week.

Key issues

- *50-year-old man*
- *Mid-life crisis*
- *Diagnosed with depression*
- *Financial worries*
- *Long-term relationship breakdown*
- *Feeling low*
- *Negative thoughts*
- *Poor past relationships*
- *Dwelling on past events*
- *Does not make friends easily*

Reflect on the case study and discuss your actions with colleagues

Actions

- *Determine if he is taking medication or having other treatment.*
- *Would other treatment options be suitable?*
- *Prior to commencing CBT what will you need to discuss with him?*
- *Discuss ground rules, agreed time of session, where sessions will be held, confidentiality, nurse/patient relationship.*

- *Discuss his commitment to complete tasks.*
- *Discuss the importance of him taking responsibility.*
- *Discuss how past events have affected him.*
- *Deal with distressing events in a positive manner.*
- *Challenge negative thoughts.*
- *Help him to develop coping strategies.*
- *The impact of CBT in reducing relapse and recurrence rates.*
- *What other support networks are available to him?*

References

American Psychiatric Association (2000). Practice guidelines for the treatment of patients with major depressive disorder [Revision]. *American Journal of Psychiatry, 157*(Suppl), 1–45.

Apt, A., Lipscitz, A., Fong, R., Carpenter, D.J., Krulewicz, S., Davies, J.T., Wilkinson, C., Perera, P. & Metz, A. (March 2006). Evaluation of suicidal thoughts and behaviours in children and adolescents taking paroxetine. *Journal of Child and Adolescent Psychopharmacology, 16*(1–2), 77–90.

Babiker, L.E. (1986). Non-compliance in schizophrenia. *Psychiatric Developments, 4,* 329–337.

Beck, A.T. (1961). An inventory for measuring depression. *Archives of General Psychiatry, 4,* 561–571.

Beck, A.T. (1976). *Cognitive Therapy and Emotional Disorders.* New York: International Universities Press.

Beck, A., Rush, A., Shaw, B. & Emery, G. (1979). *Cognitive Therapy for Depression.* New York: Guildford Press.

Biddle, S., Fox, K., Boutcher, S. & Faulkner, G. (2000). *The Way Forward for Physical Activity and the Promotion of Psychological Well Being.* London: Routledge.

Birks, M. (2007). The benefits of salsa classes for people with depression. *Nursing Times, 103,* 32–33.

Blenkiron, P. (1998). The management of depression in primary care: A summary of evidence based guidelines. *Psychiatric Care, 5*(5), 172–177.

Blumenthal, J.A., Babyak, M.A., Moore, K.A., Craighead, W.E., Herman, S., Khatri, P., Waugh, R., Napolitano, M.A., Forman, L.M., Applebaum, M., Doraiswamy, P.M. & Krishnan, K.R. (1999). Effects of exercise training on older adults with major depression. *Archives of Internal Medicine, 159,* 2349–2356.

BMA/RPSG (British Medical Association and the Royal Pharmaceutical Society of Great Britain) (2003). *British National Formulary.* London: BMA/RSPG.

Bocking, C.L., Schene, A.H., Spinhoven, P., Koeter, M.W., Wouters, L.F., Huyser, J. & Kamphuis, J.H. (2005) Preventing relapse/recurrence in recurrent depression with cognitive therapy: A randomised controlled trial. *Journal of Consulting and Clinical Psychology, 7,* 647–657.

Bradley, E., Wain, P. & Nolan, P. (2008). Putting mental health nurse prescribing into practice. *Nurse Prescribing, 6*(1), 15–19.

Butler, A.C., Chapman, J.E., Forman, E.M. & Beck, A.T. (January 2006). The empirical status of cognitive–behavioural therapy: A review of meta-analysis. *Clinical Psychology Review, 26*(1), 17–31.

Clinical Standards Advisory Group (2000). *Services for People with Depression: A summary of the CSAG Report on Services for People with Depression.* London: CSAG.

Cohen, N.L., Parikh, S.V. & Kennedy, S.H. (September 2000). Medication compliance in mood disorders relevance of the Health Belief Model and other determinants. *Primary Care Psychiatry,* 6(3), 101–110.

Colom, F., Vieta, E., Martinez-Aran, A., Reinares, M., Goileolea, J.M., Benabarre, A., Torrent, C.V., Comes, M., Corbella, B., Parramon, G. & Corominas, J. (2003). A randomised controlled trial of efficacy of group psycho education in the prophylaxis of recurrences in bipolar patients whose disease is in remission. *Archives of General Psychiatry,* 60, 402–407.

Cuijpers, P., De-Graaf, R. & Van Dorsselaer, S. (2004). Minor depression: Risk profiles, functional disability, health care use and risk of developing major depression. *Journal of Affective Disorders,* 79, 71–79.

Cuijpers, P., Smit, F. & Van Straten, A. (2007). Psychological treatments of subthreshold depression: A meta analytic review. *Acta Psychiatrica Scandinavica,* 115, 434–441.

Daley, A. (2002). Exercise therapy and mental health in clinical populations: Is exercise therapy a worthwhile intervention? *Advances in Psychiatric Treatment,* 8, 262–270.

DH (2004). *Organising and Delivering Psychological Therapies.* London: DH.

DH (May 2007a). *CBT Pilots Extended.* Available at www.dh.org.uk date. Accessed 12 October 2007.

DH (2007b). *Improving Access to Psychological Therapies (IAPT) Programme.* Computerised cognitive behavioural therapy (cCBT) implementation guidance. London: DH.

DH (April 2008). *Improving Access to Psychological Therapies (IAPT) Commissioning Toolkit.* London: DH.

Dimeo, F., Bauer, M., Varahran, I., Proest, G. & Halter, U. (2001). Benefits from aerobic exercise in patients with major depression: A pilot study. *British Journal of Sports Medicine,* 35, 11–117.

Dobson, K.S. (1989). A meta-analysis of the efficacy of cognitive therapy for depression. *Journal of Consulting and Clinical Psychology,* 57, 414–419.

Donoghue, K., Lomax, K. & Hall, J. (2007). *Using Group Work to Prevent Relapse in Bipolar Disorder.* Available at www.nursingtimes.net/nursingtimes/pages. Accessed 23 May 2007.

Fava, G.A., Grandi, S., Zielezny, M., Canestrari, R. & Morphy, M.A. (1994). Cognitive behavioural treatment of residual symptoms in primary major depressive disorder. *American Journal of Psychiatry,* 151, 1295–1299.

Fava, G.A., Grandi, S., Zielenzy, M., Rafanelli, C. & Canestrari, R. (1996). Four year outcome for cognitive behavioural treatment of residual symptoms in major depression. *American Journal of Psychiatry,* 153, 945–947.

Fechner-Bates, S., Coyne, J.C. & Schwenk, T.L. (1994). The relationship of self-reported distress to depressive disorders and other psychopathology. *Journal of Consulting and Clinical Psychology,* 62, 550–559.

Ford, S. (March 2008). *Antidepressants Have Little Effect.* Available at www.s.ford@emap.com.

Geler, B. (August 2006). Comparing suicide risk with antidepressants in children and adults. *Journal of Watch Psychiatry,* 63, 865–892.

Gensichen, J., Beyer, M. & Muth, C. (2006). Therapeutics. Review: Case management in primary care improves symptoms and drug adherence in people with major depression. *Evidence Based Mental Health Care,* 9, 79. Available at http://ebmh.bmjjournals.com/cgi/content/full/9/3/79. Accessed 16 October 2006.

Gibbons, R.D., Hur, K., Bhaumik, D.K. & Mann, J.J. (February 2005). The relationship between antidepressant medication use and rate of suicide. *Archives of General Psychiatry*, 62(2), 165–172.

Goyder, E., Dibben, C., Grimsley, M., Peters, J., Blank, L. & Ellis, E. (2006). Variations in prescribing fro anxiety and depression: A reflection of health inequalities, cultural differences or variations in access to care? *International Journal for Equity in Health*, 206(5), 4. Available at http://www.equityhealthj.com/content/5/1/4. Accessed 10 April 2008.

Gunnell, D. & Ashby, D. (July 2004). Antidepressants and suicide: What is the balance of benefit and harm? *BMJ*, 329(7456), 34–38.

Halliwell, E. (2005). *Up and Running: Exercise Therapy and the Treatment of Mild to Moderate Depression in Primary Care*. Available at www.mentalhealth.org.uk. Accessed 23 May 2007.

Hull, S.A., Aquino, P. & Cotter, S. (2005). Explaining variation in antidepressant prescribing rates in East London: A cross sectional study. *Family Practitioner*, 22, 37–42.

Hull, S.A., Cornwall, J., Harvey, C. & Eldridge, S. (2001). Prescribing rates for psychotropic medication amongst East London general practices: Low rates where Asia populations are greatest. *Family Practitioner*, 18, 167–173.

Jarrett, R.B., Kraft, D., Doyle, J., Foster, B.M., Eaves, C.G. & Silver, P.C. (2001). Preventing recurrent depression using cognitive therapy with and without a continuation phase: A randomised clinical trial. *Archives of General Psychiatry*, 58, 381–388.

Jick, H., Kaye, J. & Jick, S. (2004). Antidepressants and the risk of suicide behaviours. *JAMA*, 292, 338–343.

Keller, M.B., Klerman, G.I., Lavori, P.W., Coryell, W., Endicott, J. & Taylor, J. (1984). Long-term outcome of episodes of major depression: Clinical and public health significance. *JAMA*, 252, 788–792.

Kennedy, S.H., Lam, R.W. & Morris, B. (2003). Canadian network for mood and anxiety treatments. (CANMAT) Depression Work Group. Clinical guidelines for depressive disorders. Summary of recommendations relevant to family physicians. *Canadian Family Physician*, 49, 489–491.

Kessler, R.C., Zhao, S., Blazer, D.G. & Swartz, M. (1997). Prevalence, correlates and course of minor depression and major depression in The National Comorbidity survey. *Journal of Affective Disorders*, 45, 19–30.

Kiloh, L.G., Andrews, G.A. & Neilson, M. (1998). The long-term outcome of depressive illness. *British Journal of Psychiatry*, 153, 752–757.

Kisely, S., Scott, A., Denney, J. & Simon, G. (2006). Duration of untreated symptoms in common mental disorders: Association with outcome. International Study. *British Journal of Psychiatry*, 189, 79–80.

Kirsch, I. (2008). *Antidepressants Have Little Effect*. Public Library of Medicine. Available at s.ford@emap.com. Accessed 24 April 2008.

Lawlor, D.A. & Hopker, S. (2001). The effectiveness of exercise as an intervention in the management of depression. Systematic review and meta-regression analysis of randomised controlled studies. *BMJ*, 322, 763–767.

Ma, S.H. & Teasdale, J.D. (2004). Mindfulness-based cognitive therapy for depression: Replication and exploration of differential relapse prevention effects. *Journal of Consulting and Clinical Psychology*, 72, 31–40.

McEovy, J.P., Apperson, L.J. & Applebaum, P.S. (1989). Insight in schizophrenia. Its relationship to acute psychopathology. *Journal of Nervous and Mental Disease*, 177, 43–47.

Medinfo (2004). Available at http://medinfo.co.uk/conditions/depression.html. Accessed 15 July 2006.

MIND (2007). Available at http://www.mind.org.uk/Informaton?Booklets/ Understanding/Understanding+depression. Accessed 24 April 2007.

Moore, K.A. & Blumenthal, J.A. (1998). Exercise training as an alternative treatment for depression among older adults. *Alternative Therapies in Health and Medicine*, 4(1), 48–56.

Moreno, C.A., Arango, C., Parellada, M., Shaffer, D. & Bird, H. (2007). Antidepressants in child and adolescent depression? Where are the bugs? *Acta Psychiatrica Scandinavica*, 115, 184–195.

Moussavi, S., Chatterji, S., Verdes, E., Tandon, A., Patel, V. & Ustun, B. (September 2007). Depression, chronic diseases and decrements in health: Results from the World Health Organization surveys. *The Lancet*, 30(9590), 851–858.

NICE (2003). *Depression NICE Guidelines. Second Consultation*. London: NHS.

NICE (2004). *Depression: Management of Depression in Primary Care*. NICE Guidance (CG23). London: NHS.

NICE (2007). *Treating Severe Depression with Electromagnetic Stimulation of the Brain*. NICE Guidance (CG 242). London: NHS.

National Institute for Mental Health England (NIMHE) (2008). Available at http://www.nhchoice.csip.org.uk. Accessed 17 April 2008.

Nolan, P., Haque, M.S., Badger, F., Dyke, R. & Khan, I. (2001). Mental health nurses' perceptions of nurse prescribing. *Journal of Advanced Nursing*, 36(4), 527–534.

Office National Statistics (ONS) (2006). *Survey of Psychiatric Morbidity Among Adults in Great Britain*. Available at http://www.statistics.gov.uk/CCI/nugget.as?ID. Accessed 25 May 2007.

Olfson, M., Marcus, S.C. & Shaffer, D. (2006). Antidepressant drug therapy and suicide in severely depressed children and adults: A case–control study. *Archives of General Psychiatry*, 63(8), 865–872.

Parker, G. & Fletcher, K. (2007). Clinical overview. Treating depression with evidence based psychotherapies: A critique of the evidence. *Acta Psychiatrica Scandinavica*, 115, 352–359.

Patka, A.A., Pae, C. & Masland, P. (2006). Transdermal seligiline: The new generation of mono amine oxidase inhibitors. *CNS Spectrums*, 11(5), 363–375.

Paykel, E.S. (2007). Cognitive therapy in relapse prevention in depression. *International Journal of Neuropsychopharmacology*, 10, 131–136.

Paykel, E.S., Hart, D. & Priest, R.G. (1998). Changes in public attitudes to depression during the defeat depression campaign. *British Journal of Psychiatry*, 173, 519–522.

Paykel, E.S., Scott, J., Cornwall, P.L., Abbott, R., Crane, C., Pope, M. & Johnson, A.L. (2005). Duration of relapse prevention after cognitive therapy in residual depression: A follow up of controlled trial. *Psychological Medicine*, 35, 59–68.

Paykel, E.S., Scott, J., Teasdale, J.D., Johnson, A.L., Garland, A., Moore, R., Jenaway, A., Cornwall, P.L., Hayhurst, H., Abbott, R. & Pope, M. (1999). Prevention of relapse in residual depression by cognitive therapy: A controlled trial. *Archives of General Psychiatry*, 56, 829–835.

Preisig, M., Merikangas, K.R. & Angst, J. (2001). Clinical significance and comorbidity of sub-threshold depression and anxiety in the community. *Acta Psychiatrica Scandinavica*, 104, 96–103.

Ramana, R., Paykel, E.S., Surtees, P.G., Melzer, D. & Mehta, M. (1999). Medication received by patients with depression following the acute episode: Adequacy and relation to outcome. *British Journal of Psychiatry*, 174, 128–134.

Renton, C.A., Affleck, J.W. & Carstairs, G.M. (1963). A follow-up of schizophrenia patients in Edinburgh. *Acta Psychiatrica Scandinavica, 39*, 548–600.

Reynolds, C.F., Dew, M.A., Pollock, B.G., Mulsant, B.H., Frank, E., Miller, M.D., Houck, P.R., Mazumdar, S., Butters, M.A., Stack, J.A., Schlernitzaur, M.A., Whyte, E.M., Gildengers, A., Karp, J., Lenze, E., Szanto, K., Bensasi, S. & Kpfer, D.J. (March 2006). Maintenance treatment of major depression in old age. *New England Journal of Medicine, 354*(11), 1130–1138.

Scott, J., Palmer, S., Paykel, E., Teasdale, J. & Hayhurst, H. (2003). Use of cognitive therapy for relapse prevention in chronic depression: Cost effectiveness study. *British Journal of Psychiatry, 182*, 221–227.

Simon, G.E. & Savarino, J. (July 2007). Suicide attempts among patients starting depression treatment with medication or psychotherapy. *American Journal of Psychiatry, 164*, 1029–1034.

Staines, R. (March 2008). *Drug Guidelines to be Tightened Following Seroxtat Probe.* Available at www.r.staines@emap.com. Accessed 24 April 2008.

The Mental Health Foundation (2005). *Exercise and Depression. Exercise Referral and the Treatment of Mild or Moderate Depression.* Information for GP's and healthcare practitioners. London: The Mental Health Foundation. Available at www.mentalhealth. org.uk. Accessed 10 July 2008.

Teasdale, J.D., Segal, Z.V., Williams, J.M., Ridgeway, V.A., Soulsby, J.M. & Lau, M.A. (2000). Prevention of relapse/recurrence in major depression by mindfulness-based cognitive therapy. *Journal of Consulting and Clinical Psychology, 68*, 615–623.

Tobin, M. (February 2007). Psychopharmacology column. Why choose Selegiline transdermal system for refractory depression? *Issues in Mental Health Nursing, 28*(2), 223–228.

United Kingdom Committee on Safety of Medicines (June 2003). *Seroxat Must not Be Used for Treatment of Children.* United Kingdom Medicines and Health Care Products Regulatory Agency: Department of Health press release. Available at http://www.mhra.gov. uk/news/2003/seroxat10603.pdf.

Wagner, H.R., Burns, B.J., Broadhead, W.E., Yarnall, K.S.H., Sigmon, A. & Gaynes, B.N. (2000). Minor depression in family practice: Functional morbidity, co-morbidity, service utilisation and outcomes. *Psychological Medicine, 30*, 1377–1390.

Whittington, C.J., Kendall, T., Fonagy, P., Cottrell, D., Cotgrove, A. & Boddington, E. (April 2004). Selective serotonin reuptake inhibitors in childhood depression: Systematic review of published versus unpublished data. *The Lancet, 363*(9418), 1335.

Wieden, P.J., Shaw, E. & Man, J. (1986). Causes of neuroleptic non-compliance. *Psychiatric Annals, 16*, 571–578.

Williams, C. & Garland, A. (2002). Identifying and challenging unhelpful thinking. *Advances in Psychiatric Treatment, 8*, 377–386.

World Health Organization Collaborating Centre for Research and Training for Mental Health (eds) (2000). *Who Guide to Mental Health in Primary Care.* London: Royal Society of Medicine Press.

Chapter 9

Ethnicity and depression and mental health and learning disabilities

Introduction

The first part of this chapter will highlight the importance of recognizing depression in people from different ethnic and cultural backgrounds, whilst the second part of the chapter will discuss the importance of recognizing mental health needs in people with learning disabilities. Both are of equal importance when caring for people from diverse backgrounds with mental health care needs.

MIND (2006) expressed concern by the Chief Executive of the Commission for Health Improvement that mental health services were not responding to the needs of Black and ethnic minority people. However, there is evidence that Black and ethnic minority groups are being supported by a variety of agencies including NIMHE England, ICAR (2005), Diverse Minds (2006) and DH (2007a) enabling them to access appropriate mental health services and treatment. There have been a variety of reasons given as to why Black and ethnic minorities do not access health care services. These include health care staff misinterpreting the symptoms of depression due to cultural differences. Another reason described by Shah *et al.* (1998) was that some older ethnic people did not accept referral to secondary mental health services and Hutchinson and Gilvarry (1998) suggested that some Black people perceived care workers as being racist. However, this has been challenged by Marhawa and Livingston (2002) who found little evidence of perceived racism. What is evident is that all health and social care practitioners need to be aware of identifying psychological distress in people from diverse cultures and backgrounds.

Prevalence of depression by race or ethnicity

Ethnic groups frequently share geographical origins, culture, religious traditions and language. Helman (2000) suggested that culture incorporates shared ideas and rules and is a person's perception and understanding of the world around them, whilst Livingson and Sembhi (2003) suggested that race is often identified by a person's colour or physical appearance.

Whatever race or culture a person belongs to, it is important to establish the prevalence of depression. The prevalence of depression was studied in America. A National Health and Nutrition Examination survey was conducted between 1988 and 1994 in America by the National Centre for Health Statistics.

Following on from this study Riolo *et al.* (2005) used the data to examine prevalence of major depressive disorder and dysthymic disorder in the American population by race and ethnicity.

A diagnostic interview schedule was given out to 8449 people between the ages of 15 and 40 years. An excellent response rate of 96.1% was achieved. The study findings demonstrated that the prevalence of major depressive disorder was significantly higher in White people than in African Americans and Mexican Americans. However, the findings demonstrated the opposite for dysthymic disorder. Poverty appeared to be a significant risk factor for major depressive disorder amongst racial and ethnic groups. Some of the non-English-speaking people were less educated and may not have understood the questions asked, thus their responses did not give a true indication of their experiences. Riolo *et al.* (2003) also recognized that race and ethnicity were important factors to consider when seeking help for mental health issues, accessing mental health services and also using medication.

Ethnicity and diversity

Ethnicity is classified in census data where individuals identify with a particular ethnic group. However, the Kings Fund (2006) recognized that by grouping people together in categories that cultural and ethnic backgrounds were not always captured accurately in the data. Cultural differences such as different religions may not always be recognized due to people being associated with a label from a particular ethnic grouping.

Keating *et al.* (2003) undertook a report for the Kings Fund on ethnic diversity and mental health in London. They acknowledged that local policy initiatives were not meeting needs despite national campaigns and policies to improve race equality in mental health services.

They highlighted particularly the lack of provision for the needs of Irish people in London areas. It was difficult to maintain the healthy action zones where partnership working was encouraged despite these initiatives being supported initially. There was also some concern about acute mental health care for Black and Ethnic Minorities (BEM) due to inappropriate treatment options and also the lack of support for their families and carers. Women were particularly highlighted due to the a high number of African Caribbean and mixed race women in the mental health care system. Another concern was the higher incidence of self-harm and suicide amongst Asian women, young Afro-Caribbean people and Irish people. The report acknowledged that more research was needed to gain information about the mental health needs of BEM women in care services, the criminal justice system including those prone to suicide.

Adams and Boscarino (2005) considered the impact of mental health outcomes upon ethnic minority groups following a disaster. They studied differences in mental health outcome amongst Whites, African Americans and Hispanics a year after the World Trade Centre terrorist attacks. Adams and Boscarino (2005) collected data from a random sample of 2368 city residents. The study concluded that there was no significant evidence to support the view that Latinos or African Americans consistently suffered from poorer physical and mental health following these traumatic events compared to Whites.

This highlights the importance of considering both cultural aspects and ethnicity when assessing for depression amongst ethnic minorities. Dratcu *et al.* (1987) expressed concern about diagnosing and assessing depression from a cross-cultural perspective. They advocated the Montgommery–Asberg Depression rating Scale (MADRS) as a standardized instrument of evaluation when assessing depressed people. They compared the MADRS scale with The Hamilton Depression rating Scale and the self-rating Visual Analogue Mood Scale. This study was undertaken in Brazil and concluded that the MADRS scale was a useful tool in assessing depression in cross-cultural studies of depression. What became evident was that once depression had been diagnosed it was important to monitor it appropriately.

Monitoring ethnicity and inequality

MIND (2006) suggested that there was evidence of inequity amongst Black and ethnic minorities with the mental health care system. They argued that BEM's were more likely to be treated in secure settings, more likely to be given higher doses of medication and less likely to be offered psychological therapies. This perception had been supported previously by the Mental Health Act Commission (2001) who acknowledged that ethnic monitoring within mental health care was poor. However, The National Health Service Executive (NHSE, 1994) has recorded and monitored the ethnicity of both inpatients and staff since the early 1990s.

There are things that clearly need to be considered after gathering data to record ethnicity. These include developing policies which when implemented will address the inequity of service accessibility and poor provision for people from Black and ethnic minorities.

Depression in immigrants and ethnic minorities

People from different cultures may present with different symptoms of depression. Thus, it is very important to ensure that appropriate assessments are undertaken in these groups of people when assessing for depression.

Probst *et al.* (2007) explored race and ethnicity differences when reporting depressive symptoms to GPs and other practitioners. They explored whether participants had told a doctor or health practitioner about their problems. The findings showed that Whites and Hispanics were more likely to inform practitioners than African Americans. This highlights the importance of all practitioners being aware of the needs of depressed people from ethnic and diverse backgrounds as this has a major impact on referral and treatment options.

Livingson and Sembhi (2003) stated that some depressed people present with feelings of sadness and low mood whilst others present with pain and somatic symptoms. African American responses may appear to underestimate their distress when compared with a more structured diagnosis. Currently, there is little research available in the UK on depression in the older immigrant population, however studies have been undertaken in America.

There appeared to be little difference between rates of depression in Black and White older people in research studies undertaken in the 1990s (Blazer *et al.*, 1998; Lindesay, 1998; McCracken *et al.*, 1997). However, different methodologies were used to gather data. Comparative studies comparing like with like are needed. What is evident is that ethnic elders who were vulnerable to depression were more likely to live in deprivation.

There have been many research studies undertaken with the Irish immigrant population. Merril and Owens (1988) stated that the Irish population were more likely to be admitted to mental health institutions incorporating the highest rates of both attempted and actual suicides.

High rates of depression are evident in other ethnic groups. Livingson *et al.*'s (2002) study demonstrated that there was a higher rate of depression amongst older Cypriots and concluded that some of the reasons for this may be due to poor physical ill health, poor understanding of the English language and poor education. Despite presenting to health services they were less likely to complain about heir psychological symptoms and were also less likely to be diagnosed with depression or obtain treatment.

There are also associated links between depression and stroke in ethnic minorities. A study undertaken by Stewart *et al.* (2001) found an association between stroke and depression in older African Caribbean people living in south London. What is evident from studies undertaken into depression in ethnic older people is that future studies need to ensure comparability by considering variables that impact on particular ethnic groups such as social disadvantage and physical illness, language and cultural interpretation when assessing for depression. Researchers also need to use appropriate and consistent methodologies and screening tools.

There have been conflicting findings from studies undertaken into suicide amongst older ethnic people. There is evidence to suggest that older men are more likely to commit suicide; however, little research is available regarding immigration and ethnicity as key risk factors for suicide.

Self-harm as well as suicide needs to be considered in ethnic minorities. Bhugra *et al.* (1999) found that even though young Asian women were more likely to self-harm it was not as evident amongst older Asian people. International studies on suicide in older people have been undertaken as demonstrated by Cattell (2000) who found that older White men in America were more likely to commit suicide and Johansson *et al.* (1997) who found that older Swedish immigrants were most likely to commit suicide.

Thus, the mental health of immigrant populations must be considered. Ryan *et al.* (2006) examined the association between poorly planned migration and depression in Irish-born people living in London. This built on from previous studies undertaken by Weich *et al.* (2004) which identified that Irish-born people living in England experienced higher rates of mental distress than any other migrant group. Merril and Owens (1988) demonstrated that Irish migrants were more likely to experience higher rates of self-harm, whilst Neeleman *et al.* (1997) demonstrated that Irish migrants had higher than average rates of suicide. However, there may be reasons for this as Howes (2004) identified that the Irish were one of the largest minority ethnic groups in the UK. There was also evidence of differences of adaptability between younger and older migrants.

Ryan *et al.* (2006) highlighted that younger men and women who had migrated since the 1960s had a less well-planned migration than older people. Ryan (2003) had previously suggested that this was because older Irish migrants adapted better to life in the UK and perceived their migration more positively. This highlights how individual perception can influence illness. When depression has been diagnosed it is important to discuss treatment choices.

Treatment of depression

Treatment acceptability varies amongst depressed Black, White and ethnic minority people. Cooper *et al.* (2003) undertook a telephone survey which consisted of 829 adult patients in a primary care setting in America with patients who had been diagnosed with depression. They included 659 non-Hispanic Whites, 97 African Americans and 73 Hispanics.

The study concluded that African Americans were less likely than White people to accept antidepressants as a treatment for depression. Hispanics were less likely to accept antidepressants but were more likely to consider counselling an appropriate treatment.

Cultural and social experiences are very important factors to consider when discussing treatment options with depressed people. This was also demonstrated in the findings of a more recent study by Givens *et al.* (2007). The study by Givens *et al.* (2007) described ethnic differences in attitudes towards depression. It also considered treatment for depression, stigma and preferences for depression treatment which included both counselling and medication options.

The study was undertaken by a cross-sectional internet survey and included 78 752 people with severe depressive symptoms. This was a large study which included 3596 African Americans, 2794 Asians/Pacific islanders and 3203 Hispanics. Compared to White people the above three groups were more likely to prefer counselling as opposed to antidepressant treatment. This is where belief systems and individual perceptions about the causes of depression are important as these groups believed that counselling and prayer were much more effective as treatment for depression than medication which they perceived to be addictive. This highlights that response to preferences for depression treatment will enable individuals from other cultures to seek help sooner and enable them to access appropriate mental health services earlier.

Earlier intervention may also support them to adhere and comply with treatment regimes. This could potentially help to reduce side effects and reduce the perception that all medication is addictive.

Service providers need to consider this when working in partnership with patients. However, it also needs to be acknowledged that some severely depressed people may require medication initially before considering other alternative treatments.

Byrne *et al.* (2005) expressed concern regarding the poor quality of mental health care received by Black and ethnic minorities. This resulted in an analysis of the quality of mental care provided for ethnic minorities. The response and tolerability of the drug paroxetine amongst ethnic minority patients with mood or anxiety disorders was considered. It demonstrated that Hispanic and Asian responders had a slightly lower response rate whilst Asians had higher rates. The overall conclusion was that there was little difference between medication response and tolerability amongst Black and ethnic minorities and that generally the use of medication in ethnic minorities was not perceived as negative.

Where and how ethnic minorities access health care is also important. Gallo *et al.* (2005) suggested that Black Americans were more likely to get mental health care from a primary care doctor than from mental health care specialists.

Gallo *et al.*'s (2005) cross-sectional survey of 355 older adults found that older Black patients were less likely than older white patients to be diagnosed with depression. They also found that depression in older Black people was less likely to be actively managed in the 6 months prior to the interview. This study highlighted how ethnicity can determine how depression is identified and managed in older primary care patients.

Physical health, ageing and depression

Braam *et al.* (2005) recognized the importance of sociological factors when understanding the impact of physical health and depression in older people. Cole and Dendukuri (2003) acknowledged that poor physical health, bereavement and cognitive decline were the most likely risk factors which differentiated depression in late life from early onset depression. Braam *et al.*'s (2005) study examined the association between physical health and depressive symptoms in older people across Western Europe. Data was analysed from nine European countries from 22 570 people aged 65 years and above. The study concluded that the association between physical health and depressive symptoms in later life were consistent with Western Europe. It was also evident that functional disability was associated with depressive symptoms in later life and appropriate assessment and management of disability was required prior to treating depression in older people.

Many older people have lived in the UK for years arriving here as immigrants following the World Wars and in more recent years having been recruited here to work have become part of the UK ageing population. Livingson and Sembhi (2003) stated that about 6% of older people in the UK were immigrants and that this figure would continue to rise. If this number is to increase then the causes of depression in these groups may also increase. Rait *et al.* (1996) highlighted that ethnic older people were more likely to suffer from depression due to their socio-economic situation, immigrant status and age; however, researching this population can be difficult due to cultural, educational and language difficulties. This highlights the importance of promoting mental health and well-being in the ageing immigrant population.

Supporting race equality

The Social Care Institute for Excellence (SCIE, 2008) developed resource guide 10 focusing on commissioning services and the provision of mental health advocacy for African and Caribbean men. It promotes advocacy services by aiming to prevent social exclusion and discrimination.

This guideline was developed as a result of a literature review and practice surveys undertaken with African and Caribbean men who had discussed relevant issues. The findings developed into key guidelines of the SCIE Knowledge Review 15. These guidelines have addressed issues identified by Caribbean and African men. This was important as these groups were considered to be over-represented in mental health services and they were reported as having the most negative mental health care experiences. Despite raising awareness of the needs of Caribbean and African men, SCIE Knowledge Review 15 did not address the specific needs of African and Caribbean women. What this demonstrates is that womens mental health needs must also be considered and that as well as ethnic issues there are also be gender issues that need addressing.

This information is particularly relevant for commissioners of mental health services, mental health service managers, African and Caribbean service users and their relatives, Black and ethnic minority community workers and advocacy providers.

The NIMHE (2006) through the Care Service Improvement Partnership (CSIP) developed the Delivering Race Equality in Mental Healthcare Programme (2005). This is a 5-year action plan which aims to achieve equality and tackle discrimination in mental health services in England. This includes Black and ethnic minorities (BME) including Irish, Mediterranean and Eastern European migrants. In the future it could also support BME older people, children, young people, refugees and asylum seekers.

The three main objectives of the NIMHE (2006) include:

■ Engaging with communities
■ Gathering and providing better information on people who use mental health services
■ Supporting more appropriate and responsive mental health services
(NIMHE, 2006).

NIMHE (2006) has identified future priorities which include involving service users and carer involvement and working in partnership. All of this will impact positively upon the future provision of services.

Provision of services

The Kings Fund (2006) stated that the NHS is under a legal and moral obligation to provide services to people of all ages, genders and ethnic backgrounds. However, there were some concerns about the service provision for Black and ethnic minorities especially following the death of David Bennett. The document Delivering Race Equality in Mental Health Care (DRE; DH, 2005) was developed as a result of the death of David Bennett who was a 38-year-old African Caribbean patient who died in October 1998 in a medium secure unit after being restrained by staff. The report and further guidance promotes National Standards across mental health services. Building on from these guidelines another report was developed by the DH (2007a) to improve and reform mental health services for people from Black and ethnic minority communities in England. This document was entitled *Inside Outside*.

The three main objectives of this report are to:

■ Reduce and eliminate ethnic inequalities in mental health service experience and outcome
■ Develop cultural capability of mental health services
■ Engage with the community to build capacity through community development workers

(DH, 2007a).

These reports and guidelines have raised awareness and put forward actions ensuring that the mental health needs of BME are of equal importance to any other group of people requiring mental health services in the UK.

Another publication published in February 2007 by the DH (2007b) was entitled *Positive Steps* offering support and advice regarding the needs of BME.

This is part of the government's 5-year plan to deliver race equality in mental health care and includes religious and cultural needs for South Asian, African and Caribbean people. It is evident that the needs of BME people are being considered in relation to mental health care.

Other organizations such as the Kings Fund (2006) investigated the progress of the NHS in improving access to health care. They evaluated the effectiveness of interventions and identified barriers to progression.

A person's ethnicity is important because the NHS needs to be responsive to all people's needs. The DH (2007a) recognized that language, culture, lifestyle and different faiths were all important when responding to individual's health needs. They also recognized that some ethnic minority groups had poorer health than others creating potential health inequalities. Inequity of access to services was also demonstrated by poorer access to services and poorer quality of the service provided.

To prevent inequity of service provision for mental health, Ward and Palmer's (2005) a report highlighted the importance of mapping the provision of mental health services for asylum seekers and refugees in London. They acknowledged that refugees and asylum seekers were more likely to suffer from psychiatric disorders including depression, suicide and posttraumatic stress disorder. Many of these people had suffered from trauma, torture or imprisonment prior to arriving in the UK and were at risk of suicide as a result of their experiences. Thus, practitioners in both health and social care services need to be aware and trained to support asylum seekers and refugees in acknowledging these difficulties and support them to lead healthy fruitful lives.

The second part of this chapter recognizes the importance of promoting mental health care in people with learning disabilities. It focuses initially on depression in people with learning disabilities.

Depression in people with learning disabilities

Learning disability covers a wide range of disabilities and severities, some may be mild whilst others are more severe. Some people with learning disabilities may find it difficult to express themselves verbally, so one of the first signs of depression may include a change in their behaviour. The Royal College of Psychiatrists (1998) highlighted that it was important to recognize that people with learning disabilities have feelings but may express themselves in different ways. Even though they will experience similar symptoms of depression as other people, these symptoms may not be recognized due to communication difficulties.

Some identifiable signs of depression in people with learning disabilities include the following:

- Sudden or gradual changes in usual behaviour
- Loss of skills
- Loss of ability to communicate
- Physical illness
- Outbursts of anger, destructiveness or self-harm
- Seeking reassurance
- Loss of bowel or bladder control

- Complaining of aches or pains
- Wandering or searching
        (Royal College Psychiatrists, 1998).

There are a number of factors which can potentially lead to depression in people with learning disabilities which include:

- Bereavement or loss
- A change in their circumstances
- Physical illness
- The effect of any long-term disability
- Side effects of medication
- Abuse
    (Royal College Psychiatrists, 1998).

Caton *et al.* (2007) undertook research to identify responsive services for people with learning disabilities from minority ethnic communities. Azmi *et al.* (1997) recognized important factors including improved communication to enable carers to become more aware of services and ensuring that staff had appropriate language skills to support their clients. There also needed to be more culturally sensitive staff recruited into this field and lastly more flexibility in the service provided to meet the needs of carers.

Caton *et al.* (2007) sent out postal questionnaires to learning disability services in the Northwest of England. They found that changes in the law had helped to improve services for some ethnic minorities with learning disabilities, however, local policies needed to be developed to support service providers. It was apparent from the findings from the questionnaires that local services for ethnic minorities with learning disabilities needed to be constantly on the agenda for commissioners of services. People with learning disabilities may not always have the voice to vocalize their specific needs and it is evident that the law may need to be used to ensure that the needs of ethnic minorities with learning disabilities are met.

Low self-esteem in people with learning disabilities

Some people with learning disabilities experience low self-esteem resulting in them may underestimating their own ability and experiencing this negative perceptions. Caine and Hatton (1998) suggested that some people with learning disabilities will have experienced stigma, failure, institutionalization, unemployment and lack of close friendships. Abela (2002) suggested that this in itself can lead to depressive symptoms and feelings of low self-worth. A small study was undertaken by Whelan *et al.* (2007) with a group of people with learning disabilities who had low self-esteem. They used cognitive behavioural therapy (CBT) to help them feel more positive about themselves. All the people in the study had experienced severe mental health problems and had all been sectioned under the Mental Health Act. One of the interesting issues was that they were all aware that their lives had followed a different pathway to their peers and siblings. Goldberg *et al.* (1995) stated that this was important as awareness of a different life cycle contributed to low self-esteem. The Royal College of Psychiatrists (2004) acknowledged that CBT was the most frequently used psychological treatment use for people with learning disabilities.

Leaning disabilities and self-harm

For some people with learning disability, their behaviour takes on a different perspective and it is through this behaviour that self-harm or self-injury becomes more evident. Much of the literature focuses upon people with specific mental health problems but does not address people specifically with learning disabilities who self-harm. However, there are many people with learning disabilities who have self-harmed or self-injured throughout their life cycle.

There are a variety of reasons why people with learning disabilities self-harm. Warner (2000) identified childhood abuse whilst Walsh (1987) recognized neglect or loss through separation or parental illness as key factors. In addition to these early factors, grief and anger in later life can lead a person with learning disabilities to self-harm. The important issue is that people with learning disabilities need to be supported to cope with these feelings of low self-worth and shame as this may ultimately determine whether these feelings are transferred into self-harming behaviour. Sineson (1992) highlighted that there was a lack of knowledge and understanding regarding people with learning disabilities, and their general understanding of the world thus their behaviour was often misinterpreted.

However, this view was challenged by Babiker and Arnold (1997) who believed that reasons why people with learning disabilities self-harmed were no different to people without learning disabilities.

Professionals must not judge people with learning disabilities by expecting the self-harming behaviour to be a normal part of their learning disability. This highlights that all carers need to become more aware of the communication and behaviour of individuals with learning disabilities. As with many other conditions, some symptoms are part of recognized conditions whilst others are unique to that individual. This is about holistic care not just about labelling a person with a disability and expecting them to display a certain behaviour.

Learning disabilities and self-injury

Self-injury can be distinguished from self-harm when a person purposely injures themselves without any suicidal intent. This behaviour causes conflict amongst many practitioners as they try to understand the rationale for this behaviour and often feel that they are criticised when people in their care self-harm, yet they may have little control over the person's self-injurious behaviour. What is evident is that practitioners need to try to understand the reasons behind this behaviour rather than judging them in a negative manner. Babiker and Arnold (1997) described how being incarcerated in an institution without knowledge of being released can cause feelings of powerlessness and frustration. This could occur as a result of being sectioned under the Mental Health Act or being sent to prison or from being sent to any long-term care facility. Some clear findings were established from a study undertaken by Duperouzel and Fish (2007) of staff caring for clients with learning disabilities in a medium secure in Lancashire. The clients had all undertaken self-injurious behaviour and felt that staff did not understand why they did it. Communication with staff was considered very important. What was interesting was that many clients and staff believed that the client should be allowed to self-injure without the staff being blamed.

This chapter has recognized the importance of depression in people from Black and ethnic minority populations and immigrants both in the UK and internationally. It has also discussed the relevance of depression and mental health needs in people with learning disabilities.

Conclusion

This chapter has discussed the mental health needs of BEM populations. Concerns have been raised regarding the accessibility of services and actual service provision for BEM populations in the UK.

This has been discussed with reference to relevant DH policy documents, reports and guidelines which have acknowledged the importance of reducing inequalities and improving mental health services for BEM people. The prevalence of depression has been discussed in relation to race and ethnicity as well as the importance of monitoring ethnicity and inequalities.

The importance of identifying depression in immigrant and ethnic minority populations has also been highlighted with particular reference to the ageing immigrant population acknowledged in a study by Livingson and Sembhi (2003). The difficulties in studying immigrant populations can be due to different definitions of race and ethnicity, prevalence of depression, risk factors of socio-economic deprivation, immigrant status and old age and the risk of suicide. Treatments options have also been reviewed with particular reference to acceptability of treatment for depression amongst ethnic minority patients, Cooper et al.'s (2003). The future provision of services is very important for BEM populations as shown by Ryan et al. (2006) who studied depression in Irish migrants living in London.

This chapter concludes by discussing the mental health needs of people with learning disabilities. Particular reference has been made to the signs of depression and factors which lead to depression as highlighted by the Royal College of Psychiatrists (1998). Low self-esteem is a major factor and has been reviewed in relation to Whelan et al.'s (2007) study. Finally, self-harm and self-injury in people with learning disabilities have been discussed. The chapter concludes by discussing both practitioners' and clients' perceptions of self-injury and discussess preventing practitioners feeling guilty when people with learning disabilities self-injure. What was particularly relevant from studies cited was the difference between self-harm and self-injury in this client group where suicidal intent was not always the reason for the behaviour shown.

Reflection and discussion

Why is it important to consider culture and diversity when providing care for people with depression?

- *Ethnic groups frequently share geographical origins, culture, religious traditions and language.*
- *Culture incorporates shared ideas and rules and is a person's perception and understanding of the world around them.*
- *Cultural differences such as different religions may also not be recognized as people become associated with the label from a particular ethnic grouping.*
- *People from different cultures may present with different symptoms of depression.*

Why is it important to consider treatment options for ethnic minorities?

- *Treatment acceptability can vary amongst depressed Black, White and ethnic minority people.*
- *Cultural and social experiences need to be considered when discussing treatment options with depressed people.*

What factors need to be considered in relation to physical health, ageing and depression?

- *Sociological factors needed to be considered when understanding the impact of physical health and depression in older people.*
- *Poor physical health, bereavement and cognitive decline were the most likely risk factors which differentiated depression in late life from early onset depression.*

How can race equality be ensured in mental health care?

- *By engaging with communities.*
- *By gathering and providing better information on people who use metal health services.*
- *By having more appropriate and responsive mental health services.*

What factors need to be considered in relation to people with learning disabilities who self-harm or self-injure?

- *Self-harm*
- *Childhood abuse*
- *Neglect*
- *Loss through separation*
- *Parental illness*
- *Grief and anger in later life*
- *Self-injury*

References

Abela, J.R.Z. (2002). Depressive mood reactions to failure in the achievement domain: A test of the integration of the hopelessness and self esteem theories of depression. *Cognitive Therapy Research*, 26, 531–532.

Adams, R.E. & Boscarino, J.A. (2005). Differences in mental health outcomes among Whites, African Americans, Hispanics following a community disaster. *Psychiatry*, 68(3), 250–265.

Azmi, S., Hatton, C. & Emmerson, E. (1997). Listening to adolescents and adults with intellectual disability in South Asian communities. *Journal of Applied Research in Intellectual Disabilities*, 10, 250–263.

Babiker, G. & Arnold, L. (1997). *The Language of Injury: Comprehending Self-Mutilation*. Leicester: The British Psychological Society.

Bhugra, D., Desai, M. & Baldwin, D.S. (1999). Attempted suicide in west London. Rates across ethnic communities. *Psychological Medicine*, 5, 1125–1130.

Blazer, D.G., Landerman, L.R., Hays, J.C., Simonsick, E.M. & Saunders, W.B. (November 1998). Symptoms of depression among community dwelling elderly African-American and White older adults. *Psychological Medicine*, 28(6), 1311–1320.

Braam, A.W., Prince, M.J., Beekman, A.T.F., Delespaul, P., Dewey, M.E., Geerlings, S.W., Kivella, S.L., Lawlor, B.A., Magnusson, H., Meller, I., Peres, K., Reischies, F.M., Roelands, M., Schoevers, R.A., Saz, P., Skoog, I., Turrina, C., Versporten, A. & Copelan, J.R.M. (2005). Physical health and depressive symptoms in older Europeans. Results from EURODEP. *British Journal of Psychiatry*, 187, 35–42.

Byrne, R., Perera, P., Pitts, C.D. & Christi, J.A. (October 2005). Paroxetine response and tolerability amongst ethnic minority patients with mood or anxiety disorders: A pooled analysis. *Journal of Clinical Psychiatry*, 66(10), 1228–1233.

Caine, A. & Hatton, C. (1998). Working with people with mental health problems. In: Emerson, E., Hatton, C., Bromley, J. & Caine, A. (eds) *Clinical Psychology and People with Intellectual Disabilities*. Chichester: John Wiley and Sons, pp. 210–230.

Cattell, H. (2000). Suicide in the elderly. *Advances in Psychiatric Treatment*, 6, 102–108.

Caton, S., Starling, S., Burton, M., Azmi, S. & Chapman, M. (2007). Responsive services for people with learning disabilities from minority ethnic communities. *British Journal of Learning Disabilities*, 35, 229–235.

Cole, M.G. & Dendukuri, N. (2003). Risk factors for depression among elderly community subjects: A systematic review and meta-analysis. *American Journal of Psychiatry*, 160, 1147–1156.

Cooper, L.A., Gonzales, J.J., Gallo, J.J., Rost, K.M., Meredith, L.S., Rubenstein, L.V., Wang, N.Y. & Ford, D.E. (2003). The acceptability of treatment for depression among African-American, Hispanic, and white primary care patients. *Medical Care, 41*(4), 479–489.

Delivering Race Equality in Mental Health Care (2005). Available at http://www. action-dre.org.uk. Accessed 2 June 2008.

DH (January 2005). *Delivering Race Equality in Mental Health Care: An Action Plan for Reform Inside and Outside Services and the Government's Response to the Independent Inquiry into the Death of David Bennett.* London: DH.

DH (February 2007a). *Inside Outside. Improving Mental Health Services for Black and Minority Ethnic Communities in England.* London: DH.

DH (February 2007b). *Positive Steps. Supporting Race Equality in Mental Healthcare.* London: DH.

Diverse Minds (2006). *Race and Mental Health.* Available at www.mind.org.uk/News+ploicy+and+campaigns/Policy/RMH.htm.

Dratcu, L., da Costa Ribeiro, L. & Calil, H.M. (1987). Depression assessment in Brazil. The first application of the Montgommery-Asberg Depression Rating Scale. *British Journal of Psychiatry, 150,* 797–800.

Duperouzel, H. & Fish, R. (2007). Why couldn't I stop her? Self injury: The views of staff and clients in a medium secure unit. *British Journal of Learning Disabilities, 36,* 59–65.

Gallo, J.J., Bognor, H.R., Morales, K.H. & Ford, D.E. (2005). Patient ethnicity and the identification and active management of depression in late life. *Archives of Internal Medicine, 165*(17), 1962–1968.

Givens, J.L., Houston, T.K., Van Voorhees, B.W., Ford, D.E. & Cooper, L.A. (May–June 2007). Ethnicity and preferences for depression treatment. *General Hospital Psychiatry, 29*(3), 182–191.

Goldberg, D., Magrill, L., Hale, J., Damaskinidou, K. & Paul, J. (1995). Protection and loss: Working with learning disabled adults and their families. *Journal of Family Therapy, 17,* 263–280.

Helman, C.G. (2000). *Culture, Health and Illness.* Oxford: Butterworth-Heinemann.

Howes, E. (2004). *2001 Census Profiles: The Irish in London.* London: London Greater Authority.

Hutchinson, G. & Gilvarry, C. (1998). Ethnicity and dissatisfaction with mental health services [Letter]. *British Journal of Psychiatry, 172,* 95c–96c.

Johansson, L.M., Sundquist, J., Johansson, S.E., Bergman, B.O., Quist, J. & Traskman-Bendz, L. (1997). Suicide among foreign born minorities and native Swedes: An epidemiological follow up study of a defined population. *Social Science and Medicine, 44,* 181–187.

Keating, F., Robertson, D. & Kotecha, N. (2003). *Ethnic Diversity and Mental Health in London.* Recent developments. Kings Fund Working Paper August 2003. London: Kings Fund.

Kings Fund (2006). *Access to Healthcare and Minority Ethnic Groups.* Available at http://www.kingsfund.org.uk/publications/briefings/access_to_health.html. Accessed 28 May 2008.

Lindesay, J. (1998). Diagnosis of mental illness in elderly people from ethnic minorities. *Advances in Psychiatric Treatment, 4,* 219–226.

Livingson, G., Leavey, G., Kitchen, G., Manela, M., Sembi, S. & Katona, C. (2002). Accessibility of health and social services to immigrant elders: The Islington study. *British Journal of Psychiatry, 180,* 369–374.

Livingson, G. & Sembhi, S. (2003). Mental health of the ageing immigrant population. *Advances in Psychiatric Treatment*, 9, 31–37.

Marhawa, S. & Livingston, G. (2002). Racism, stigma or choice. Why do ethnic elders avoid psychiatrists? *Journal of Affective Disorders*, 72(3), 257–265.

McCracken, C.F., Boneham, M.A., Copeland, J.R., Williams, K.E., Wilson, K., Scott, A., McKibbin, P. & Cleave, N. (1997). Prevalence of dementia and depression among old people in Black and Ethnic Minorities. *British Journal of Psychiatry*, 171, 269–273.

Mental Health Act Commission (2001). *Ninth Biennial Report 1999–2001*. London: The Stationary Office.

Merril, J. & Owens, J. (1988). Self-poisoning among four immigrant groups. *Acta Psychiatrica Scandinavica*, 77, 77–80.

National Health Service Executive (1994). *Collection of Ethnic Group Data for Admitted Patients*. EL (94) 77. Leeds: NHSE. Available at www.dh.gov.uk/Publications AndStatistics.

Neeleman, J., Mak, V. & Wessley, S. (1997). Suicide by age, ethnic group, coroner's verdicts and country of birth: A three year survey in inner London. *British Journal of Psychiatry*, 171, 463–467.

NIMHE (2006). *Delivering Race Equality*. Available at http://www.actiondre.org/index.php?option=content&task. Accessed 2 June 2008.

Probst, J.C., Laditka, S.B., Moore, C.G., Harun, N. & Powell, M.P. (2007). Available at http://www.springerlink.com/content/a57131282v528062/. Accessed 28 May 2008.

Rait, G., Burns, A. & Chew, C. (1996). Age ethnicity and mental illness: A triple whammy. *BMJ*, 313, 1347.

Riolo, S.A., Nguyen, T.A., Gredon, J.F. & King, C.A. (June 2005). Prevalence of depression in race/ethnicity. Findings from the National Health and Nutrition Examination Survey 111. *Research and Practice. American Journal of Public Health*, 95(6), 998–1000.

Riolo, S.A., Nguyen, T.A. & King, C.A. (2003). Antidepressant medication use by age and gender: Nationally representative data. *Poster Presented at 50th Annual Meeting of the American Academy of Child and Adolescent Psychiatry*, 16 October 2003, Miami, FL.

Royal College of Psychiatrists (1998). *Depression in People with Learning Disability*. Available at www.rcpsych.ac.uk. Accessed 22 May 2008.

Royal College of Psychiatrists (2004). *Psychotherapy and Learning Disability – The Present Position and Options for Future Development*. London: Royal College of Psychiatrists Report.

Ryan, L. (2003). Moving spaces and changing places: Irish women's memories of emigration to Britain. *Journal of Ethnic and Migration Studies*, 29, 67–82.

Ryan, L., Leavey, G., Golden, A., Blizard, R. & King, M. (2006). Depression in Irish migrants living in London: A case control study. *British Journal of Psychiatry*, 188, 560–566.

SCIE (March 2008). *Resource Guide 10: Commissioning and Providing Mental Health Advocacy for African and Caribbean Men*. Available at http://www.scie.org.uk/publications/resourceguides/rg10/index.asp. Accessed 2 June 2008.

Shah, A., Lindesay, J. & Jagger, C. (1998). Is the diagnosis of dementia stable time in elderly immigrant Gujaratis in the UK (Leicester). *International Journal of Geriatric Psychiatry*, 7, 440–444.

Sineson, V. (1992). *Mental Handicap and the Human Condition: New Approaches from the Tavistock*. London: Free Association Books.

Stewart, R., Prince, M. & Mann, A. (2001). Stroke, vascular risk factors and depression: a cross sectional study in a UK Caribbean town population. *The British Journal of Psychiatry*, 178, 23–28.

Walsh, W. (1987). *Adolescent Self Mutilation: An Empirical Study.* Unpublished Doctoral Thesis. Boston College graduate School of Social Work.

Ward, K. & Palmer, D. (March 2005). *Mapping the Provision of Mental Health Services for Asylum Seekers and Refugees in London: A Report.* London. Available at www.sparc@hcct.org.uk. Accessed 25 May 2008.

Warner, S. (2000). *Understanding Child Sexual Abuse: Making the Tactics Visible.* Gloucester: Handsell Publishing.

Weich, S., Nazoo, J., Sproston, K., McManus, S., Blanchard, M., Erens, B., Karlsen, S., King, M., Lloyd, K., Stansfeld, S. & Tyler, P. (2004). Common mental disorders and ethnicity in England. The EMPIRIC study. *Psychological Medicine, 34,* 1543–1551.

Whelan, A., Haywood, P. & Galloway, S. (2007). Low self esteem: Group cognitive behavioural therapy. *British Journal of Learning Disabilities, 35,* 125–130.

Chapter 10

Managing depression in primary and secondary care and evidence-based practice

Introduction

This chapter covers five key areas in relation to depression and mental health care provision. Firstly, the importance of recognizing, diagnosing and treating depression in primary care is discussed with reference to evidence-based practice. It is evident from reviewing policy and guidance that it is imperative for depression to be managed appropriately in all care sectors. Many of the current policy documents aim to improve the mental health of the population and indeed the nation. The patient's experience of depression is considered in relation to the role of the expert patient. Secondly, the patients safety in mental health is discussed with reference to best practice and risk management National Patient Safety Agency guidance. Preventing suicide in the community is highlighted in relation to good practice guidelines and root cause analysis (RCA). The third area considers treatment in relation to evidence-based practice with particular reference to medicine management and improving access to cognitive behavioural therapy (CBT). The fourth area covered in this chapter is mental health policy which makes reference to the National Service Framework for adult mental health (DH, 2000) and Louis Appleby's report on *Mental Health Reform Ten Years On* and the updated Care Programme Approach (CPA) (BACP, 2008b). Reporting of suicide by the media is also highlighted by BACP (2008a) as well as the National Suicide Prevention Strategy (DH, 2007). Finally, the chapter concludes by promoting mental health research.

Evidence-based care for depression in primary care

Most people with chronic conditions and mental illness choose to be cared for in their own homes and in their own communities. Goldberg and Huxley (1992) suggested that more than 90% of people with a mental illness were managed in primary care. They need to be managed in an appropriate manner supported by a range of health and social care providers. Shared care helps to ensure that people with mental illness are assessed, diagnosed, treated and managed in the most appropriate environment. Most people with depression and other mental illness are cared for in the primary care setting with the support of secondary care services. Some people will require inpatient or outpatient services to support them throughout their illness following stressful life events which can occur at times throughout the lifespan.

The World Federation for Mental Health (2005) focused on an international survey published in Atlanta in America entitled *The Painful Truth Survey*. The findings from this survey identified that people with mental illness waited more than 11 months to see a doctor and were diagnosed with depression only after having visited the doctor on five occasions.

These people were experiencing physical symptoms which included unexplained headaches, general aches and pains and back and gastric pain. What was recognized was that undiagnosed physical symptoms could lead to depression. This led to concern as a delay in the diagnosis of depression leads to a delay in treatment. The survey results reported a high prevalence of painful physical symptoms in people with depression. As a result of this survey the World Federation for Mental Health (2005) promoted an educational programme for doctors which raised awareness of painful physical symptoms in people with depression.

After raising awareness of depression it is important that doctors are able to screen for depression in the primary care setting. This was highlighted by Ansseau *et al.* (2005) who suggested that depression was quite a common disorder in people in primary care. Bunevicius *et al.* (2007) were concerned about the instruments used to screen for depression and anxiety as they were not all suitable when detecting depression in primary care. Their study was undertaken in the primary care setting to assess the effectiveness of the Hospital Anxiety and Depression Scale (HADS). The study was undertaken in Lithuania and included 503 primary care patients. They chose to use HADS as it was a diagnostic tool suitable for detecting depression in non-psychiatric medical populations. Bunevicius *et al.* (2007) tested the effectiveness of HADS when using the MINI International Neuro-psychiatric Interview in primary care patients. The findings from the study showed that HADS was a sensitive and accurate screening tool for diagnosing major depression in primary care patients when a cut off score of six or above was used. However, the study highlighted that other screening tools needed to be used to detect minor depression and dysthymia in primary care settings.

A report was undertaken by Pincus *et al.* (2005) which was entitled *Depression in Primary Care: Bringing Behavioral Health Care into the Mainstream*. This report was produced for the Robert Wood Johnson Foundation which aimed to link depression care with the management of other chronic conditions. This enabled it to be integrated into the quality improvement agenda of purchasers and providers without being submerged into mainstream health care.

Pincus *et al.*'s (2005) report was undertaken in America; however, the issues included within it are relevant across the UK and the international community. Some key issues identified included:

- Depression is a serious and often chronic condition in primary care patients
- Depression in primary care often goes unrecognized and is inconsistently treated despite evidence-based practice
- Some chronic disease models have been effective in treating patients with depression in primary care
- Barriers within the primary care system prevent these models being sustained
- Difficulty can occur due to the number of clinicians and operational systems in place
- These include patients, providers, purchasers, stakeholders, practices and planning agendas

(based on Pincus *et al.*, 2005).

Another challenge for primary care practitioners were competing demands upon their time. Pincus *et al.* (2005) raised concerns that there were no financial incentives to manage depression, thus it may not be seen as a priority.

One of the main challenges in implementing effective evidence-based care for depressed people in the primary care setting is a co-coordinated approach based upon best practice.

Rubenstein *et al.* (1999) undertook a collaborative approach to improve the care of depression in a variety of primary care practices in America. This approach helped to create partnerships between health care organizations and researchers. Reasons for the lack of progress in caring for depressed primary care patients included complex behaviour changes. These require proactive systems to detect and manage depression. Patients with depression are less likely than patients with non-depression to seek help, partially due to fatigue and low confidence and due to the stigma of being labelled as mentally ill.

Rubenstein *et al.* (1996) suggested that time needed to be spent with the patient following a diagnosis for depression. They recommended that following an initial half-hour assessment that active treatment was needed and follow-up care for up to a year maybe required.

However, many practitioners only had a 15-minute consultation in the practice which caused conflict due to the lack of time spent with the patient. There was also little evidence of mental health specialist integration in primary care. As a result of these issues, Katon *et al.* (1996) developed a multifaceted intervention to improve the treatment of depression in primary care. This was advocated by collaborating of care through a team approach by transferring the role of assessment, education and treatment monitoring to non-medical practitioners. A variety of factors and variables can prevent this from happening efficiently which include different team working, different roles, lack of resources and different management structures and support.

Some of these findings are supported in the UK by the DH (2000) National Service Framework for Mental Health. It highlights seven key standards which focus upon the planning and delivery of UK mental health services. Standard two stated that people with severe mental health needs should have their needs met by shared care with local mental health Trusts. This would enable anyone who accessed primary care services with a mental health problem to be assessed and treated appropriately and referred to an appropriate mental health secondary service provider if required. Management of depression is important and there needs to be collaboration between primary and secondary services.

Management of depression in primary and secondary care

The National Institute for Clinical Excellence (NICE, 2004) developed Clinical Guideline 23 referring to the management of depression in primary care. These guidelines apply the step care model which aims to match the needs of people with depression with the appropriate services. The step care model demonstrates that the higher the step the more intense intervention will be required.

Step 1: Recognition in primary care and general hospital settings.
Step 2: Treatment of mild depression in primary care.
Step 3: Treatment of moderate to severe depression in primary care.
Step 4: Treatment of depression by mental health specialists.
Step 5: Inpatient treatment for depression.

(NICE (2004) Clinical Guideline 23).

Step 1 is where GPs, practice nurses and care providers in general hospital settings are responsible for care. General hospital settings are important as inpatients in general hospitals may become depressed due to physical illness, disability or dementia. Depression in dementia is often missed due to the patient's confused state. Thus, it is important to recognize the symptoms of depression in all patients regardless of their age, gender, physical or mental capacity. They also need to consider whether the side effects of medication are causing the depression. The care provider's role is to assess for the signs, symptoms, causes and level of depression. During the assessment, patients need to be asked the following two questions:

- During the last month, have you been bothered by feeling down, depressed or hopeless?
- During the last month, have you been bothered by having little interest or pleasure in doing things?

Responses to both these questions will help determine the extent to which the person is feeling depressed.

Step 2 is the responsibility of the primary care team and primary care mental health services and is where mild depression is often diagnosed. Sometimes no intervention is necessary and the patient may not wish to have treatment. A variety of interventions may be offered which could include exercise, psychological interventions, CBT or guided self-help. Not all patients will attend outpatients or follow-up appointments. However, the role of primary care practitioners would be to have some contact with the patients diagnosed with mild depression who do not attend follow-up appointments. This would prevent potential further crisis and also acknowledge those patients who had recovered. It may also highlight those patients who may require support and treatment in the future by helping them to develop their own coping strategies.

Step 3 is also the responsibility of the primary care team and primary care mental health workers and is provided when moderate to severe depression has been diagnosed. Appropriate interventions would include medication, psychological intervention and social support. It is very important to monitor the risk of these patients and if a high risk has been identified then the choice of medication may need to be reconsidered. Also, the amount of medication given may need to be assessed to prevent overdose and additional support may need to be provided. CBT or interpersonal therapy may be provided for patients with moderate to severe depression who refuse medication.

However, the assessment of the patient and compliance with treatment are key factors when managing moderate to severe depression. Support networks or telephone contacts should also be put into place.

Step 4 is the responsibility of mental health specialists and crisis intervention teams. Their prime focus would include depressed people who are at significant risk of suicide or self-harm, recurrent depression, atypical and psychotic depression and treatment-resistant depression. Crisis resolution teams provide intervention for severely depressed people in primary care who are considered to be at risk. Medication is usually prescribed by a consultant psychiatrist and the ultimate aim is to provide care in the community with appropriate treatment maintenance.

Step 5 is the responsibility of inpatient mental health services and crisis intervention teams. This provision would include depressed people who are at severe risk of self-neglect, suicide or self-harm or who are considered a risk to themselves or others. Electroconvulsive therapy (ECT) may be given to achieve rapid improvement from severe symptoms of depression when other treatments have been ineffective or when the depression is considered to be life-threatening. These steps have been developed as a result of trials and expertise based upon evidence-based practice (NICE, 2004 Guideline 23).

National guidance for depression in children and young people

Another guideline has been developed by the National Institute for Clinical Excellence (2005b) for depression in children and young people in primary, community and secondary care. Key priorities include recording social, educational, family and relationship issues during the assessment of a young person with depression. This would help to ensure better provision of coordinated care.

When treating children with depression, professionals need to consider whether the parents have mental health problems. If they have been diagnosed with a mental illness this needs to be treated in parallel with the child's treatment. Thus, links with adult mental health services need to be achieved. From the depressed child's perspective, liaison with educational and social care is essential to achieve a holistic approach. A step approach has been advocated in the NICE (2005b) guidelines.

Step 1 identified detection and risk profiling. This acknowledged that health professionals in primary care, schools and community settings needed to be trained to recognize the symptoms of depression and to assess children and young people who were potentially at risk of depression. The training could be provided by regular links with Child and Adolescent Mental Health Services (CAMHS).

Step 2 supports the training of CAMHS staff in using interview-based instruments to improve their diagnostic skills.

Step 3 states that mild depression in children should not be treated with antidepressants as an initial treatment.

Steps 4 and 5 are considered in relation to moderate to severe depression and suggest that these children should be offered psychological treatments or family therapy for a 3-month period as the initial treatment. Antidepressants should only be considered with psychological therapies and when prescribed they should be monitored on a regular basis.

With regard to services for children a recent study was undertaken by BACP (2008b) on behalf of the Welsh Assembly Government (WAG) regarding counselling services in schools for children and young people. The aim of counselling in schools is to promote emotional health and to address mental health issues. Twelve different models of school counselling were found to be operating in schools across Wales. Differences occurred as a result of service provision and different roles and job descriptions of the counsellors. One of the main aims of the BACP (2008b) study was to develop good practice counselling guidelines for schools in Wales. The study highlighted the importance of involving teachers, parents and children as well as health and social care agencies. School counsellors provide a useful role when mental health problems are apparent. However, interventions need to be undertaken earlier e.g. peer education to promote mental health and well-being. Discussion around mental health issues will help to reduce the stigma of mental illness.

Guidance on posttraumatic stress disorder in adults and children

Another guideline produced by NICE (2005a) was the management of posttraumatic stress disorder (PTSD) in adults and children in primary and secondary care. Clinical Guideline 26 was developed in March 2005. PTSD occurs following catastrophic traumatic events resulting in the person re-experiencing the symptoms of the event. Other specific symptoms include hyper-arousal and emotional numbing. Some people experience the symptoms immediately after the event whilst others have delayed symptoms. Depression is often co-morbid with PTSD. The depression can be helped by treating the PTSD. Professionals must consider the element of risk when assessing people with PTSD who may be at risk of suicide or self-harm. When people with PTSD are so severely depressed they may require treatment for the depression prior to treatment for the PTSD. Other people may have lost family or friends through sudden or unnatural circumstances and experience traumatic grief. In these circumstances it may be better to treat the PTSD first.

Children suffering from PTSD after a traumatic event need to be treated appropriately by professionals in emergency departments. The parents will also need guidance to support the child.

When the management of the adult or child is shared between primary and secondary care, the CPA should be implemented to ensure consistent monitoring and support, as Dinan (1999) suggested people with depression have higher morbidity and mortality rates than the general population.

It is evident from these guidelines that there has been a major focus on managing depression in both primary and secondary care. What needs to also be considered is the patient's experience of depression.

Patient's experience of depression and the expert patient

Wilson et al. (2003) undertook a 5-year follow-up study of general practice patients experiencing depression. They found a high proportion of patients were prescribed antidepressants during the 5-year period studied and concluded that most GPs who diagnosed depression prescribed antidepressants. This suggests that they were prescribing for minor as well as moderate and severe depression. Minor depression could have been treated with alternative treatments such as psychological therapies. However, Jorm et al. (1997) and Angermeyer and Matschinger (1996) found from previous community studies that most patients with depression preferred to be treated with non-drug treatments. The study concluded that depression was a chronic illness which was treated by GPs with high amounts of prescription antidepressants for short periods of time. One of the main concerns was that the prescription periods for some depressed patients should have been for much longer. These findings recommended that GPs needed information about alternative treatments for depression.

People's perception of the care they receive is very important as it can influence their ability to get better. Badger and Nolan (2007) study determined how people who were treated for depression perceived their care. Lockwood (2004) had previously identified that much of the research undertaken did not acknowledge patients' perspectives. Both Grime and Pollock (2003) and Shooter (2003) recognized the importance of addressing personal, social and housing needs. They considered these issues to be of equal importance as providing treatment for people with depression when promoting recovery. Badger and Nolan (2007) identified a lack of basic information about depression amongst recently diagnosed people. It was important to provide them with information about depression to them and for practitioners to inform them that they would get better with treatment.

Once a diagnosis has been made, depressed people can be helped to deal with their illness by developing coping strategies. They may also need to be helped to deal with the stigma about mental illness.

The expert patient

It is very important to ensure that the patient's experience of living with a long-term condition is recognized and that the patient journey from prediagnosis to aftercare is acknowledged by practitioners in both primary and secondary care. Mayor (2006) suggested that one way of offering support to patients is through an Expert Patient Programme (EPP). Initially, many patients do not perceive a long-term condition (LTC) as having too much impact on their general health. However, it is evident from speaking to patients with LTCs that reliance on their family, friends and carers and health and social care services that it has an enormous impact upon their health and well-being. Patients may join self-help groups which Zabalegui *et al.* (2005) suggested helps to improve psychological health by having a positive effect upon quality of life. Whatever happens with the provision of services for mental illness, the safety of mental health patients is paramount.

Patient safety in mental health

The DH (2006b) acknowledged Professor Louis Appleby's concerns regarding overall patient safety in mental health services. With reference to suicide and deliberate self-harm, Professor Appleby highlighted the importance of the Suicide Prevention Strategy and Twelve Points to a Safer Service (2008).

Another important document was published by the DH (2007) in June entitled *Best Practice in Managing Risk*. It provided principles based upon evidence-based practice which need to be considered when assessing and managing risk to self and others in mental health services. It is hoped that practitioners will benchmark their practice against these principles and utilize tools for risk assessment and risk management into their practice.

The four key underlying principles required to balance care needs against risk needs are:

- Encouraging positive risk management
- Promoting collaboration with service users and carers
- Ability to recognize and build on service users' strengths
- Awareness of the organization's role in risk management in line with individual practitioners

(DH, 2007).

National patient safety agency

Due to concerns regarding patient safety incidents a review of systems within organizations was undertaken. This acknowledged how incidents were identified and how they were dealt with. Two approaches identified by the National Patient Safety Agency (NPSA, 2007) included a person-centred approach and a system approach. They highlighted that organizations who used a person-centred approach may consider individuals to be careless by blaming them for the mistakes made and believing that by removing the individual from their job or from the organization the problem would be solved. Some organizations that use the system approach have also set people up to fail. This is because they have focused upon the system rather than also considering the individual. Both approaches in isolation do not necessarily address the issues within the organization and will not prevent future patient safety incidents occurring. One way of addressing this issue is by Root Cause Analysis RCA.

Root cause analysis

The approach used by RCA addresses the following key questions:

- What happened?
- How did it happen?
- Why did it happen?
        (NPSA, 2007).

What happened refers to the actual incident and needs to consider the events leading up to the incident in chronological order. How it happened needs to consider whether the incident occurred as a result of unsafe practice or inappropriate care delivery and often includes actions or omissions in care.

This could include forgetting to risk assess a patient for suicide or self-harm or giving a patient the wrong medication.

Why the incident happened needs to consider any other contributing factors, which could include poor communication, lack of staff education and training or inappropriate delegation of a task to a practitioner who does not have the skills to deal with the situation. Other contributing factors could include staff shortages, lack of resources or appropriate equipment, unpredictable patient behaviour or staff not coordinating care appropriately.

The NPSA (2007) recognized that once the root cause of the incident had been identified then the problem could be resolved quickly within the organization. However, this will depend upon the ability of the organization to resolve the issues.

Some problems that occur within organizations include poor risk assessment, poor care planning, not using the CPA, poor documentation or failure to provide continuity of care between inpatient and community services. All of these are instrumental in providing quality of care to patients.

Organizations can undertake two approaches when preventing patient incidents which can be either reactive or proactive. A reactive approach would include reflection on the incident after the event and identifying barriers that could have been put into place to prevent the incident occurring. An example of this would be improved monitoring of patients or improved staffing ratios. Proactive approaches can be addressed by barrier analysis.

Barrier analysis

The NPSA (2007) identified barriers which they described as control measures to prevent harm to buildings, organizations, people and communities. The NPSA (2007) suggested that proactive approaches identify possible hazards before they occur and as result solutions to these possible hazards can be identified. Some examples would include developing local guidelines and protocols, clinical supervision with staff which may identify risks or undertaking training and development. They also recognized that there are barriers to implementing good practice.

There are a variety of barriers which include:

■ Human action
■ Administrative
■ Physical environment
■ Natural causes
        (NPSA, 2007).

With regard to human action what needs to be considered is to what extent the person or the organization can prevent patient incidents.

There will always be some element of human error; however, organizations need to consider whom they employ and whether they have the right skills and ability to do the job required. This will then form part of the proactive approach.

Administrative barriers can be addressed by putting in place policies and procedures and training to help prevent incidents which are part of an administrative function. With regard to the physical environment managers can risk-assess the environment to ensure as best as possible whether it is safe? For example, on an inpatient unit the organization needs to ensure that patients are observed appropriately. From a natural cause perspective the position of where new buildings are built may need to be considered.

Suicide prevention: good practice guidelines

A recent report undertaken by the University of Manchester into the National Confidential Inquiry into Suicide and Homicide by People with Mental Illness (2008) highlighted that there had been an overall reduction in suicide rates in the general population in the UK; however, the rates in Scotland remained twice as high as those in England and Wales. One concern was that the rates were particularly high in the younger age group. If unsuccessful suicide attempts could potentially remain with them into old age, thus raising the rate of potential suicide rates in all ages of the population.

It was also evident that homicide rates in Scotland amongst younger males were higher than in England and Wales and that drugs and alcohol were a major contributing factor. Many of these young men did not have a mental illness and recommendations needed to address service interventions and treatments for alcohol and drug abuse as well as for mental illness.

The report also recognized that the prevention of risk by mental health services needed to be improved in many situations. With regard to abuse of alcohol and drugs, the report recognized that better were required between addiction teams and services providing care for dual diagnosis. The National Confidential Inquiry (2008) discussed suicide rates in inpatients. It suggested that increased supervision was needed in acutely disturbed patients soon after admission and increased observation of patients who were likely to abscond by controlling entry and exit to the ward.

Another key time of particular risk was prior to discharge where patients may be returning to stressful situations. Loss of contact with mental health services was a major factor in patients who had been discharged back into the community. This is an area that is under-researched and more robust studies would be beneficial to add to the evidence base.

The Chief Medical Officer/Chief Nursing Officer (2008) issued guidelines from WAG on the safe management of mental inpatients. It highlighted five key areas of guidance in relation to patient safety.

- Patient observation
- Physical intervention
- The National Confidential Inquiry into suicide and homicide by people with mental illness
- Good record keeping

All of the above are relevant in relation to people with depression; however, of particular relevance is patient observation when reducing risk. The National Confidential Inquiry is also important as it has implications for service managers for the service delivery. Service providers need to review findings and recommendation in order to improve future service provision for patients with mental illness. Of particular importance is suicide prevention in inpatient services and also sudden unexplained death of inpatient mental health patients. Record keeping is fundamental to practice as it enables events to be recorded in the interest of the patient and maintains communication with other members of the team. As well as addressing these aspects of care it is important that the care provided is based upon sound evidence.

Evidence-based practice

Sackett *et al.* (1996) suggested that by looking at the evidence and by evaluating research on treatment that best practice will be achieved. It is clear that studies which review evidence-based research consider many more patients or cases than any one individual practitioner could in their career. As a result of reviewing the evidence, practitioners are able to weigh up the risks and benefits and make decisions in a more balanced way. However, Chassin and Galvin (1998) recognized that it can be difficult to keep up to date as new information is being published almost daily. Thus, there are still a variety of approaches and differential treatments used for a variety of conditions across the UK. National guidelines and protocols can also be interpreted from a local perspective assisting practitioners in their day-to-day management of people with mental health problems.

There are a variety of factors that need to be considered when basing decisions upon research studies. Practitioners need to consider who has undertaken the research, how many patients were studied, under what conditions were they studied and whether the findings can be generalized to other populations and also the limitations of the study.

Even though some published research studies may have small numbers of participants, the findings may be very relevant to the practitioner's own practice enabling them to undertake replicate studies with larger sample sizes or to use different methodologies. This highlights the importance of evolving and developing practice rather than basing practice upon what has always been seen to be effective.

Evidence-based practice is relevant for all practitioners and as recently highlighted by the DH (2008a) the report on medicine management has helped to highlight that medicine management is everybody's business.

Medicine management

The DH (2008a) medicine management report is relevant in mental health care today as doctors, nurses and pharmacists are currently prescribing medication. Mental health care is delivered by multidisciplinary teams and any member of that team may be asked questions from service users about their medication, thus the title of the report is everybody's business. Service users have requested impartial advice on medication which will enable them to make informed choices. It is important that patients are given full information regarding the type of medication which is best suited to them, the different dosages and potential side effects. It may be that due to them taking medication for other conditions alternative mental health treatments are advocated which are in the best interest of that individual.

When a particular treatment has not been effective, sequential treatment may be implemented. One example of this would be if CBT has not worked, antidepressants may then be commenced. This was demonstrated by Stewart *et al.* (1993) who recognized the relevance of using the antidepressant imipramine when CBT had been ineffective. Another example would be if all other treatments have failed, then ECT may be commenced as a last resort. It is a similar approach to treating pain where prescribing starts at the lower end of the pain ladder then leading onto more intensive pain medication. Fava *et al.* (2005)

highlighted the relevance of sequential treatment for mood and anxiety disorders. However, there is also evidence that prescribing two treatments together can be effective for some patients. Rush *et al.* (2006) and Nelson (2006) considered acute and long-term outcomes in depressed outpatients who required one or more treatment steps.

This study included 3671 patients from 41 care facilities in America. Out of these 41 areas, 18 of them were primary care facilities. More than 75% of patients suffered from recurrent or chronic depression and 61% had a psychiatric diagnosis. After taking flexible doses of SSRIs and citalopram only 28% of the patients studied remained in remission. One of the reasons given for this was that many of the patients had co-morbidity with other conditions, particularly anxiety. Fava (1999) suggested that often co-morbidity is only recognized when the most severe symptoms of the original diagnosis have abated.

As discussed in earlier chapters, patient compliance with medication is an important factor to consider. Basco and Rush (1995) suggested that the rate of non-compliance for long-term medication is about 40%. This figure will be determined and influenced by the support given by the health and social care professionals as well as the information and knowledge attained by the patient.

Segal *et al.* (2002) suggested that the alternative therapy approach was very expensive and when given alone had little impact for depressed people. Thus, a combination of therapies described as sequential treatment, which consists of both psychotherapy and medication, appears to be the most appropriate method of treating major depressive disorder. Another factor which may have influenced this approach is the lack of availability or access to CBT.

Improving access to cognitive behavioural therapy

The DH (2008c) developed a toolkit in partnership with NHS commissioners. This toolkit aimed to improve access to psychological therapies was developed after consultation with the National Institute for Mental Health in England (NIMHE) and also the Care Services Improvement Partnership (CSIP).

A commissioning cycle for psychological therapies was developed and included the following important stages:

- Understanding the benefits
- Stakeholder engagement
- Needs assessment and gap analysis
- Service model and care pathways
- Workforce planning and development
- Understanding the market
- Commissioning for outcomes

(DH, 2008c).

The overall aim of this commissioning cycle was to help primary care services to implement NICE guidelines and to improve access to psychological therapies for people with depression and anxiety.

Mental health policy

National Service Frameworks have been developed to offer guidance to practitioners dealing with a variety of key illnesses and conditions. Many of them have been adapted and developed to meet the needs of the four nations in the UK. Within Wales, the Revised Adult Mental Health Service Framework and Acton Plan for Wales was developed by the Welsh Assembly Government (WAG, 2005).

The WAG framework (2005) had four main principles which were:

■ Equity of mental health services irrespective of gender, race, ethnicity, physical disability or sexuality
■ Empowerment of carers and people with mental illness to ensure they have input into the planning, development and delivery of mental health services
■ Effective interventions to improve quality of life
■ Efficient use of resources and collaborative working between health, social services and the voluntary sector

(WAG, 2005).

Having reviewed the previous NSF, four themes became the priorities for mental health services in Wales. These included:

■ Service and workforce reform including crisis resolution/home treatment services and improving inpatient mental health environments
■ Systems development
■ Care programme approach
■ Mental health promotion and social inclusion

(WAG, 2005).

National suicide prevention strategy

The DH (2002) initially published the *National Suicide Prevention Strategy for England*. The National Institute for Mental Health in England (2006) produced an annual progress report in the *National Suicide Prevention Strategy for England*. The report was acknowledged by Professor Louis Appleby, National Director for Mental Health and highlighted that as there was no single approach for suicide prevention, a broad strategic approach was more suitable which incorporated health, social care agencies, voluntary and private agencies and government departments. Progress was evaluated in many key areas which included the Suicide Audit in Primary Care (CSIP, 2006b) which helped primary care trusts to undertake audits on suicides and open verdicts. The DH (2006a) also published a resource entitled *Help Is at Hand for People Bereaved by Suicide and other Traumatic Deaths*. The CSIP (2006a) also published guidance on action to be taken at suicide hotspots. This demonstrates that in England much has been achieved with regard to suicide prevention.

Scotland also have strategies which are effective in suicide prevention; however, there is an increase in suicide in young men which is also related to social circumstances and alcohol and drug abuse. In Ireland, the Information Analysis Directorate (2006) reported suicide rates between 1991 and 2003. It reported that the male suicide rate in Northern Ireland was increasing whilst the female suicide rate had remained constant.

Within Wales, the WAG (2008) have developed Talk to Me, a national action plan to reduce suicide and self-harm in Wales (2008–2013). It states that between 1996 and 2006 approximately 300 people died as a result of suicide in Wales. Suicide is one of the highest causes of death in young people in Wales. Approximately, 21:100,000 men died from suicide compared with 6:100,000 women in Wales.

The National Confidential Inquiry into Suicide and Homicide by People with Mental Illness (2008) advocated 12 points to a safer service. It highlighted the increased number of suicides occurring during the immediate discharge period from hospital and also the increased number of depressed inpatients who committed suicide whilst absconding from the ward. It also highlighted the number of depressed people who had a history of violence or self-harm who were not receiving higher levels of care through the CPA.

Care programme approach

The DH (2008b) revised previous approaches of care with the development of new guidance entitled *Refocusing the Care Programme Approach*. It is evident that person-centred individual care needs to be provided to all people with mental illness and that those people who are considered higher risk need to have a much higher level of care intervention. The CPA supports partnership working across all relevant agencies with the allocation of a care co-coordinator. The role ensures that assessment and care planning improve the outcome for service users and their carers.

The CPA involves assessing, planning, implementing and evaluating care. For patients who are at risk of depression, the assessment process will include screening for depression.

Screening for depression

Depression may not always be recognized or diagnosed by health care professionals in primary care. Gilbody *et al.* (2005) undertook a Cochrane review to determine the evidence for screening for depression. Gilbody *et al.* (2006) believed that screening could become part of health policy in England and Wales where doctors received rewards for providing enhanced services for people with depression as part of the quality and outcome framework. However, concern was expressed about screening people unless the evidence demonstrated its effectiveness. Thus, the National Screening Committee (2003) developed criteria for assessing the viability, effectiveness and appropriateness of screening for depression. The evidence showed that screening alone would not improve either the management or outcome of depression. The most effective approach was to use screening as part of a package of care for depressed patients in primary care.

Progress on mental health reform

Professor Louis Appleby (2008) reported on the 10-year programme of health care reform in mental health services which was launched in 1999. There have been many improvements during that time period in community services. Of particular relevance is the increase in crisis resolution teams, assertive outreach teams and early intervention teams.

There has also been an increase in the number of mental health practitioners providing care for people with mental health problems. Treatments have focused more upon psychological therapies with the development of computerized CBT and overall there has also been a reduction in the suicide rate.

Future policy initiatives include reducing stigma of mental illness and reducing social exclusion, increasing the availability of psychological therapies, improving services for ethnic minorities and implementation of the Mental Health Bill which aims to treat high-risk patients in the community.

Media reporting on suicide

There have been various perceptions from the public regarding the media's reporting of suicide. One perception may be that high profile reporting and publicity on the television, radio and newspapers led to an increase in suicides amongst younger people. This may be because the young people see their friend's photographs displayed in the papers and on the television and feel that they can no longer cope. The media have a professional obligation to ensure that they report accurate information and should ensure that what is reported is sensitive to those close to the people who have committed suicide. Sadly, on some occasions the priority may be selling papers rather than considering the feelings of distressed people. Maybe the families and loved ones and close friends should be consulted on their view of media reporting and as a result new protocols on reporting on suicide developed. This has been advocated by BACP (2008a) who have requested the urgent media guidelines on the reporting of suicide. Concern was raised after the sensational media reporting following the youth suicides in Bridgend in Wales.

BACP (2008a) recommended that guidelines should be developed to guide journalists reporting on suicide in the media. This should include reporting suicide as a completed suicide rather than as a successful suicide.

They also recommended that journalists should provide helpline numbers and not publish photographs or report the actual methods of suicide. One of the criticisms of the media is that they tend to sensationalize the suicide which may influence other young people to try it themselves. To support the reduction of suicides in Wales, the WAG has advocated the Scottish initiative Choose Life strategy. The WAG (2008) action plan to reduce suicide and self-harm has also a commitment to work with the media to ensure a more sensitive approach when reporting on mental health and suicide issues.

Mental health research

There are a variety of initiatives being developed across the country regarding mental health research. The National Institute for Health Research (NIHR) (2008) acknowledged that 40% of the UK population experience mental health issues and that one in four adults in the UK will be diagnosed with a mental health problem every year. What is evident is that research must inform and influence practice. Another aspect of the NIHR is the UK Mental Health Research Network (MHRN), which was developed in 2003 and is a component of the UK Clinical Research Network (UKCRN). Its prime aim is to include service users and staff in mental health research. The NIHR has a Health Technology Assessment programme which is currently supporting clinical trials in mental health. The majority of research has been funded in primary care, secondary care and clinical trials.

The HealthAcorn Report (2007) highlighted the association between poor physical and poor mental health and within Wales mental ill health has become a major economic concern. This led to the publication of the document (Designed for Life, 2005), which aimed to improve the mental health and well-being of the people of Wales. The Wales Mental Health in Primary Care Network (WaMH in PC, 2007) was established to develop Gold Standards for Primary Care Mental Health in Wales and also a Welsh Declaration for Mental Health and Well-Being. One of the key aims of the network is to promote research and development based upon evidence. This will then support mental health and well-being in Wales. The All Wales Mental Health Promotion Network (2008) was officially launched on 14 March 2008. The network is supported by health, social care, age concern, MIND and a variety of other multi-agencies. A variety of research projects have also been undertaken which include the More than a Number campaign which studied young people's experiences of mental health services in rural Wales. This was supported by the big Lottery Fund and looked at the barriers experienced by 18- to 40-year olds when accessing mental health services.

What is evident is that wherever people live in the UK and across the world, mental health has a major impact upon them as individuals and upon the society they live in.

Conclusion

This chapter has identified how depression can have an impact upon both the individual and society at any time throughout the lifespan. The importance of basing care upon evidence has been a key focus throughout this chapter. Discussion has centred upon the management of depression in primary and secondary care using national guidance. It is essential that the patient is the key focus of all care provided, ensuring they become true partners in their care. This can be achieved by providing knowledge and understanding of the condition and enabling them to make decisions about treatment and management options. Mental health promotion can be achieved by giving the individual some responsibility for their mental health. The patient's experience of depression has been highlighted as well as the importance of the role of the expert patient.

Patient safety is a key issue and has been discussed in relation to the National Patient Safety Agency. Patient safety has been explored by using RCA and barrier analysis. Suicide prevention and good practice guidelines have also been developed to enable policy makers to format strategies for suicide prevention.

Evidence-based practice and evidence-based medicine have been discussed in relation to medicine management and cognitive behaviour therapy. Mental health policy is an integral part of this concluding chapter where national suicide strategies have been explored.

The CPA has also been discussed and highlighted in relation to the management of care in both primary and secondary care services. Screening for depression in primary care is important; however, it is not to be used in isolation and a package of care is needed to ensure that the patient is supported to receive the correct treatment and care.

Progress on mental health reforms over the past 10 years have been reviewed as well as some future plans for mental health provision. BACP (2008a) highlighted the importance of guidelines for journalists when reporting suicide as currently the reporting can be sensationalized resulting in potentially other young people committing suicide. Finally, the chapter has considered research that is currently being undertaken within mental health.

Reflection and discussion

Using a step approach/model where should depressed people be treated?

Step 1: Recognition in primary care and general hospital settings.
Step 2: Treatment of mild depression in primary care.
Step 3: Treatment of moderate to severe depression in primary care.
Step 4: Treatment of depression by mental health specialists.
Step 5: Inpatient treatment for depression.
(NICE (2004) Clinical Guideline 23).

What two key questions should be asked when assessing people for depression?

- *During the last month, have you been bothered by feeling down, depressed or hopeless?*
- *During the last month, have you been bothered by having little interest or pleasure in doing things?*

What four key underlying principles need to be considered when balancing care needs against risk needs?

- *Encouraging positive risk management*
- *Promoting collaboration with service users and carers*
- *Ability to recognize and build on service users' strengths*
- *Awareness of the organization's role in risk management in line with individual practitioners*

(DH, 2007).

What key questions does root cause analysis ask?

- *What happened?*
- *How did it happen?*
- *Why did it happen?*
  (NPSA, 2007).

Name four barriers to managing risk?

- *Human action*
- *Administrative*
- *Physical environment*
- *Natural causes*
  (NPSA, 2007).

Share four examples from your clinical practice with your team. Discuss with your colleagues policies and strategies in relation to suicide and self-harm in your organization

References

All Wales Mental Health Promotion Network (2008). Available at www.publichealth.org. Accessed 25 May 2008.

Angermeyer, M.C. & Matschinger, H. (1996). Public attitudes towards psychiatric treatment. *Acta Psychiatrica Scandinavica*, 94, 326–336.

Ansseau, M., Fischler, B., Dierick, M., Mignon, A. & Leyman, S. (2005). Prevalence and impact of generalized anxiety disorder and major depression in primary care in Belgium and Luxemburg: The GADIS study. *European Psychiatry*, 20, 229–235.

Appleby, L. (2008). *Mental Health Ten Years On: Progress on Mental Health Care Reform.* Available at www.dh.gov.uk. Accessed 24 January 2008.

BACP (2008a). *BACP Media Centre. BACP Calls for Media Guidelines on Reporting Suicide.* Available at http://www.bacp.co.uk/media/index.php?cat=2. Accessed 6 May 2008.

BACP (2008b). *Counseling in Schools: A Research Study into Services for Children and Young People.* Commissioned by the Welsh Assembly Government. Executive summary. Available at www.bacp.co.uk/reserch/School_Counselling.php.

Badger, F. & Nolan, P. (March 2007). Attributing recovery from depression. Perceptions of people cared for in primary care. *Journal of Nursing and Healthcare in Chronic Illness, 16*(3a), 25–34.

Basco, M.R. & Rush, A.J. (1995). Compliance with pharmacology in mood disorders. *Psychiatric Annals, 25,* 269–279.

Bunevicius, A., Peceliuniene, J., Mickuviene, N., Valius, L. & Bunevicius, R. (2007). Research article. Screening for depression and anxiety disorders in primary care patients. *Depression and Anxiety, 24,* 455–460.

Chassin, M.R. & Galvin, R.W., for Institute of Medicine National Roundtable on Health Care Quality. (1998). The urgent need to improve health care quality. *JAMA, 280*(11), 1000–1005.

Chief Medical Officer/Chief Nursing Officer (June 2008). *Letter Regarding the Safe Management of Mental Health in-Patients.* Cardiff: WAG.

CSIP (2006a). *Guidance on Action to be Taken at Suicide Hotspots.* Available at http://www.csip-plus.org.uk/Rowan/Docs/SuicideHotspots.pdf. Accessed 12 June 2008.

CSIP (2006b). *Suicide Audit in Primary Care Trust Localities.* Available at http://csip-plus.org.uk/RowanDocs/SuicideAuditTool. Accessed 12 June 2008.

Department of Health (2000). *The National Service Framework for Mental Health.* London: DH.

Designed for Life (May 2005). *Creating World Class Health and Social Care for Wales in the 21st Century.* Cardiff: Welsh Assembly Government.

Dinan, T.G. (1999). The physical consequences of depressive illness [Editorial]. *BMJ, 318,* 826.

DH (September 2002). *National Suicide Prevention Strategy for England.* London: DH. Available at http://dh.gov.uk/Publications. Accessed 12 June 2008.

DH (2006a). *Help Is at Hand: A Resource for People Bereaved by Suicide and other Sudden, Traumatic Death.* Available at http://www.dh.gov.uk/assetRoot/04//13/90/07/04139007.pdf. Accessed 12 June 2008.

DH (July 2006b). *Patient Safety in Mental Health Services.* Letter to Chief Executives from the National Director for Mental Health. Gateway Reference: 6895.

DH (June 2007). *Best Practice in Risk Managing Risk: Principles and Evidence for Best Practice in the Assessment and Management of Risk to Self and Others in Mental Health Services.* London: DH.

DH (January 2008a). *Medicines Management: Everybody's Business. A Guide for Service Users, Carer's and Health and Social Care Practitioners.* NIMHE National Workforce Programme. London: DH. Available at www.dh.gov.uk/publications. Accessed 25 June 2008.

DH (March 2008b). *Refocusing the Care Programme Approach. Policy and Positive Practice Guidelines.* London: DH.

DH (April 2008c). *Improving Access to Psychological Therapies (IAPT) Commissioning Toolkit.* London: DH.

Fava, G.A. (1999). Subclinical symptoms in mood disorders. *Psychological Medicine, 29,* 47–56.

Fava, G., Ruini, C. & Rafanelli, C. (2005). Sequential treatment of mood and anxiety disorders. *Journal of Clinical Psychiatry, 66,* 1392–1400.

Gilbody, S.M., House, A.O. & Sheldon, T.A. (2005). Screening and case finding for depression. *The Cochrane Database of Systematic Reviews,.* Issue 4, CD002792.

Gilbody, S.M., Sheldon, T. & Wesseley, S. (April 2006). Should we screen for depression? *BMJ*, *332*, 1027–1030.

Goldberg, D. & Huxley, P. (1992). *Common Mental Disorders: A Biosocial Model*. London: Routledge Press.

Grime, J. & Pollock, K. (2003). Patients ambivalence about tasking antidepressants: A qualitative study. *The Pharmaceutical Journal*, *271*, 516–519.

HealthAcorn Report CACI and TNS (January 2007).

Information Analysis Directorate (2006). *Section 75 Analysis of Suicide and Self Harm in Northern Ireland (2000–2005)*. Belfast: DHSSPSNI.

Jorm, A.F., Korten, A.E., Jacomb, P.A., Rodgers, B., Pollitt, P., Christensen, H. & Henderson, S. (1997). Helpfulness of interventions for mental disorders: Beliefs of health professionals compared with the general public. *British Journal of Psychiatry*, *171*, 233–237.

Katon, W., Robinson, P., Von Korff, M., Lin, E., Bush, T., Ludman, E., Simon, G. & Walker, E. (1996). A multifacted intervention to improve treatment of depression in primary care. *Archives of General Psychiatry*, *53*(10), 924–932.

Lockwood, S. (2004). 'Evidence of me' in evidence based medicine? *BMJ*, *329*, 1033–1035.

Mayor, V. (February 2006). Long term conditions. 3. Being an expert patient. *British Journal of Community Nursing*, *11*(2), 59–63.

National Confidential Inquiry into Suicide and Homicide by people with Mental Illness. (June 2008). Available at http://www.manchester.ac.uk/nci. Accessed 26 June 2008.

National Institute for Clinical Excellence (NICE) (December 2004). *Depression: Management of Depression in Primary and Secondary Care*. Clinical Guideline 23. London: NICE.

National Institute for Clinical Excellence (NICE) (March 2005a). *Post-traumatic Stress Disorder. The Management of PTSD in Adults and Children in Primary and Secondary Care*. Clinical Guideline 26. London: NICE.

National Institute for Health and Clinical Excellence (NICE) (2005b). *Depression in Children and Young People. Identification and Management in Primary, Community and Secondary Care*. Clinical Guideline 28. London: NICE.

National Institute for Health Research (NIHR) (2008). Available at www.hta.ac.uk.

National Institute for Mental Health in England (2006). Annual Report on Progress 2006. In: *National Suicide Prevention Strategy for England*. London: NIHME.

National Screening Committee (2003). *The UK National Screening Committees Criteria fro Appraising the Viability, Effectiveness and Appropriateness of a Screening Programme*. London: HMSO.

Nelson, J.C. (2006). The Star*D Study. *American Journal of Psychiatry*, *163*, 1864–1866.

NPSA (2007). *National Patient Safety Agency*. Available at http://www.npsa.nhs.uk/patientsafety/improvingpatientsafety/. Accessed 25 June 2008.

Pincus, H.A., Houtsinger, J.K., Bachman, J. & Keyser, D. (2005). Depression in primary care: Bringing behavioral health care into the mainstream. *Health Affairs*, *24*(1), 271–276.

Rubenstein, L.V. et al. (1996). *Partners in Care Clinician Guide to Depression and Management in Primary Care Settings*. Santa Monica, CA: RAND.

Rubenstein, L.V., Jackson-Triche, M., Unutzer, J., Miranda, J., Minnimu, K., Pearson, M.L. & Wells, K.B. (September/October 1999). Evidence based care for depression in managed primary care practices. *Health Affairs*, *18*(5), 89–105.

Rush, A.J., Trivedi, M.H. & Wisniewski, S.R. (2006). Acute and longer term outcomes in depressed out patients requiring one or several treatment steps: A STAR*D Report. *American Journal of Psychiatry*, *163*, 1905–1917.

Sackett, D.L., Rosenberg, W.M., Gray, J.A., Haynes, R.B. & Richardson, W.S. (1996). Evidence based medicine: What it is and what it isn't. *BMJ*, *312*(7023), 1–2.

Segal, Z., Vincent, P. & Levitt, A. (2002). Efficacy of combined, sequential and crossover psychotherapy and pharmacotherapy in improving outcomes in depression. *Journal of Psychiatric Neuroscience*, *27*, 281–290.

Shooter, M. (2003). The patients' perspectives on medicines in mental illness. *BMJ*, *327*, 824–826.

Stewart, J.W., Mercier, M.A., Agosti, V., Guardino, M. & Quitkin, F.M. (1993). Imipramine is effective after unsuccessful cognitive therapy. *Journal of Clinical Psychopharmacology*, *13*, 114–119.

Twelve Points to a Safer Service (2008). Available at http://national-confidential-inquiry.ac.uk. Accessed 12 June 2008.

Wales Mental Health in Primary Care Network (WaMH in PC) (2007). Available at http://www.rcgp.org.uk.

Welsh Assembly Government (WAG) (October 2005). *Adult Mental Health Services. Raising the Standard. The Revised Adult Mental Health National Service Framework and an Action Plan for Wales.* Cardiff: WAG.

Welsh Assembly Government (WAG) (2008). *Talk to Me. A National Action Plan to Reduce Suicide and Self Harm in Wales, 2008–2013.* Cardiff: WAG.

Wilson, I., Duszynski, K. & Mant, A. (2003). A 5-year follow up of general practice patients experiencing depression. *Family Practice*, *20*(6), 685–689.

World Federation for Mental Health (2005). *Depression: The Painful Truth.* News embargoed for release: 26 May 2005. Available at http://www.wfmh.com/Painful truth survey.htm. Accessed 9 October 2006.

Zabalegui, A., Sanchez, S., Pablo, D. & Juando, C. (2005). Nursing and cancer support groups. *Journal of Advanced Nursing*, *51*(4), 369–381.

Index